T0057243

DESPERATE

AN EPIC BATTLE FOR CLEAN WATER
AND JUSTICE IN APPALACHIA

KRIS MAHER

SCRIBNER

NEW YORK   LONDON   TORONTO   SYDNEY   NEW DELHI

Scribner
An Imprint of Simon & Schuster, Inc.
1230 Avenue of the Americas
New York, NY 10020

First Scribner trade paperback edition October 2022

SCRIBNER and design are registered trademarks of The Gale Group, Inc.,
used under license by Simon & Schuster, Inc., the publisher of this work.

For information about special discounts for bulk purchases,
please contact Simon & Schuster Special Sales at 1-866-506-1949
or business@simonandschuster.com.

The Simon & Schuster Speakers Bureau can bring authors to your live event.
For more information or to book an event, contact the Simon & Schuster Speakers Bureau
at 1-866-248-3049 or visit our website at www.simonspeakers.com.

Map copyright © 2021 by David Lindroth, Inc.

Frontispiece photo by Roger May

Manufactured in the United States of America

1   3   5   7   9   10   8   6   4   2

Library of Congress Cataloging-in-Publication Data has been applied for.

ISBN 978-1-5011-8734-6
ISBN 978-1-5011-8735-3 (pbk)
ISBN 978-1-5011-8736-0 (ebook)

For the people
of the Forgotten Communities

"It is a region of black riches concealed under green velvet."
—Oliver F. Holden, mining engineer, September 1921

CONTENTS

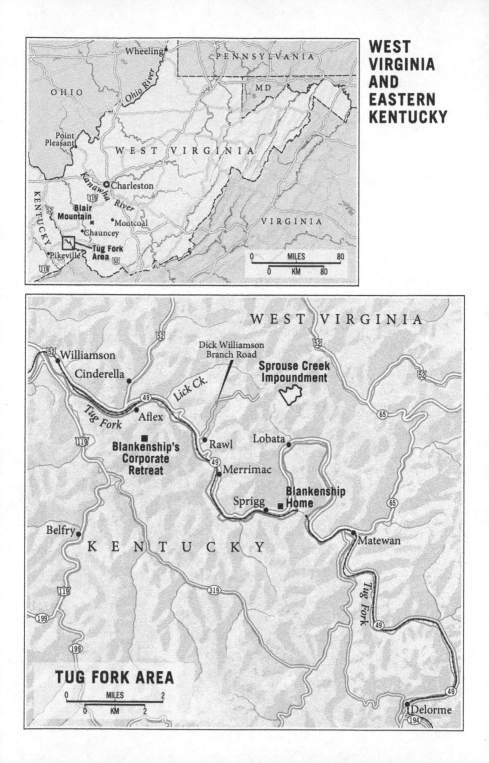

WEST
VIRGINIA
AND
EASTERN
KENTUCKY

PART I

BLACK WATER

FEBRUARY 2004–MAY 2005

CHAPTER 1

Kevin Thompson had been hunting for evidence all afternoon. A lone figure trekking through a rolling three-thousand-acre property in Mingo County, West Virginia, the forty-year-old attorney had climbed over barbed-wire fences and hiked up and down ridges on behalf of a client who was suing Arch Coal, one of the nation's biggest coal companies, for contaminating his land. With his tan floppy hat, a backpack stuffed with topographic maps, and binoculars strung around his neck, Thompson looked more like a reality-TV explorer than a lawyer. For safety reasons, he was wearing steel-toe boots and carrying a hard hat. He knew he probably should have told the coal company that he would be out on his client's property that day but he wanted to cover the ground without interference. A quarter of a mile away, beyond a rise, bulldozers and giant rock trucks were moving dirt on a flattened ridge, and coal that had been buried for millions of years lay black as velvet in the sun.

As he hiked up a valley fill, a steep slope of churned-up dirt, Thompson scanned the ground for signs that the workers hired by an Arch subsidiary had illegally dumped fuel and machinery there. On previous visits, Thompson had found tainted water seeping out of the ground. As an environmental engineer had recently told him, black water meant diesel was oozing to the surface, and red water came from rusting equipment. While hiking higher, he listened for the beeping of trucks on the other side of the ridge. He knew that as long as the miners were moving coal around, he didn't have to worry about rocks raining down on him from another blast on the mountain.

Thompson's client James Simpkins was a prominent local businessman who sold lumber and mining equipment. He supported mining on his remote spread and had even mined large tracts of it himself, slopes that were now covered with thick grasses where his prized

Angus cattle grazed. But he believed the coal company had been negligent and contaminated his property with fuel and machinery. He'd hired Thompson a few months earlier after watching him win a sizable settlement against Arch for an adjacent landowner. Simpkins told people he admired the young man's hustle. He liked Thompson, he said, even if he was a lawyer.

Thompson had a full head of light auburn hair, a resonant baritone voice, and an occasional stutter when too many thoughts crowded his brain. He also had a wife and daughter at home in New Orleans, where he rowed crew on the bayous to keep in shape. In the 1990s, he had built a successful litigation consulting business there and narrowly missed making a fortune when a chance to sell it fell through. But then an undeniable urge had led him to stake a claim as an environmental lawyer in southern West Virginia. After years of working as a consultant, he found he was drawn to the detective work of litigation as much as he was to arguing before a judge in a courtroom. And the coalfields were only a two-hour drive south from his hometown of Point Pleasant, close enough that he could stay there and keep an eye on his aging mother.

It was February 2004, and after working for a year and a half on two contamination lawsuits against Arch, Thompson was still getting his footing in the coalfields. He hadn't found any new evidence on the valley fill that day, but before climbing down he stopped to take in the view. The series of ridges around Simpkins's property was called Mystery Mountain. And that seemed appropriate enough—this part of the state was still largely a mystery to Thompson. Now the gray and ocher ridges of the Appalachian Plateau, still bare from winter, stretched into the blue distance like swells in a choppy sea. "It's the most amazing view you've ever seen," he often told people. "It's crazy up there."

On his way to his car, Thompson remembered he had an appointment with three potential clients: a preacher named Larry Brown, his brother Ernie Brown, and another man named B.I. Sammons. He had a scrap of paper with directions to a church nearly an hour away. He threw his gear into his Ford Explorer and realized he had just enough time to make it. He thought about stopping to clean up—his right hand, which he'd snagged on a fence, had dried blood on it and his pants were caked with dirt—but he decided showing up on time was more important. All he knew about the three men who wanted to meet him were their names and that they lived in a place called Rawl. It didn't strike Thompson as a complicated matter. B.I. had simply said that their wells had gone bad. As he drove down Route 49 beside the Tug Fork, a winding tributary of the Big Sandy River on West Virginia's rugged border with Kentucky, Thompson figured a coal company must somehow be involved.

When Thompson turned onto Dick Williamson Branch Road, he found an old coal-mining community set in a hollow between low hills. The square houses with porches and newer double-wide homes were crowded close to a single lane of pavement, their tiny yards hemmed in by chain-link fences. Thompson slowed as a few barking dogs trotted into the road. At the top of the hollow, which was already in shadow, he came to a plain white church with a steeple. He noticed an ancient coal company house next to it that was weathered and gray. Then Thompson saw bright plastic toys in the yard and realized a family was living there.

Inside the Rawl Church of God in Jesus Name, more than fifty people filled the pews, and at first Thompson thought he had interrupted an evening service. The last of the sunlight was hitting imitation stained-glass windows: a white dove and a ray of yellow light against a scattering of abstract blue and green shapes. A few heads turned when Thompson entered, and then a tall man with narrow shoulders and large, silver-framed glasses approached him and asked if he was a lawyer.

"I'm not dressed like one, but I am," Thompson said. The man introduced himself as Larry Brown, pastor of the church, and Thompson realized that all the people in the pews had been waiting for him. Larry Brown brought Thompson over to his brother Ernie, who had dark-brown hair and looked about twenty pounds heavier and ten years younger. Then Larry introduced Billy Sammons Jr., who went by B.I. and wore a plain white trucker hat over his white hair. Ernie Brown and B.I. seemed eager to talk, but Larry hushed them. "This is the fella we want to hear from," he said.

Brown walked Thompson up the blue-carpeted aisle to an altar that looked more like a stage set for a high school band concert, with microphones, acoustic guitars, and a drum kit. A seven-foot-tall white cross, with a wooden crucifix at its center, hung on the wall. "Just tell the people a little about yourself," Larry Brown said.

Thompson looked out on the room full of people. After spending the day wandering around with only his own thoughts, it took him a few seconds to adjust to the crowd. But once he started talking, the words came easily. He introduced himself and said he focused on cases involving contamination from mines and other sites, and then he cut the tension in the room by apologizing for his appearance.

"I've been tramping through bushes and climbing over and under fences, looking for evidence, and I'm embarrassed to be tracking mud through your church here," Thompson said. His own slight drawl loosened the more he spoke. He explained that he was from Point Pleasant, that he'd gotten his undergraduate degree from Marshall University in Huntington and his law degree at Tulane University in New Orleans. He shared with them that he split his time between Louisiana and West Virginia and that he had sued oil and gas companies that contaminated property. Not shy about selling himself, he said that he had just won a big settlement against Arch Coal and that he'd been out that afternoon in the county for a second case against the company.

"I'm not against coal miners," Thompson said, knowing he had only one chance to win over the crowd, many of whom looked as though they had come directly from mining or construction jobs. "I love coal miners." He also knew that in West Virginia, making such a statement could sound like checking a box. But, he went on to say, he believed that coal companies had devastated the state for too long. With his voice rising, he said coal barons, most of whom had never set foot in the state, had oppressed West Virginia for more than a hundred years and left miners and their families with a poisoned land and water. A few voices mumbled in agreement. Others seemed less receptive to that message, but he couldn't care about that now.

Standing before the people, he saw faces that looked weary and distrustful, others that looked angry, and a few that were already staring up at him with hope. He leaned in and said he wanted to find out more about people's water. "Can someone tell me about your wells and the water in your homes?"

In the back of the church, Larry Brown leaned toward his wife, Brenda, and said, "We're going to hire this guy." Over the past few weeks, he and his brother and B.I. had invited other lawyers, including one from Washington and another from New York, to Rawl. They had shown up wearing expensive suits and promised they could win a lawsuit but said the people would have to get themselves organized first. So far, Thompson hadn't promised anything. But he spoke with more passion than the other lawyers. And he already seemed to know more about coal and West Virginia than the other attorneys had. Brown saw Thompson's muddy boots and the dried blood on his hand and believed the young lawyer wasn't afraid to get dirty looking for evidence. It was exactly the kind of commitment the people in Rawl needed.

Thompson later recalled that Brown asked how many people in the crowd had had gallbladder and kidney problems and that a smattering of hands went into the air each time. He asked how many people had had rashes. More hands went up. Many people hadn't discussed their health problems with their neighbors. But now people began speaking over each other, expressing their worries and asking Thompson questions all at once. Four or five people had brought jars of gray and rusty-looking water they'd filled up at their taps.

"Massey's been poisoning us," Larry's brother Ernie said.

Thompson had of course heard of Massey Energy—it was the biggest coal company in West Virginia. But he didn't know much about its operations. He learned that day that Massey's Rawl Sales & Processing subsidiary had a preparation plant that cleaned coal on the other side of the ridge above Rawl. Some people thought the company's impoundment—a man-made reservoir created to store coal slurry, the liquid waste from the plant—had been leaking deep into the ground.

Residents were attributing a wide range of problems to their water. Thompson heard stories of broken water heaters, corroding pipes, and filter systems that burned out in a month. Larry Brown told Thompson that he had gotten boils on his legs that he believed were caused by bathing in the water. He said his wife had gotten them too, and that his daughter had had two miscarriages.

"Good Lord, I'm sorry to hear that," Thompson replied.

After the meeting wound down, Larry Brown explained that some of his neighbors had been wary of attending. People along Route 49—not just in Rawl, but in the three neighboring communities of Lick Creek, Merrimac, and Sprigg—had been living with bad water for years. Some were afraid they or a family member could lose their job at Rawl Sales or another coal company if they publicly criticized Massey. Whenever Brown organized a community meeting, he said, he feared that some attendees were there just to listen in and report back to Massey. As Thompson stood listening, several people mentioned Massey's CEO, Don Blankenship, with a mixture of defiance and fear, and said he was to blame, without offering a clear reason. Working on his cases against Arch Coal, Thompson had heard Blankenship's name come up. But he could tell that it carried a different weight in Rawl.

Thompson told Larry, Ernie, and B.I. that he would discuss what he'd seen and heard with some lawyers he'd been partnering with, but that it looked like the people in the community might very well have a strong case if the water showed contamination from mining. He knew he needed a more detailed picture of people's health conditions, and after the church meeting he gave Ernie and B.I. a health survey and asked them to get as many filled out as they could.

When he left, Thompson thought about one thing Larry Brown had said about Massey.

"People are scared of the company," Larry had said. "We have no confidence in them, because of the things that's happened in the past. We been done like that in the past." But he'd said the time had come for the people to stand up.

Thompson had been staying at his mother's house in Point Pleasant, and when he got back that night, he was still buzzing. He called his wife, Kathleen, at home in New Orleans and told her about the jars of gray and rust-colored water, the long list of health problems, the concerned faces in the crowd. He was moved, but it was hard to put his exact feeling into words. He had felt the anger in the room and that the people were ready to fight. All they needed was an advocate.

"There could be a couple hundred or more plaintiffs," Thompson said. He realized he could threaten a class action. Based on his recent experience with Arch Coal, he believed Massey was likely responsible for the water contamination in these four communities and that he could force the company to settle within six months to a year.

"We're going to make twenty million dollars," he said, guessing at what he thought Massey would have to pay in a settlement.

Kathleen, who had managed litigation for an insurance company before marrying Thompson, told him that the case sounded compelling—and horrifying. She was more right than she knew.

In his excitement, Thompson had no inkling that over the next seven years the case would come to dominate his life, eventually threatening his marriage, his finances, and his safety. That by taking it on, he would become deeply involved in the lives of hundreds of people in Rawl and its neighboring communities along Route 49. Or that the conflict would pit him against one of the nation's most powerful coal companies and its CEO, just as the industry was about to go through a series of historic shocks, plunging Thompson into one of the most important environmental issues of the day: the struggle of ordinary citizens to hold companies and elected officials accountable for failing to protect their drinking water.

Over the next few weeks, Thompson kept in contact with Larry, Ernie, and B.I., but a visit to Ernie and Carmelita Brown's house made the strongest impression on him. The couple lived alongside Route 49, just west of Rawl, in the middle of a tight curve in the road. It was a picturesque spot. Across the two-lane state road, a grove of trees in a hollow sloped down toward the Tug Fork. Thick woods surrounded the Browns' property. To the right, set back in the trees and partly camouflaged by overgrowth, there was an abandoned wooden house that was easy to miss from the road, another sign of the area's coal-mining history hidden in plain sight. When Thompson parked at the Browns' for the first time, their own house, with its reddish-brown beams, reminded him of a Swiss chalet. A set of wooden stairs led to a side door that opened onto the kitchen on the second floor, where Thompson was hit with a smell of rotten eggs that choked his throat and made his eyes water.

The odor was so severe that Thompson couldn't believe that the Browns were moving around the place without seeming to notice it themselves. But as they explained, they had stopped being able to smell it.

Ernie and Carmelita walked Thompson down a hallway to their bathroom, where Carmelita had first seen the water turn black. That was all the way back in about 1983, she said. Some twenty years later, neither could remember the exact date. But Carmelita vividly recalled turning the faucet on to draw a bath for herself one evening and watching with alarm as dark-gray water with fine black particles in it filled the tub. Not knowing what to do, she had called Ernie into the room and they stood together, waiting to see if the water would run clear again. For months, the water did seem to return to normal. But then it turned gray again, and the episodes became more frequent over time.

Ernie brought up the big impoundment—the one Thompson had heard about at the church meeting—on the other side of the mountain. Thompson knew little about slurry or what went into cleaning coal at a preparation plant. But he listened to Ernie's theories about the potential link between the Rawl Sales operation and the family's well.

A former Massey miner, Ernie said that at first he had thought the impoundment was too far away to affect their well, which was 220 feet deep and partly cased in cement. But he came to suspect that slurry was escaping from the impoundment and making its way under their house. Ernie also believed that blasting by a contractor for Rawl Sales in the early 1980s had cracked the earth under the impoundment. At the time, the blasts had felt like small earthquakes, knocking pictures from walls and cracking windows in their neighbors' homes. The Browns had sensed the ground move beneath their own house. "We figured it was the coal company doing something somewhere, up to no good," Ernie said.

Some twenty years after Carmelita first noticed the water changing, their bathtub and sink and toilet bowl were all stained black. Steam from the shower had given the pink walls a grayish tint. Ernie hauled out old plumbing fixtures he'd had to replace when the water had eaten through them. He said he had even been forced to replace electrical outlets, after they had been corroded by the gas permeating the house. Carmelita said she had discovered that if she left a new penny on a table in the washroom, the top side would turn black after a few days while the unexposed side remained shiny. "If it's doing all this, what do you think it's doing to us?" Ernie asked.

Ernie wore his dark-brown hair neatly parted to the side and kept his mustache carefully trimmed. His toughness and punctiliousness both came through when he spoke. He had grown up in Lick Creek, less than a mile away from Rawl, and his mining career had ended in 1989, when he'd badly injured his back while operating a cutting machine for a contractor in a Massey mine. Since then, he had been forced to live off disability insurance. Years of frustration over their water had left him jaded when it came to Massey. Now he sat at the kitchen table and read his Bible every evening, looking for passages to speak on at the Sprigg Freewill Baptist Church, where he and Carmelita were active members. Like his brother Larry, he had a deep faith that he had begun practicing later in life.

Carmelita, who went by Carm, had grown up in a small hollow called Road Branch about ten miles north of Williamson that was later cleared to make way for Route 119, the four-lane highway. Her brown eyes had shadows under them that gave her oval face a melancholy cast. But she seemed less weighed down by life than her husband, and she laughed when she recounted growing up in Mingo County. As a young girl, she had helped her father, a moonshiner friendly with the county's corrupt politicians, tend to his stills, carrying leaves in burlap sacks into the hills to cover up the equipment he had partially buried in locations he kept secret from everyone but his daughters and a partner of his. She said her father gave jars of moonshine to officials at the county courthouse and kept a stash under her grandfather's church on a hill, and that he sometimes crawled under the building and listened to the service going on above him. "Dad would lay back under there and drink moonshine while they was up there preaching," Carmelita said, smiling at the image. "So he got the Word preached to him."

She had met Ernie in 1973 when he was eighteen and she was fourteen, though at the time she'd lied and told him she was fifteen, because she was jealous that her older sister was getting all the attention from boys in the area. It was something the couple laughed about now. After dating Ernie for a year, Carmelita dropped out of the tenth grade to marry him, and the couple had been inseparable ever since.

For years now, the bad water had cast a cloud over every aspect of the Browns' lives, from their health to their finances. Carmelita handed Thompson folders full of medical bills and letters she had written to a congressman when she couldn't get health coverage. She had suffered her first bout of kidney stones in 1993 and the cycle repeated itself, sending her to the hospital every few years. She and Ernie blamed the water for the stones and a host of other problems: headaches, diarrhea, itchy red patches on their backs, necks, and arms.

Even though they had stopped drinking water from their well, Carmelita had continued doing their laundry in the water. They took short showers but sometimes had to grab a wall afterward, because the steam made them dizzy and burned their eyes. All these years later, the water still ran black on random days. Carmelita showed Thompson a spiral notebook she kept above the kitchen sink in which she kept track of every time the water was bad. "Water turned black and has bad smell. Water getting blacker. 11:30 p.m.," read a recent entry.

The couple's two children, Christopher and Charity, had suffered from rashes and diarrhea growing up. Christopher had nosebleeds, stomachaches, and a poor appetite from a young age. As a girl, Charity had allergies and a bout of difficulty breathing that required her to be in an oxygen tent for a week.

More recently, Charity and her husband had stopped coming over for dinner on Sundays, because they and their two young children got sick after every visit. They complained that Carmelita was serving them rotten food. She was mortified. Then it dawned on her and Ernie that they'd been putting ice cubes from their refrigerator's ice maker in everyone's pop. "It was stinking up our house, and we'd let them eat the ice," Ernie said bitterly.

Thompson was moved by how much Carmelita and Ernie had been through. Before he stood up to leave he promised to help them. In just a few hours, the couple had opened their lives to him, after welcoming him into their home, which he now viewed as one giant piece of evidence.

CHAPTER 2

When he started practicing law in West Virginia in 2002, Thompson formed a partnership with an attorney named Marty Smith in Charleston, the state capital. But he rarely used their office. His environmental cases had drawn him to Mingo County, a ninety-minute drive south on Route 119, and to be near his clients he started working out of an old hotel in Williamson, the county seat. The city of 3,300 lay in a bowl surrounded by hills with uneven ridges, and one side was lined by a concrete flood wall next to the Tug Fork. The dusty streets and weathered brick buildings gave the city the washed-out look of a patient whose life had been draining away for years. Most storefronts along East Second Avenue, the city's most vibrant stretch, had been taken over by lawyers, including one who promoted himself as "The Car Wreck King!" At one end of the avenue was a Goodwill and a concrete bridge that crossed into Kentucky. At the other end, trees of heaven grew inside the walls of an old bottling plant and Norfolk Southern trains loaded with coal eased out of town from a rail yard that was one of the largest on the railroad's Ohio-to-Virginia line.

Whenever he was in Williamson, Thompson booked room 309 at the Mountaineer Hotel. The tan-brick, five-story hotel had a blue-neon Art Deco sign on its awning and a ground-floor barbershop. A local lawyer named Mark Mitchell had recently bought the 1920s-era building and planned to restore it to its former brilliance. In the meantime, it was a faded gem—the hallways had no carpeting, many rooms didn't have heat, and there were few guests other than visiting railroad employees. For Thompson's purposes, however, the Mountaineer was ideal. Mitchell charged him forty dollars a night, and Thompson didn't mind the bare-bones accommodations or the fact that practically no one stayed there. The city's other hotel, the Sycamore Inn, attracted more business, but its owner had politely asked Thompson not to eat at the restaurant, fearing some of his customers wouldn't be happy with him serving an environmental lawyer. Thompson was obsessed with security, and he also liked that Mitchell had installed keypad locks at the hotel's front and side entrances.

The Mountaineer was only a few yards from the Mingo County Courthouse, a limestone building from the 1960s with flat, stylized columns on its facade. Between the two was the Coal House, built during the Great Depression from sixty-five tons of locally mined coal to showcase the region's best-known industry. The rectangular structure with an arched entrance housed the Tug Valley Chamber of Commerce. Out in front, a statue of Chief Logan, an eighteenth-century Cayuga leader affiliated with the Mingo tribe, stood in an aqua-blue fountain, frozen midstride in his buckskins and gazing across East Second Avenue toward the Mountaineer's parking garage, where Mark Mitchell often parked his silver DeLorean.

Thompson's first two lawsuits in Mingo County each involved a single landowner and simple claims of ground contamination, and he'd partnered with a lawyer from New Orleans and another from West Virginia. After a few visits to Rawl, it was obvious to him that he would need even more backing for the case against Massey. Only a big firm would be able to shoulder enough of the workload and costs. At a minimum, the case was going to require engineering and medical experts and law associates to review West Virginia case law on proving a toxic tort, a lawsuit in which people claim that their exposure to a chemical or dangerous substance caused their illness.

Thompson persuaded Van Bunch, a partner at Bonnett, Fairbourn, Friedman & Balint, PC, to drive five and a half hours to Williamson from his home in Signal Mountain, Tennessee, a suburb of Chattanooga, to meet with Ernie and Carmelita. Bunch was a liberal, a runner, and a committed environmentalist—he had been a founding member of the Green Party of Tennessee. A Deadhead since his first Grateful Dead show, in 1977, at the Fox Theatre in Atlanta, he was also a highly respected class-action litigator whose firm, based in Phoenix, had won billion-dollar settlements against the nation's biggest insurance companies. Thompson himself had once worked with Bunch on an insurance-related case in New Orleans. They were little more than friendly acquaintances by now, but Thompson knew Bunch's reputation, and he hoped that after years of high-stakes cases against the insurance, real estate, and securities industries, the prospect of representing people in rural West Virginia, some of whom lived at or below the poverty line, would appeal to him.

On a chilly, overcast day in April, about three months after Thompson's first visit to Larry's church, the two lawyers drove to Ernie and Carmelita's house. In borrowed coveralls, they climbed onto two four-wheelers behind Ernie and B.I., who had his white hat on again. The four-wheelers scrambled up a rocky trail behind Ernie's house, maneuvering around switchbacks and climbing up the mountain until B.I. cut his engine to point out thin plumes of smoke rising through some leaves. An underground mine fire had been consuming a coal seam for years, he and Ernie explained. Thompson had brought along a video camera, and he taped the smoke coming out of the ground, panning across the hillside.

At the top of the ridge, the men joined a network of trails that had been carved by ATV riders, weaving between the scrubby vegetation of a former surface mine. There were no other riders out. Ernie and B.I. drove to the northeast-facing side of the ridge and turned off their engines. Down in the valley was a tall, green, windowless building and a cluster of smaller ones. This industrial complex was the Sprouse Creek Processing Co. coal-preparation plant, a part of Rawl Sales, where the company cleaned the coal from area mines so that it could be shipped to customers. To the west of the plant, at a slightly higher elevation, was the impoundment, which resembled a dark-blue lake, with one side supported by an earthen dam with terraces down the valley. Tucked among the hills, the entire operation was invisible from Rawl and the other three communities along Route 49.

To Thompson, the impoundment seemed far away from Rawl, but he had no idea how far slurry could travel underground. He added that to the list of questions he planned to ask the environmental engineer and consultant he'd been working with since 2002: Scott Simonton, a former Marine with degrees in civil and environmental engineering who now taught at Marshall University in Huntington, an hour and a half north of Williamson.

Ernie and B.I. didn't think that leaks from the impoundment alone had caused the area's water contamination. As they took the two lawyers around, both Ernie and B.I. suggested that Rawl Sales had directly pumped coal waste from its processing plant into the hills. To Thompson, the final stop on the tour was the most intriguing. Ernie and B.I. drove to a place in the woods where two eight-inch-diameter pipes were sticking out of the ground. Ernie had heard a rumor that the company had drilled holes around the banks of the impoundment to drain slurry so the reservoir wouldn't become full. But these pipes were nowhere near the impoundment. B.I. believed that they were, in fact, slurry injection sites and that the company had covered the mountains with them. He said he had once been out hunting when he surprised two security guards for the company patrolling the area with AK-47s.

Thompson didn't quite know what to make of these theories. Ernie's sounded possible; B.I.'s was more outlandish. Thompson and Bunch searched the surrounding area for any pipes that might have transported slurry all this way, but they found nothing. For all Thompson knew, these holes might have been drilled by a natural gas company, or been used by Rawl Sales for some other purpose. Why would the company pump slurry into the hills when they'd built an impoundment to store it?

Back at the Browns' place, Ernie and Carmelita gave Bunch the same tour they had given Thompson. The house still had the same pungent rotten egg smell, and Thompson watched as Bunch's face registered astonishment when he walked in. In the kitchen, with its pink countertops, Carmelita showed Thompson and Bunch a collection of mason jars filled with her tap water lined up on the windowsill. When she gave the jars a shake, black particles rose up and turned the water gray. She unscrewed a lid, and the water still had a chemical odor. Thompson had already confirmed on his own that other homes had similarly bad water that came out oily and gray or rust-brown.

Sitting around the kitchen table and hearing about the Browns' problems with their water, Bunch began to see the mason jars—and the Browns' house itself—as evidence, just as Thompson had. Bunch had grown up in Tennessee, and his voice still had some Appalachia in it as he looked at Ernie, Carmelita, and B.I. and said: "I'm going to help y'all. I'm going to help y'all get clean water."

• • •

Back in Williamson, the lawyers traded notes at Starters, a sports bar half a block from the courthouse. The Rawl Sales operation was clearly the only industrial site in the area, and so far, the company's impoundment was the prime suspect for the contaminated wells, though it was hard to see how slurry from that distant lake could end up in the jars above the Browns' kitchen sink. One thing had stunned Bunch, and he mentioned it to Thompson: the mountain was on fire. If there were hidden fires, could there also be hidden slurry?

Bunch told Thompson he would talk to his partners and, if they gave the green light, he'd have an agreement drawn up for how Thompson's and Bunch's firms would split costs. They both thought the lawsuit should be filed as a class action. Eventually they could sign up as many people as possible in the four communities, but, to start, they would need only a few named plaintiffs on a complaint. That left plenty to do. They had to get several sets of well tests, collect medical records and property deeds, take depositions. Hire experts in mining, toxicology, and epidemiology, as well as someone who could calculate economic losses, such as the decline in value of a house without drinkable water.

As they ate chicken tenders and salads and drank beers, Bunch tempered Thompson's enthusiasm, reminding him that the litigation could take several years and that he still needed approval from his partners to invest staff and resources in the case. Even though Bunch was more sober-minded, he had seen enough to make him think there could be a strong case. Bunch suspected his partners in Phoenix would like the idea of going after Massey, a company with billions of dollars in annual revenue that could afford to pay for the inconvenience and suffering it had caused along Route 49.

Thompson said the company could start by doing something it had so far refused to do: give people bottled water to drink. In his view, the situation at the Browns in particular was dire. "Priority number one is clean fucking water," he said.

On April 23, 2004, with the support of Larry, Ernie, B.I., and a few others, Thompson sent a letter to Massey's headquarters in Richmond, Virginia, demanding replacement drinking water for the four communities within twenty-four hours. The letter asked Massey to provide a clean, permanent water supply, to regularly test the communities' water, to treat any coal slurry leaking from the impoundment, and to put out the mine fires in the area. Finally, Thompson requested that Massey set up a medical monitoring program to protect residents from "ill health effects" they might develop from the contaminated water.

"My clients and their families depend for their daily existence on water drawn from wells that have been contaminated by the mining operations of Rawl Sales and Processing," Thompson wrote. "The contaminated water table in the Rawl, Lick Creek, Merrimac, and Sprigg communities presents a threat to the environment and human health. I hope that we can work together to abate this dangerous public nuisance."

The letter was bold in its demands, given that Thompson was just starting to gather evidence. But the letter did something else: it took the years of frustration and the growing fears of health problems in the communities and focused them into a single threat of litigation the company couldn't ignore.

About a week later, a faxed version of Thompson's letter reached Don Blankenship's desk at his office in Belfry, Kentucky, along Route 119 south of Williamson. It was the CEO's habit to write instructions on faxes. As Thompson would later learn, Blankenship wrote a single word in the margin of his letter: "Shane."

Shane Harvey, Massey's general counsel, replied to Thompson on May 10. Harvey, who was in his thirties but had the sober demeanor and close-cropped hair of a recent ROTC cadet, claimed to share Thompson's sense of urgency. "Please contact me immediately with your proof that the water is unsafe and your proof that the water has been contaminated by Rawl Sales & Processing," Harvey wrote. "We take this matter seriously and encourage you to be open and forthcoming in providing the information necessary to evaluate the issues you have raised."

Harvey's request for proof laid bare Thompson's biggest challenge. To force any action from Massey, he needed to present clear evidence that the company was responsible for the water contamination and likely had been negligent in letting it happen.

Even then, Massey was sure to put up a fight.

CHAPTER 3

Thompson soon learned that many of the 700 or so people living in 250 homes between the hills along Route 49 had been trying to get clean drinking water for so long that they had given themselves a name: the Forgotten Communities.

One of his first guides through this history was B.I. Sammons, who lived in Lick Creek, four miles east of Williamson. Thompson almost missed the turnoff where the road had been rerouted years ago. Around a tall stand of bushes, there were trailers and other homes along a paved road. A creek ran down the middle of the hollow, and Thompson had to cross a concrete slab bridge to park at B.I.'s home. The two-story house, yellow with brown trim, would have fit in on any suburban street. But as he walked up to the front door, Thompson saw that the paint was flaking and the brick steps he stood on were crumbling. Inside, a stuffed fox with a squirrel in its mouth collected dust on a shelf, and three or four trucker hats, all white, were lined up on the back of the living room couch.

Thompson never knew what to make of the older man's conspiratorial stories. One of B.I.'s most lurid tales involved bodies being dropped from helicopters into the Rawl Sales impoundment to cover up murders. B.I.'s own past wasn't spotless. A former deputy sheriff, he had been indicted in the 1980s, along with more than fifty other local officials and residents of the town of Kermit, when federal prosecutors cracked a drug ring and exposed widespread corruption in the county. B.I. had pleaded guilty to taking a five-hundred-dollar bribe, and court records showed that he had spent some time at a minimum-security prison camp for nonviolent offenders in Terre Haute, Indiana. The lawyer seeking clemency for him at the time had been Michael Thornsbury, who was now the county's circuit court judge. In the mid-1990s, while working as a coal truck driver, B.I. had fallen from a truck onto

19

his back and suffered a concussion and memory loss—he had no recollection of being arrested and serving time.

A good deal of what B.I. said about the water, however, Thompson couldn't dismiss. B.I.'s wife, Deborah, was a nurse, and her records of the family's many health problems matched B.I.'s descriptions: headaches, rashes, infections, and diarrhea that she attributed to "being in the water," as well as trips to the emergency room for their son and daughter, who suffered from fevers and infections. Their dentist had said their children "had the softest teeth he had ever seen," she recalled. B.I. didn't spare any details. One night his son had woken up with a fever, screaming in pain. He had pus coming out of his penis. A doctor had confirmed the boy had a urinary tract infection.

B.I. said his water had gone bad in the early 1990s but that people had known about risks well before that. He told Thompson about a morning in 1984 when he woke up to find the creek in front of his house flooded with coal slurry. This story also sounded far-fetched to Thompson at first, but others corroborated the accident. Somewhere above Lick Creek, a slurry line had ruptured in the night and by morning black sludge filled the length of the hollow and was flowing into the Tug Fork. Rawl Sales had brought backhoes and other equipment to clean up the spill, but the creek wasn't the same afterward. B.I. said he used to catch "minners" at the edge of his yard to use for bait, but after the spill the fish never came back. It was clear this loss pained him, on top of everything he believed his family had been through as a result of the water. Some of B.I.'s friends told Thompson he could believe about half of what B.I. said. But even that, Thompson had come to realize, was an alarming amount of suffering.

By the late 1980s, other people living along Route 49 found that their water occasionally began to smell and look rusty or gray. Those who could afford it bought cases of bottled water at Walmart or Big Lots, and others filled jugs at a spring off Route 49. Thompson was stunned to learn that many people had been forced to pay for bottled water for years, replace filters frequently on their wells, and buy new dishwashers and water heaters that wore out quicker because of the water. One man had replaced his water heater three times in twelve years. Mingo County was one of the poorest counties in the nation; in 1990, nearly a third of its 33,500 residents lived below the poverty line.

Thompson told people he met with in the four communities to pull together any receipts they had kept for bottled water, water filters, and plumbing fixtures.

People had complained to Rawl Sales, but the company had apparently always denied that any of its mining activities or coal processing had affected any wells. Back in the 1980s, Carmelita had called Rawl Sales and asked a mining engineer to test their well. An employee came to take water samples periodically but never gave her any results. In 1987, Ernie was so frustrated that he and Carmelita had never received any information that he chased the man from their property and told him not to return.

B.I. took Thompson to the home of his neighbor Maude Rice, a widow with a white perm who lived in a double-wide with wood paneling and deep-carpeted floors. Polite but tough, Rice explained that she had sued Rawl Sales in 1995, alleging that its mining activities had contaminated her well water, which had started to smell like sulfur. Her complaints, along with B.I.'s, prompted the state to send a geologist to study about three dozen wells in Lick Creek that year. The geologist found that Rice's well was likely affected by an abandoned mine in the Pond Creek seam, and another well at the home of Julius Cooper had probably been affected by an abandoned mine in the Alma seam. The mines were in two of the nine major coal seams—layered like the icing in a cake—that had been mined extensively in the area since the early 1900s. Bacteria that converted sulfates into hydrogen sulfide likely accounted for the rotten egg odor in many of the area's wells, he noted.

The state expert concluded that only Cooper's well had been affected by pre-1977 mining, which would make Cooper eligible, under the Surface Mining Control and Reclamation Act of 1977, to receive federal money to get a new well or replacement water. Thompson didn't know whether Cooper was ever able to tap those funds, but he doubted it because he later found a letter from December 1995 in which Cooper had appealed directly to Don Blankenship to help him pay for a new well.

Still, the state report gave Thompson the first hard evidence of slurry injection. The geologist had noted that Rawl Sales had pumped slurry into the abandoned Pond Creek mine works through a single hole at the head of Lick Creek in the early 1980s, and he mentioned the slurry spill there in 1984. He had concluded that the slurry in the old mine likely hadn't affected most wells he sampled. Thompson wasn't so sure.

By the mid-1990s, B.I. and a handful of his neighbors were determined to get help from the county or state to pay for a municipal water line that would carry clean drinking water from Williamson or Matewan, ten miles to the southeast. But for years, they got nowhere. One of B.I.'s allies in the campaign for clean water was James "Bo" Scott, another former Massey miner who lived in Rawl. A towering man with a beard of gray stubble, Bo explained to Thompson that Massey would never admit that its operations had contaminated drinking water— even if the cost was minimal. This was how the company maintained its dominance in the coalfields, he said.

"Massey has always been this way. I will spend ten thousand dollars just to keep from paying you a hundred dollars," Bo said. "To show you that I can beat you."

Bo spoke from experience: he'd spent years fighting Massey over injuries he'd received in 1996, when he had been a foreman at a mine across the border in Kentucky. A state inspector had shut the mine because the sandstone roof was unstable. The company was using a dangerous technique known as retreat mining, in which miners work their way out of the mine, removing coal pillars and letting the roof collapse in stages behind them. This allowed the company to extract more coal, but there was nothing left to hold the mountain up. As Bo told it, a supervisor ordered him and two contractors to reenter the mine and see what repairs were needed for the mine to reopen. After they went in, the roof caved in. One rock crushed Bo, pinning him down and severing an artery in his left leg. After he was freed, he was rushed to Williamson Memorial Hospital for emergency surgery. Doctors put thirty-two stitches and sixteen clamps into his leg. "I like to bled to death," he said. The first visitor in his hospital room was the mine's superintendent, Bo said, and he made it clear the company wouldn't take responsibility for sending the men underground again. Massey fought Bo for more than five years over his workers' compensation benefits, until he had finally prevailed at the Supreme Court of Kentucky.

Bo walked with a limp and had lost feeling in his damaged leg, and now he stayed busy preaching at area churches. Bo had been friends with Ernie Brown since they were kids, and he still had a photo of students from different grades standing on the steps of the elementary school in Cinderella, another nearby coal camp. With their buzz cuts and sharp plaid shirts, the two friends wear big smiles, as does a young Larry Brown, two grades higher. All these years later, Ernie and Bo had both suffered disabling injuries in Massey mines. And all three men now had tainted water running through their homes.

In the late 1990s, the *Williamson Daily News* carried articles in which Bo argued that blasting on Rawl Sales' surface mine above the hollow had contaminated people's wells. From 1998 to 2002, he wrote letters to the county's three commissioners, as well as to his congressman and West Virginia's two senators, but they offered little or no assistance.

On February 23, 2000, Senator Robert Byrd, known as the "King of Pork" for bringing billions of dollars to West Virginia for the dozens of buildings, bridges, and expressways that bore his name, replied that he'd help if an appropriate sponsor contacted him. "Most Americans take safe drinking water for granted," Senator Byrd wrote. "Unfortunately, we in West Virginia know all too well that safe drinking water is not one of life's certainties." That same year, when the state failed to approve a Small Cities Block Grant to fund a water line to Lick Creek, the county's commissioners wrote to Governor Cecil Underwood. "These people are desperate for a safe, potable water supply now, not in the future," the commissioners wrote. "We do not know where to turn from here."

In 2001, the state hired a civil engineering firm to study the need for a municipal water line to the four communities. The report found "severe problems with ground water sources within the study area" caused by the decades of coal mining prior to 1977, rather than Rawl Sales' more recent activities. The "only acceptable and viable resolution," the firm concluded, was a water line from Williamson at a cost of nearly $2.7 million, or about $10,692 per household. That was the price for safe drinking water. The project would be eligible for federal funds, because the firm concluded that the water had been degraded by mining that took place decades earlier. Yet when Thompson read the report, he noticed there were no references to "slurry" or "injection," even though a Rawl Sales official was listed as having been interviewed.

But still no water came. When the state failed to take action, Bo and B.I. were so exasperated that they threatened to secede from the state of West Virginia and join Kentucky. B.I. told a reporter for the *Lexington Herald-Leader* he would have no trouble getting 750 people in the communities to sign a petition to leave West Virginia. No elected official on either side of the Tug Fork took the men seriously. On January 24, 2002, Joe Manchin, then West Virginia's secretary of state, wrote to Bo and said he admired his "true *Mountaineer* spirit," but he couldn't intervene.

In a final act of desperation, someone—all these years later, it wasn't clear exactly who—had a six-foot-wide, red-and-white sign printed. The person planted their plea in the weeds near the turnoff to Lick Creek:

COMMUNITIES FORGOTTEN
PLEASE SUPPORT
LICK CREEK - RAWL
MERRIMAC - SPRIGG
GETTING A WATER SYSTEM

It was a sign that Don Blankenship himself would have passed regularly, coming from his home in Sprigg, a few miles to the east on Route 49.

CHAPTER 4

Thompson had a long way to go to prove that Rawl Sales was responsible for the discolored water coming out of his clients' taps. But he had plenty of evidence that Massey had been having problems with other slurry impoundments in the region.

One of the worst environmental disasters in US history had struck just after midnight on October 11, 2000, when a Massey impoundment in Martin County, Kentucky, ruptured and sent more than 300 million gallons of coal slurry through old mine workings and out the side of a hill. Slurry was sucked from the reservoir like bathwater draining from a tub, until workers finally plugged the hole. The sludge polluted more than a hundred miles of streams, killing fish and other aquatic life. Hours after the accident, slurry lining creeks and coating streets and properties looked like a vast flow of lava. In one neighborhood, the sludge rose to the rim of a basketball hoop. Massey called the impoundment breakthrough "an act of God." But perhaps the only divine action was that no one was killed or seriously injured. The federal Mine Safety and Health Administration, or MSHA, part of the Department of Labor, then headed by Elaine Chao, the wife of Kentucky senator Mitch McConnell, fined Massey $110,000. A Kentucky judge cut that to $5,600. (Massey paid $3.5 million in state fines and $46 million for the cleanup, both of which were covered by its insurance companies.)

Thompson knew the devastation had raised alarms about the dangers of impoundments across the Appalachian coalfields. Several groups, including the Ohio Valley Environmental Coalition (OVEC), set up the Sludge Safety Project to help communities affected by impoundments and coal slurry and to press for stronger government oversight. When activists learned that people in Rawl with contaminated wells were living near another Massey impoundment, they went to meet with B.I., Larry Brown, and others. It was Vivian Stockman, the head of OVEC, who'd first suggested to B.I. in early 2004 that he call Thompson, after she heard about his settlement with Arch Coal.

A few months earlier, a stream ecologist from Wheeling Jesuit University, Ben Stout, had driven down from the state's northern panhandle to find out what was happening with people's water in Mingo County. Stout, a wiry man with a bright smile and an earnest face weathered from fieldwork, was arguably the foremost expert in West Virginia on coal slurry impoundments and the effects of mining on streams. He tracked impoundment accidents on a poster in his lab classroom in Wheeling. The first entry was the infamous Buffalo Creek disaster in 1972: a Pittston Coal slurry dam in Logan County had burst, and 132 million gallons of slurry swept through a hollow, killing 125 people. Massey Energy had been responsible for more than half of the fifty-three smaller spills that had occurred since, Stout had found.

Thompson heard from Ernie and Carmelita Brown that Stout had knocked on their door just a few weeks before Thompson himself visited them. Carmelita wouldn't let Stout in at first, because she thought he might work for Massey. But she changed her mind when she saw a female graduate student, Jomana Papillo, with him—Carmelita didn't think Massey would hire a woman as an engineer. Stout took samples of the Browns' well and sent them to an independent lab. The results revealed high levels of iron, manganese, arsenic, and sodium, and lower levels of barium and aluminum. The levels varied widely on different days; each sample was like a snapshot of the metals in the water at that moment. Stout was also disturbed by the levels of hydrogen sulfide permeating their home, which he determined were higher than the federal limits for workplaces. He spent days taking water samples from another dozen homes, from the creeks that ran through Rawl and Lick Creek, and from the Tug Fork. When he got those results back from a lab, he called all the families and warned them not to drink the water or use it for any purpose, if they could help it.

Thompson was eager to see what Stout would find across the four communities. In the meantime, he continued to interview people about their water and their health. OVEC's organizing had given Thompson a head start, and Ernie and B.I. went door-to-door, asking people to fill out a detailed health survey. They eventually brought him more than a hundred responses. He knocked on doors and met with people in their homes. Most welcomed him, but some regarded him with suspicion, referring to him when he wasn't around as "the lawyer from Louisiana." What residents wanted most, Thompson came to realize, was to protect their family's well-being. Though they appreciated the help of young activists, few members of the community saw themselves as environmentalists. For them, taking on Massey wasn't about saving a mountain. It was about making a coal company do the right thing.

As much as people took pride in coal mining, there was also distrust toward coal companies that went back generations. Larry Brown told Thompson about his grandfather, who had come to the area seeking work in the 1920s and had taken a job manning a conveyor system that hauled coal over the hills above Rawl. After his grandfather was struck in the head on two occasions by a heavy piece of machinery, the company fired him without providing any benefits. "They treated people like they were nobodies, just dumb hillbillies," Larry said. In the next breath, he said he *was* a hillbilly. In the early 1970s, he and Brenda had moved away to try life elsewhere, and he took a job as a laborer for the navy building nuclear submarines in Connecticut. But after a year, the couple returned to the place that was home. If the word "hillbilly" had any meaning at all, Larry seemed to say, it meant someone who loved living among these hills.

He and Brenda had paid a high price for coming home. Normally a fast-talker with a mischievous side, Larry got serious when he blamed his well water for the boils and rashes and stomach problems they'd been enduring. He said he wondered now if the water had caused his daughter's miscarriages or the seizures his son had growing up. Brenda's niece Chastity Dawn Prince had died at age four of a rare kidney cancer. The girl had visited Larry and Brenda several times a week, sleeping over and drinking their well water along with the rest of the family. Thompson told Larry he would look into filing a wrongful death claim on her behalf if he found a link between the water and her cancer. The scope of the case, Thompson was starting to realize, could extend to people who'd lived in the communities in the past, and others who had visited regularly.

Thompson knew that as one of the most respected members of the community, Larry would be a key plaintiff. Larry said he wasn't afraid of suing Massey; his faith had made him fearless. He'd been born again one afternoon in 1977, when he was working on a crew paving roads in Williamson. As he bent down to take a drink at a water fountain, a voice told him to pray. As Larry told it, the world around him became more vibrant, and all his interactions with people took on deeper meaning. Soon with the help of his family and neighbors, he built the church next to his double-wide. Now on Wednesday and Friday evenings, he played guitar for a handful of people who sang along and stood up to testify. He lit up when he recalled taking people down to the river to baptize them anytime they were willing, day or night. "I been there when it's thundering and lightning and storming," Larry said. "People say, 'Ain't you scared?' I say, 'What you scared of? If He's going to take us, man, what a way to go! We're in His Will.'"

In order to build his case, Thompson needed to go beyond people's health and find out how the water had affected their property and work lives. He also needed to become more familiar with the history of mining in the area and how interwoven it was with his clients' lives. He met other former miners like Frank Coleman, who lived at the mouth of Rawl in a gray house with a cinder-block first floor. Coal miners would have the most credibility in front of a jury, Thompson reasoned, because they would be perceived as being the least likely people to bring a frivolous water contamination lawsuit against a coal company. They also knew more intimately than anyone how coal was mined and cleaned. Years after he quit working underground, Coleman said he could hear trains go by on the other side of Route 49 and know from the sound of the wheels if the cars were loaded with coal or not.

Coleman had thinning reddish hair and the watchful eyes of someone who had been in his share of fights. "Been fightin' all my life," he said in a husky voice. He had grown up poor and white in Matewan, in a community that was referred to at the time as the "colored coal camp," a reminder of the days when coal companies segregated miners. Most of his quarrels growing up were with his older brother, and another boy who challenged him to fights until Coleman knocked him out one day. He moved out of his mother's house and started working in local mines before he was old enough to drive. Then, when he was still a teen, he left on a train from Matewan to serve in Vietnam. He told a cinematic tale of being captured by North Vietnamese soldiers, escaping, and finally getting shot while serving as a machine gunner on a Huey helicopter. After his discharge, he returned to Mingo County restless and full of anger and worked in the mines cutting coal. For a long time, the only peace he could find, he said, came from lying back in a canoe and floating down the Tug Fork.

Coleman had worked for a number of companies, including Massey, and like Ernie Brown, he had permanently injured his back. He took painkillers and, when he watched TV, propped his feet up on a coffee table to ease his discomfort. He thought his well water might have caused his stomach and kidney problems. One day, after cutting his lawn, he used his garden hose to cool off and let the water run over his face. When his eyes became infected, he blamed that on the water too. Another time, while he was cleaning a spill in his basement, some liquid from his hot water heater got into a cut on his right hand. An infection required several surgeries. Now the scars on the back of his hand turned white when he made a fist.

Thompson saw signs of the area's mining past everywhere. Coleman explained that a flat rectangle in his yard marked the place where a company store had once stood. Across Dick Williamson Branch Road was a fenced-in property owned by Rawl Sales. A mine had closed there in the 1980s, Coleman said. During the 1977 flood, the Tug Fork had risen so high that the water came over Route 49 and covered the first floor of Coleman's house, which Rawl Sales had owned at the time. Farther upstream, the company had put train engines on a bridge to keep it from being swept away. Coleman said hogs from Kentucky had been carried across the river and pulled into the old Rawl Sales mine.

Even residents who had prospered working for Massey often had complicated relationships with the company, as was the case with another former miner in Rawl, Donald Dillon. Well into his sixties but still sharp and fit, Dillon had worked for Massey as an electrician, a high-paying job in the mines. He had earned enough to buy two houses in Rawl and build a third that was the biggest in the hollow. Even so, Dillon didn't trust Massey. He believed the company had fired him from a job when he was a few months short of the full vesting of his pension so it could save money. The decision had cost him about four hundred dollars every month since his retirement.

Dillon had the same self-reliant streak Thompson had seen in other people in the area. He said he'd been hot-tempered in his youth but he'd become more forgiving after he was born again and started attending church with his wife, Mary. Even so, he still carried a pearl-handled Derringer with two bullets in his front pocket.

Dillon also understood the effects of the water firsthand. He had grown up drinking from a well in Rawl, and he recalled that the water then was clean and "so cold it hurt your teeth." Now it wasn't fit to drink. He had burned through his share of water heaters and plumbing fixtures. And he was worried about Mary. She had been suffering from heart disease and cirrhosis of the liver, among other conditions, and she had been growing frailer each year. The affable Dillon became reticent when the subject of her health came up, and Thompson could feel his concern.

Dillon offered to drive Thompson around so the lawyer could better understand the terrain. Up until the 1980s, he explained, men living in Rawl had been able to get up in the morning and walk with a meal bucket to a mine portal, as two generations of miners had done before them. After their shifts, they washed at the mine's bathhouse and walked back home for supper. Dillon had his own stories about slurry injection. In the 1980s, a crew of men had been forced to evacuate a Rawl Sales mine when slurry started flooding the active section. He said that another time the superintendent at the processing plant had been nearly killed when a slurry line blew up. Thompson took notes, and realized his own clients knew as much about the area's mining as any experts he might find.

From Rawl, Dillon followed Route 49 south toward Merrimac. The narrow bumpy road hugged the mountain, with a wall of rock to the left and a bent guardrail on the right, the only thing keeping one from tumbling down to the river below. At Merrimac, houses and trailers were spread out on flat land near the river. Then they continued east toward Sprigg, where there was a cluster of homes tucked into a hill. The farthest one they came to belonged to Thelma Parsley. Through her kitchen window, Parsley could see the fairway-like lawn, the black electric gate beside Route 49, and the long drive up to the bright-green house where Don Blankenship lived. The old superintendent's house had stood there since 1914, when it was built by U.S. Steel for an executive who founded the Crystal Block mining companies. Today, the property was called Crystal Acres.

Why would Blankenship continue living here, Thompson wondered, in one of the communities where people were getting sick from their well water? Parsley had the answer: she had watched construction workers lay pipe for a city water line from Matewan to the Tug Valley Country Club across the road and then to Blankenship's house, where it ended. The water line didn't reach Thelma Parsley's place—or any of the homes of the other seven hundred people living between there and Lick Creek.

On September 16, 2004, Thompson sued Massey, with backing from Van Bunch's law firm. He filed the lawsuit in Mingo County court as a class action, naming Larry Brown, B.I. Sammons, Frank Coleman, and three other residents as the plaintiffs.

Thompson had no smoking gun linking Massey to the contaminated water. Nevertheless he alleged that the company had conducted "negligent, dangerous, hazardous and/or ultra-hazardous mining activities in and around Rawl for the last 40 years." He claimed that during the construction of its impoundment, Rawl Sales had drilled holes so excess slurry would drain into abandoned mine works below, the theory he got from Ernie Brown. Thompson said Rawl Sales negligently abandoned its mines, causing underground fires that destabilized the rock strata. Blasting on Massey's property further shook the ground, he wrote. The resulting water contamination had led to diseases in his clients—B.I. Sammons and others had suffered from kidney stones, kidney failure, painful urination, chronic diarrhea, and even cancer, Thompson wrote—and rendered their properties worthless. As he had mentioned in his letter to Massey that spring, he and Bunch wanted the company to fund a medical monitoring program so doctors could screen the residents for illnesses caused by the water.

In the twenty-four-page lawsuit, Thompson claimed that Massey managers knew or should have known that their activities would result in an increased risk of disease. He alleged that the company violated the state's surface mining law; its groundwater protection act and water pollution control act; and a state law requiring the preservation of natural streams. On top of that he included a count of "tort of outrage," a count of unjust enrichment, and damages from personal injury and the loss of property, plus punitive damages for Massey's "intentional, grossly negligent and reprehensible actions."

Thompson filed the lawsuit electronically. It was like launching a stone from a distance: nothing would happen for a while. But eventually the giant would feel the blow and respond.

CHAPTER 5

Thompson's hometown of Point Pleasant, on the Ohio River 120 miles north of Williamson, was surrounded by farms, iron foundries, and power plants. It was a world away from the southern coalfields. The family's ranch house on a corner lot had a sloping gray roof and two-car garage, and the backyard ran down to some woods and a Defense Department strategic materials depot, with long single-story buildings surrounded by a double fence topped with barbed wire and under constant guard, which became a source of fascination. In the afternoons, when Thompson got home from school, he typically watched cartoons with his father, whose shift ended early. A block away, Ordnance Elementary School was surrounded by baseball and football fields, and there were always kids around for pickup games. In fifth grade, Thompson tried to stop his friends from ripping out a sapling at the edge of the fields to make way for an end zone. He later referred to the incident as his first environmental stand. He watched as his friends bent the tree down and ripped it out. "I failed to protect the landscape," he joked later. "It's bare today."

Kevin Wayne Thompson was born on May 25, 1963, at St. Mary's Hospital in Huntington, West Virginia. His father, Carl, a radiologist, and his mother, Vada, adopted him days after his birth. Thompson later said his parents told him early on that he'd been adopted, and he never had a desire to track down his birth parents. Both of Thompson's adoptive grandfathers were troopers with the West Virginia State Police—one was nicknamed Snake, the other Slim. They told stories at the dinner table about moonshining, gambling, and organized crime. The men helped instill the belief in their grandson that coal companies frequently did more harm than good. One grandfather told a story about investigating an explosion that had ripped through a coal mine. After going undercover, he learned that a manager had set the charge himself to frame the mine workers' union. The union, however, didn't fare much better in the family's estimation. Thompson learned that one of the most dangerous places for a state trooper to be was on a picket line keeping the peace between striking miners and company security guards.

From an early age, Thompson knew that coal drove the state's politics, and that the farther south one traveled in West Virginia the more sway it held. Thompson's mother, Vada Wilkerson, had been raised in a coal camp near Fayetteville, about an hour southeast of Charleston, in the 1930s. (By a strange coincidence, Fayetteville was the town where the founder of Massey Energy, A. T. Massey, had once run a coal company store. After it burned down, he moved to Richmond, Virginia, where he started a small coal brokerage that would go on to become one of the nation's biggest coal companies.) She often told her son stories about the local coal company's influence in the town. Even though her father was a state trooper, Vada was lower in the social order than the children of the men who oversaw the local mines. She remembered that Patty Holt, whose father was superintendent of the local mine and who was thought to be related to the governor of West Virginia, Homer A. Holt, sat in front of her in junior high. Because her family didn't have indoor plumbing, Vada usually bathed once a week. At the end of one of those weeks, Patty Holt raised her hand and asked the teacher to have Vada moved farther away from her, because she smelled bad. Vada shrank inside and her face flushed. She felt the other girl had intended to humiliate her in front of her classmates. Rather than defend her, the teacher bowed to Patty Holt's wishes and asked Vada to move to a seat in the back of the classroom. Vada said nothing and moved. But the moment became frozen in time, and it never lost its power in the retelling. Thompson, who heard the story often in his childhood, held on to its message, just as his mother had: the coal industry had empowered a select group of people who often used that power, in both consequential and petty ways, to oppress others.

By the time Thompson was in high school, he was dreaming of becoming a broadcast journalist. He saw himself as a foreign correspondent reporting on terror plots in the Middle East and coups in Africa, the camera bringing his face into millions of American living rooms. As a teenager with more immediate concerns, he discovered that traveling speech competitions offered the best way to meet girls from other schools. And he was good at giving speeches off the cuff. In his junior year, he won first place in a statewide competition in the Boys Extemporaneous category. Years later, Melba Lynn Shank, who sat next to him in English and Latin classes, still recalled his thick head of hair and clear speaking voice. "I could always picture him being a broadcaster, a weatherman," she said.

Thompson studied broadcast journalism at Marshall University, but then he took the LSAT, partly because his father thought having a law degree was a good backup plan. Tulane University School of Law was the best-ranked school that accepted him, and he decided to go. Once there, Thompson fell in love with New Orleans, with its shotgun houses, narrow bayous, and vibrant nightlife. He drank hard and late into the night in uptown bars, shunning the tourist-jammed French Quarter, until, in his third year of law school, he signed up to row in a novice boat for the Tulane crew team under head coach Bob Jaugstetter. After that, he got up before dawn on rowing days. He liked the physical challenge of the sport as much as moving across the water in the early morning. He had grown up next to the Ohio River, and New Orleans, where those waters finally reached the Gulf of Mexico, felt like home.

Even as a law student, Thompson was ready to break from the traditional path most lawyers followed. Before he graduated from Tulane, he and a friend decided to start a business videotaping depositions for law firms. In the late 1980s, it was a novel idea, and the potential market—law firms across the United States—was massive. With minimal planning, Thompson and his friend Marko Markovich, a second-year MBA student, each put up $150. They checked out a video camera from the law school and hired an undergraduate communications major at $7 an hour. They walked the student through how to videotape a deposition, something neither had done before, and then they sent him out with equipment they didn't own. The trial run—it was a divorce case—was a success. The partners started charging law firms $125 an hour. They came up with a logo and business cards and called the company Legal Process.

After Thompson graduated and passed the bar in the spring of 1988, he accepted a one-year position working in the antitrust division of the Office of the West Virginia Attorney General. He thought the job offered a chance to chase white-collar criminals, but after months in a basement indexing files, he was eager to get back to his fledgling business. He and Markovich soon opened offices in Baton Rouge and Chicago, and they started providing graphics and technicians to help attorneys make presentations during trials.

Thompson also put his tech savvy to use. When he learned that videotapes contained an unused audio track, he and Markovich invented a system that made their taped depositions searchable by keywords—the kind of functionality that only became common years later with digital recording. Their invention was the size of an arcade game, a clunky cabinet with a video screen, a knob, and a keyboard. It was so heavy that two people had to push it into a courtroom. But it struck fear into opposing lawyers because it enabled Thompson's clients to challenge the testimony of a witness—sometimes while they were still on the witness stand. Thompson would type a few commands and give the knob a twist. Then he would let the jury watch the witness on the video screen say something damning or contradictory.

His consulting work let him observe hundreds of lawyers conduct depositions and handle witnesses and evidence in front of a jury. In the early 1990s, Legal Process taped some six thousand hours' worth of depositions in the wave of breast implant litigation that was sweeping the country. Thompson was also making money faster than he could spend it. He worked long hours and then stayed up drinking and partying. He took dates to see his favorite band, the Radiators, play New Orleans–infused funk and swamp rock. When Thompson heard that Kim Basinger was in the city, he decided to ask her out if he ever ran into her, even though she was married. "I had resolved that she needed to meet me and take me as a lover," he joked years later. One Saturday morning, he was at a coffee shop near his office and felt the eyes of all the women in the shop on him. He thought he must look irresistible in his new suit, which was an unusual shade of blue. Then he realized all the eyes were focused just behind him. He turned and saw Alec Baldwin, Basinger's husband, standing in his own dark-blue suit. "This was Alec Baldwin in 1994," Thompson said. "He was phenomenally handsome." Thompson gave up his quest for Kim Basinger on the spot.

"It sucks to have to wear a suit on a Saturday, doesn't it?" he recalled Baldwin saying to him.

"Kevin's always been a bit of a free spirit," another former partner at Legal Process, Dan Regard, said. "A real affable person—an optimist, a people-oriented extrovert. Not an extrovert in a hard-charging way. The person who can walk into the room and become your best friend."

At times, Thompson's life resembled a cross between an Aaron Spelling TV drama and a gonzo version of the journalism career he had once dreamed of pursuing. When he joined two college friends for a night in Tijuana, one of them, a burly lawyer named John Alderman, gave the manager of a Dunkin' Donuts five dollars to tell him where the "bad people" go. The three friends got blind drunk at a Polynesian-themed strip club, and Thompson ended up dancing naked after several women pulled him onstage. On his way out, a table of Americans handed him a baseball cap full of dollar bills. An older man in the group said, "Twenty years in the navy, and that's the best floor show I've ever seen."

Then a pair of events put the brakes on his lifestyle. In November 1994, Thompson went back to his parents' house in Point Pleasant for Thanksgiving. The next day, after playing touch football, he went with his friend Alderman to a bar across the river in Gallipolis, Ohio, and met his future wife, Kathleen.

"He's got his leather jacket on and his entourage with him and they come in and take over a table," Kathleen recalled. She and Thompson talked all evening and for their first date the next day, he drove her out to the abandoned TNT factory outside Point Pleasant. "It was one of the most bizarre first dates you could have," Kathleen said. The same night, while driving, Kevin and Kathleen saw a house on fire, and then a policeman stopped them. "He says, 'Have you seen any legs across the road?' And we're like, 'What?' He said, 'Somebody's reported somebody's dead up here with legs across the road.' And Kevin and I are like, 'Okay, that's a little weird.'"

The TNT factory, an abandoned World War II–era munitions plant, was a throwback to Thompson's childhood. In the fall of 1966, Point Pleasant was terrorized by a winged creature that young couples spotted nearby in the misty woods. Newspaper headlines fed the hysteria, and then a copyeditor gave the monster a name: the Mothman.

That same year, UFO sightings proliferated near the site, which was an ideal setting for a paranormal encounter, with toxic pools and mysterious earth-covered concrete domes where explosives had been stored. People seemed to stop seeing the Mothman only after the Silver Bridge connecting Point Pleasant to Gallipolis collapsed during rush hour on December 15, 1967, killing forty-six people. Thompson's father used to drive him through the TNT area, and the tales his sister Carlene told him about the monster gave him a thrill that never left him.

He and Kathleen never saw a dead body but they spent the night talking about growing up on opposite sides of the Ohio River. They realized that Kathleen's father, who was an orthopedist, had worked with Thompson's father. Then she realized that his sister was author Carlene Thompson, who wrote dark thrillers that she'd admired for years. Kathleen was blond and petite, with an intellect that matched Thompson's. She worked for an insurance company in Columbus, Ohio, and had a two-year-old daughter named Kelsey. On the following Monday, Thompson was back in New Orleans and called her to ask her out to dinner. When Kathleen laughed and pointed out that they were hundreds of miles apart, Thompson said, "Not if you pick me up at the airport." He booked a flight for the next day.

Two years later, the couple married on the Saturday after Thanksgiving. They bought a rambling three-story house in New Orleans that had been built in 1880 by a judge, and Kathleen filled it with books and dogs—Samson, a golden retriever, and Delilah, a Lab mix, and Thompson's favorite, a gray cairn terrier named Blue. Like Thompson, Kathleen had an independent streak. She had grown up on a farm and was comfortable around guns. She owned a .45 Magnum and a black .38 Smith & Wesson with a wooden handle that she sometimes kept under her pillow when Thompson was out of town. A few months after the couple set up their home in New Orleans with Kelsey, Thompson's father died, and the loss made him consider what direction his life should take.

From the start, Kathleen believed Thompson needed to pursue his career as a lawyer, because it made him come alive. "Kevin is at his sexiest when he's taking on a company and rattling his saber in the courtroom," she said. "Not when his hair is standing straight up on his head and he's looking a little crazed."

Instead, Thompson nearly made a deal that would've kept him out of the courtroom for the rest of his career. In 1997, Paul Orfalea, the founder of Kinko's, offered to buy out Thompson and his two partners at Legal Process for $3 million. Thompson wanted to clinch the deal, but he and Markovich couldn't agree on how to structure it. When they had formed the company, they had concocted a convoluted partnership agreement befitting a law student and a newly minted MBA. It included a nuclear clause that said that if either partner didn't agree on something, he could blow up the company after giving twenty-four hours' notice in writing. Thompson was furious, and he entered the launch codes. "I said, fuck you, I'm leaving. I'm taking my clients and forming a new company," he recalled later.

Thompson called his new company Evidence Management. He hired a team of graphic designers to help him create trial materials for clients and an executive assistant to keep his schedule and paperwork straight. Kathleen quit her job with the insurance company, and she started working at the new company. For the first time, Thompson's work and home life were in alignment. Sitting in his living room preparing some trial graphics on his laptop, he asked Kelsey, who was seven, which color to use. He started calling her the chief coloring officer.

The situation was bound to be short-lived, though, because Thompson wanted to play more than a supporting role for other lawyers. He wanted to go from taping depositions to conducting them, and be the one standing in a courtroom in front of a jury, taking on a powerful interest to make a difference in someone's life. Despite the risks—or maybe because of them—once again he was ready to strike out on his own.

If Thompson hadn't met a lawyer named Stuart Smith in 1999, he might never have started practicing environmental law. Smith had grown up in a blue-collar neighborhood in New Orleans and had retained the city's working-class accent despite the wealth he had acquired winning verdicts against the country's most powerful oil and gas companies. He had pioneered an entire field of environmental law after discovering widespread radioactive contamination in the nation's oil fields. The radioactivity was in the salt water that came up when companies drilled for oil. The water left behind a deposit called "scale" on drill pipes, and the dust then got into workers' lungs, causing cancer. Smith discovered that Big Oil had been aware of the problem but minimized it for years, never warning its own workers or the contractors who cleaned the pipes. Seven years earlier, Smith had settled a landmark case against Chevron in Laurel, Mississippi, for an undisclosed amount and started driving a Porsche coupe and living in a mansion in the French Quarter, as he recounted in his book *Crude Justice*. His modern office in a high-rise downtown had a broad view of the final miles of the Mississippi River.

In addition to being an aggressive litigator, Smith had a reputation for being difficult to work with. But when another lawyer in New Orleans told Thompson that Smith needed help with a case heading to trial, Thompson saw the six-foot-tall chain-smoking lawyer as a potential mentor. One of Smith's mottos, which he learned from another New Orleans lawyer, Jack Harang, captured his bravado: "You eat what you kill. If you don't kill, you don't eat." Another made it clear that he'd rather take his chances at trial than accept a settlement: "Settlements are like kissing your sister; it feels good but isn't very sexy." Smith had a predatory intelligence when it came to battling corporations, and Thompson was drawn to his charismatic personality. Smith was about as modest as New Orleans itself.

For his part, Smith liked Thompson from their first meeting, and more importantly, he was impressed by the kinds of graphics Thompson said he could deliver. Smith explained that they would be taking on ExxonMobil, the world's biggest oil company, with annual revenue of more than $400 billion, or more than the gross domestic product of most countries. The company earned $1 billion in profit every eight days or so, a figure Smith fixated on. He had filed the lawsuit on behalf of Joseph Grefer, a retired judge who owned thirty-three acres of irradiated land in Harvey, Louisiana, just outside New Orleans. Thompson designed graphics to show the jury the extent of the radioactivity on the land over time, when tens of thousands of pipes had been cleaned by a contractor hired by ExxonMobil.

The case, as it turned out, was another landmark, and this time Thompson had a front-row seat. ExxonMobil refused to settle, and Smith became adamant about going to trial and taking the oil giant for as much as he could. The trial lasted about five weeks. Thompson had been impressed by the scathing opening statement. Jack Harang, who partnered with Smith on the case, had said that ExxonMobil had committed "an environmental rape" and that "by their actions, by their reckless handling of this toxic waste, they have shown to us that they believed . . . they were bigger than this court . . . bigger than this state, and certainly bigger than the poor people of this property and the business that they destroyed. It's going to be up to you, ladies and gentlemen, to teach them that the cost of doing good is less than the cost of doing bad, that it's cheaper to do right than it is to do wrong."

In his no-holds-barred manner, Smith cross-examined all of ExxonMobil's witnesses and experts. He grilled the company's industrial hygienist for three days and got him to admit that the company hadn't determined if anyone in Harvey had been harmed by the radioactive material shed from the pipes. On the second day of deliberations, the jury announced its verdict. It required ExxonMobil to pay $56 million to clean up the property and $125,000 to replace the lost value of the land. Then the foreman read aloud the punitive damages to a stunned courtroom: $1 billion.

Though an appeals court later reduced the total award to $219 million, the verdict still stood as a record payout to an individual property owner, according to Smith, and it initiated a wave of pollution lawsuits throughout the oil fields in Louisiana and beyond during the early 2000s. This was the period when Thompson began looking for environmental cases of his own in West Virginia. He was, in effect, returning home and setting out on a quest at the same time.

In 2002, Thompson landed his first environmental case—the initial one against Arch Coal. The complaint had originally been brought by Marc Lazenby, a lawyer out of Princeton, West Virginia, on behalf of Clinton Daugherty, a landowner in Mingo County. Lazenby had focused on the company's failure to pay Daugherty for hauling coal across his land after mining it, known as a wheelage fee. But when the lawyer saw steel drums leaking diesel on the property, he knew he needed to bring on an environmental lawyer. Thompson's friend John Alderman recommended him for the job, and Thompson drove down to Daugherty's land and saw the mess for himself. Thompson would always remember the date: July 12, 2002. It was the start of the second phase of his career.

When Lazenby realized that the environmental claims were more significant than his wheelage case, he let Thompson take the lead.

An attempt to mediate a settlement failed. Lazenby was more cautious than Thompson, knowing there was always a chance they could lose everything at trial—get zeroed. But like his mentor Stuart Smith, Thompson never doubted the case or himself, and he wanted to roll the dice. Moments before the trial began in the Mingo County Courthouse, Thompson turned to Lazenby and whispered, "This is my first time before a jury." As the two lawyers stood to greet the judge, Lazenby panicked. But Thompson was thrilled.

Thompson gave a solid opening statement, and his performance throughout the trial put Lazenby at ease. When the final witness, Gary Bennett, president of the Arch subsidiary that mined the property, was on the stand, Thompson planned to show a video he'd taken during a tour of the property: a state regulator said on camera that it looked as if the company's waste disposal practice had been to throw it as far as possible down a hillside. A defense lawyer referred to the clip as the "Batman video," because Thompson's jacket flew up like a cape when he jumped over the berm to point to the refuse below. Judge Michael Thornsbury, Mingo County's sole circuit court judge, had allowed the video to be admitted as evidence over the defense's objections. But when Thompson went to play it, he found that a bulb had blown on his projector. Hearing whispers at the defense counsel table, he asked the judge for five minutes to get his backup projector.

Before Thompson could press play again, he felt a hand on his shoulder. "Kevin, don't do it!" an attorney for the coal company said. "We settled." While Thompson had been preoccupied, Lazenby had settled the case. Thompson was initially disappointed, but he came around once he realized that with Lazenby's help, they had won a sizable settlement for Daugherty and that his share of the fee was more money than he had ever earned from a single case.

Thompson had launched his career in the coalfields, where he was starting to believe mining companies had left a trail of devastation. To celebrate, he bought a doll to bring back to Kelsey in New Orleans. She ran up to greet him when he got home, as she always did. But the victory also meant he would be spending even more time in West Virginia.

There had been a moment a few weeks before the settlement when Thompson knew he had found his calling. He and Daugherty were at the offices of Arch's law firm, Jackson Kelly PLLC, in the Laidley Tower, a twenty-two-story office building wrapped in blue glass. Arch's lawyers had just finished deposing Daugherty, and he and Thompson were about to leave. They paused in the Holt conference room, named for one of the founding partners of the firm. Bill Powell, a partner at Jackson Kelly, saw Thompson looking up at a framed photograph from the 1930s of dozens of men in dinner jackets at the Greenbrier resort, a getaway for the state's coal elite in White Sulphur Springs. Powell was proud of the firm's heritage, and he told Thompson about some of the early partners. He noted that one of them, Homer A. Holt, the son of the founding Holt partner, had become governor in 1937.

"What are the odds of that?" Powell asked.

Thompson immediately recognized the photograph as an image of Depression-era privilege. A light clicked on in his brain, and he remembered Patty Holt, his mother's middle-school classmate, the one who'd complained of her smell. It seemed that the girl's relative had not only been the state's twentieth governor—he'd been a Jackson Kelly attorney.

As he looked around the room, Thompson realized the fine furniture and pictures had all come from coal riches. Standing before him was a lawyer in a long line of educated, well-connected men who, in Thompson's estimation, had blithely wielded their power to benefit coal companies at the expense of generations of miners and working people. The thought of it made him furious. Pointing his forefinger at Powell, Thompson backed the other lawyer against a wall, pressing his finger into the smaller man's chest. "You're nothing but a Pinkerton," Thompson said, referring to the detective agency that had employed enforcers and labor spies to crush union organizing in the early twentieth century. "You don't use guns, but you're no better than a Pinkerton."

"Come on, Kevin," Daugherty said, startled by the outburst. He pulled Thompson back. "Let's go." They left Powell standing awkwardly in the room.

Thompson called his mother that night, after he had cooled down, and told her about the encounter. She loved that he hadn't forgotten the ancient slight that had shaped her memories of growing up in a coal camp. Now, all these years later, he was finally in a position to avenge that old injustice and take an even bigger stand.

CHAPTER 6

In the fall of 2004, as Thompson waited for Jackson Kelly to respond to his first set of interrogatories—questions aimed at finding out the extent of slurry injection at Rawl Sales and who had ordered it—he sifted again through all the publicly available reports he could find on water quality in the area. He was convinced that Rawl Sales was responsible for the bad water, but he found it hard to believe that the company had secretly injected slurry or that it had posted armed sentries to keep residents from finding out about it. "That's another myth," he said. "No company would do such a ridiculous thing. You'd get in too much trouble."

A report written by Barbara Smith, an epidemiologist with the state Department of Health and Human Resources, had been prompted by a handwritten letter that B.I. had sent to the Environmental Protection Agency. He wanted an investigation to determine if people's wells had been contaminated by an old landfill, a railroad facility, or Rawl Sales' Pond Creek mine, or its nearby strip mine. The report was finalized in February 2004, the same month Thompson first visited Rawl.

Smith had brought a team to Lick Creek in the summer of 2002. They visited homes and interviewed residents. But the mandate for their health consultation didn't include performing any water, soil, or air tests of their own. To evaluate the Rawl Sales sites, Smith's team primarily relied on the 1995 findings by the state geologist who had concluded that Maude Rice's well was likely the only one affected by the abandoned Pond Creek mine, and the 2001 engineering report that had called for a municipal water line after concluding that severe groundwater problems had been caused by decades of mining activity. In her own analysis, Smith found that the levels of iron, lead, manganese, and sulfates previously found in area wells fell below exposure dose levels set by health agencies, her basis for determining health risks. In the end, the report ruled out all four sites as sources of exposure to contaminants that could cause adverse health effects in residents.

The report was a disappointment to B.I. and others. Thompson knew that to many residents it had a pro-industry flavor. Smith wrote that coal mining "can add many minerals to the groundwater," as though it did little more than sprinkle vitamins into the earth. The report addressed people's anxiety about cancer but said that the types of cancers in the four communities were consistent with those found in Mingo County as a whole, where the rate of lung cancer was more than twice that of the US. The report noted that the annual per capita income in the county was $12,445. Thompson felt the implication was that people living in Mingo County were generally sick and poor. Any complaints about the water were mostly cosmetic, the report seemed to say. It noted that residents complained of rotten egg or sulfur smells and kerosene and sewer-like odors. However, another factor for Smith was that only 42 percent of people said they used their well water for drinking. She underlined her conclusion about the three sites: "no public health hazard."

Thompson was disturbed by the apparent lack of curiosity about the slurry in the Pond Creek mine. Smith wrote that any slurry in the mine would have been diluted over time by water flowing into the mine. Thompson wondered if Smith's team had asked for records related to slurry injection, but the report seemed to indicate they hadn't. "There are no known records of what was used in this sludge and no testing data was located," Smith wrote. The report handed Massey a powerful defense against charges that it had contaminated people's wells.

On December 10, 2004, Ben Stout, the stream ecologist from Wheeling Jesuit University, faxed his own preliminary report about the area's water to Thompson at the Mountaineer. Stout had been thorough, sampling more than a dozen wells at the highest and lowest points in the four communities to see if there were differences in contaminants at different depths underground. Because people complained that their water was worse after heavy rains, he took samples months apart when the flow of groundwater was high and low.

For the first time, Stout tested the area's wells for heavy metals like lead, barium, and beryllium, and for arsenic, a metalloid, because he hypothesized that if coal slurry was impacting the wells, these constituents of slurry would be present in higher concentrations in the water. And sure enough, they were.

To anchor his findings, Stout had compared contaminant levels in Rawl, Lick Creek, Merrimac, and Sprigg to three neighboring counties in West Virginia and two in Kentucky. As Thompson both hoped and feared, Stout found that the water along Route 49 was the worst in the region's coalfields. The water in these four communities was "unquestionably poor," Stout wrote. As he had warned its residents earlier that year, the water should be considered unsuitable for drinking and, if possible, bathing. He found arsenic, a known carcinogen, in six of eight wells tested at high flow, with two samples exceeding the EPA drinking water standard of 10 parts per billion (ppb). Ernie and Carmelita's well had 340 ppb—more than thirty times the standard. He noted that these results were higher than other regional samples by state regulators. The Route 49 wells appeared to be markedly different from many others in the southern coalfields.

In the four communities, Stout found that average lead levels "greatly exceed" the average concentrations in other regional wells. Seven of eight wells he tested at high flow contained lead, with three wells exceeding the EPA standard. Iron and manganese levels were off the charts at several homes. While iron and manganese were typically not considered health threatening, Stout wrote that the high concentrations—25,089 ppb of iron in one well, compared to the EPA standard of 300 ppb—could have serious health effects, especially on the nervous system. He concluded that the likely source of contamination was coal slurry. Stout was never a paid expert for Thompson. He wanted to remain independent, do his science, and make his findings available to everyone. Thompson believed that would lend Stout's report even more credence.

Stout privately told Ernie and Carmelita that he thought the area's geology had contributed to their problems and possibly explained why they were among the first to have black water. Their house sat near the Lick Creek Syncline, a geologic fold that Stout believed had acted like a funnel, drawing contaminants toward the family's well. In more than a decade of sampling streams and wells in the state, their water was the most contaminated he had ever found.

Another of Stout's shocking findings came from Frank Coleman's water heater. It had especially high levels of arsenic, barium, and lead. The water had 557,700 parts per billion of iron, more than 1,800 times the federal standard; and 27,260 parts per billion of manganese, more than 500 times the standard. The numbers were unheard of for water inside a home. Although people weren't drinking from their hot water heaters, Stout believed the appliances concentrated the contaminants over time and that when people showered, they could be exposed to metals on their skin and in their lungs from inhaling water vapor. The manganese in the heavily contaminated hot water also explained why so many tubs and sinks had been stained black, he said.

Stout concluded: "This study supports the claims of citizens that their well water is contaminated and subject to 'blackwater' events." He said additional studies were needed to determine the exact source of the pollution. He also advised that a study of the relationship between illnesses in the communities and well water quality be conducted.

Encouraged by Stout's December report—coming nearly three months after Thompson had filed his lawsuit—Thompson filed an emergency motion in the first week of January 2005 in Mingo County court, arguing that the water in Rawl wasn't safe to drink. Thompson asked Judge Thornsbury to require Massey to provide bottled water immediately to families along Route 49. His April letter to the company demanding bottled water for his clients hadn't gone anywhere. This time, he felt he had a real chance to force Massey's hand. For emphasis, he attached a photograph of a garden hose filling a bucket with black water at Ernie and Carmelita's house. "There can be no doubt that water coming out of the taps in Rawl is toxic soup," Thompson wrote.

Judge Thornsbury heard arguments on the emergency motion on April 27, 2005, blaming the three-month delay on his busy docket. Thompson had been frustrated at having to wait to make his case in court, but when he walked in with fed-up residents from Rawl, Lick Creek, Merrimac, and Sprigg, he felt like he was on his home court after his victory against Arch Coal in the Daugherty case.

The courtroom itself wasn't big, and it had the same drab, mid-1960s furnishings and fluorescent lighting as the rest of the courthouse. But it was the primary seat of power in the county, where Judge Thornsbury, in his traditional black robes, presided over everything from petty crimes to murder trials from behind the seal of the state of West Virginia and the motto *Montani Semper Liberi*—Mountaineers Are Always Free.

Even though the brown leather chairs in the jury box were empty, the room felt electric. It was the first full hearing in the Rawl case. Thompson had previously represented two well-off landowners in front of the judge; now his clients, who numbered more than a hundred so far, were working-class residents of Mingo County. They urgently needed something as basic as safe drinking water, and several dozen of them—including Larry, Ernie, and B.I.—filled the six rows of maple-colored benches behind him.

Thornsbury had been the county's sole circuit judge since 1997, when he was appointed to the job. Many of Thompson's clients had known him since he was a lawyer on East Second Avenue. Some had even gone to high school with him. Before he won election to a full term in 1998, Ernie and B.I. had campaigned for him in the hollows along Route 49. All the same, Thompson understood that many of his clients had their suspicions about Mike Thornsbury. They were his constituents, but from long experience they believed that any elected official in the county would, in the end, choose the coal company over the people.

A few days before the hearing, Larry Brown had heard a voice tell him to go to the top of the mountain above Rawl. On the old surface mine, he had parked his four-wheeler and closed his eyes. When he opened them, the mountains had been erased by a thick fog. He had recounted his experience to Thompson, and said he wasn't afraid then or now. While he was in a meditative state, Larry said, the Lord told him that people might try to harm him for going against Massey. But he shouldn't give in to fear. He said he heard the voice say: "All these people are not serving me. But I want you to stand for every one of them. Leave none of them out." Thompson started referring to "Larry's vision," and he saw it as a sign of people's apprehension—and of their defiance. It fed his own confidence to see the preacher in the courtroom with his other core clients.

Like Arch Coal, Massey had hired Jackson Kelly to defend it. Two lawyers with the firm, Robert McLusky and Daniel Stickler, had argued in briefs ahead of the hearing that Thompson had previously "cried 'emergency'" when he sent his letter to Massey a year earlier. There was no emergency: most residents had stopped using their wells for drinking water. In February, in their written response to Thompson's latest motion, the lawyers said existing studies exonerated Rawl Sales. That included the 1995 state geologist's study of Lick Creek wells, the 2001 engineering report that found that wells had been affected by pre-1977 mining, and Barbara Smith's 2004 report. Stickler and McLusky wrote that Rawl Sales had injected slurry in the 1970s and early 1980s into abandoned sections of the Pond Creek mine near the head of Lick Creek. The tilt of that coal seam, however, would have caused the slurry to flow to the northwest, away from Rawl, Merrimac, and Sprigg, they wrote, though it might have affected a small portion of Lick Creek. Moreover, the lawyers wrote that "starting in 1984" the company constructed an impoundment "into which it then discharged slurried coal refuse." They contended that Thompson's lawsuit would likely be dismissed based on a statute of limitations argument, because "much of the well water in this region has been of exceedingly poor quality for <u>decades</u>."

Thompson thought Jackson Kelly's written arguments were weak. They were attempting to push the blame onto mining that had gone on for decades before Rawl Sales arrived on the scene. And they tried to undercut Stout's study by pointing out that he hadn't concluded that Rawl Sales itself caused any contamination. Yet in early April, Smith issued a second report that considered Stout's findings. While she discounted the cancer risk from arsenic levels in the wells, she said the lead and sodium made the water unsafe for the public, especially children. She now concluded that the water posed "a Public Health Hazard for the past, present, and future."

So far, Jackson Kelly had stated in a written response to Thompson in February that Rawl Sales had injected slurry in two locations: at the head of Lick Creek and near the Sprouse Creek processing plant. Thompson knew of two holes near Lick Creek for sure. A few weeks before the hearing, he had gone out with the environmental engineer Scott Simonton and Dan Stickler and verified that the two pipes he'd seen with Ernie and B.I. on their four-wheeler tour had, in fact, been used for slurry injection. Jackson Kelly's argument about the tilt of the area's rock strata was more problematic to Thompson, but he still believed the judge would be persuaded by the appalling condition of the water.

"Your Honor, we're going to try to do this as efficiently as possible today," Thompson said after he rose to speak. "But the core of the matter is the water at Rawl is bad, it's unsafe to drink, so we have filed this case as a class action because we believe that the scientific evidence that we're going to put on today shows we're talking about a community affected by the water caused by injection of a slurry into an abandoned mine works that ran below Rawl, Lick Creek, Merrimac, and Sprigg."

Judge Thornsbury, who had full cheeks and a thin, graying mustache, wasn't an easy read behind his tinted, rectangular glasses. He had already set a trial date for six months later, and Thompson hoped he would be eager to move the case along quickly.

Thompson spent five minutes laying out his argument. The Rawl Sales impoundment had increased the pressure on the rock strata beneath it, and the company's blasting and strip-mining above the four communities had opened fissures underground, enabling slurry to migrate from the three injection sites the company had identified. Thompson held up the same photograph he had sent to the judge for everyone in the courtroom to see. "This is a bucket of tap water poured from Ernie Brown's well," he said. "It's completely black."

Stickler and McLusky watched Thompson's performance. Stickler, who was in his late fifties, had a trim build and neat salt-and-pepper mustache and the dapper look of a 1940s-era film star. McLusky, nearly a decade younger, had a balding head and canny, hawkish eyes. Both had joined Jackson Kelly in the 1980s, and they were among the firm's top litigators, working out of its Charleston offices in the smoke-blue Laidley Tower, which Thompson had by now heard other plaintiffs' lawyers refer to as "the Death Star." Between them, the two lawyers brought decades of experience defending coal companies in all manner of cases.

Thompson called Scott Simonton, his environmental expert, to the witness stand. The balding former Marine had dressed in a jacket and tie for the occasion. "Dr. Simonton, have you studied the water at Rawl?" Thompson asked him.

"Yes," Simonton said.

"Is it healthy?"

"No."

"Is it safe to drink?"

"No." Simonton said he had also warned people not to drink their water, and he came across as genuinely troubled as he summarized Ben Stout's findings, including the high levels of arsenic and lead. Then Thompson turned to Rawl Sales' operations. Among the hundreds of pages of Rawl Sales files that Jackson Kelly had turned over so far, none indicated that the company had a permit to inject slurry underground.

"Did you conduct a record search at the Department of Environmental Protection for an injection well permit?" Thompson asked Simonton.

"Yes. No injection well permit was found." Simonton added that the state agency had told him that no injection well permits had been issued for the entire area. Thompson was aiming to prove that Massey had been caught disposing of coal waste without informing regulators.

After Thompson sat down, McLusky started questioning Simonton. It didn't take long for the defense attorney to knock Simonton back on his heels. McLusky asked if he had tested for any chemicals used in the coal-cleaning process when he sampled wells. Simonton said he hadn't. And were all the heavy metals described in Stout's report naturally occurring in the rock strata between coal seams? Simonton said they were.

"You're not here as a medical doctor, as I understand it?" asked McLusky.

"No."

"Nor as an epidemiologist?"

"No."

"Not as a toxicologist?"

"No."

"You haven't come back with any tests or independent studies on the health effects of any of these substances on people?" McLusky asked.

"No."

McLusky asked Simonton if he was willing to render a scientific conclusion that Massey's mining activities had affected the wells in the community. Simonton replied, "I suppose there is a chance that Martians could have put it there, but I'm pretty certain it was coal-mining activities."

And could he say with a reasonable degree of scientific certainty—the common standard for expert testimony—that Massey's impoundment or injection wells had put the contaminants in the people's drinking water?

Simonton hesitated. "I wouldn't bet my children's lives on it, but it strongly suggests, and I feel confident, there's a connection," he said.

With a few well-aimed questions, McLusky had exposed weaknesses in the case before the foundation had even set. If Thompson had any hope of advancing the lawsuit, he would need to find a clear link between Rawl Sales' operations and the wells of his clients. He would need to hire an epidemiologist to conduct independent health reports. Even then, McLusky and Stickler were certain to call their own experts to rip apart whatever evidence he presented.

Still, when the hearing was over, Thompson's confidence was unshaken. All he needed to do at this point was persuade the judge to require Massey to provide bottled water. He had called Larry Brown to testify, to put a human face on the situation. Larry said that he and his neighbors had been coping with bad water for more than a decade, and Thompson believed his testimony would carry weight with the judge. Larry was the most prominent leader in the community, and he had taken the most visible role in the case.

Brown had expected a tough cross-examination from McLusky and Stickler, but none came on this day. Later, when he spotted the pair of lawyers on the steps of the courthouse, he walked over to them smiling, and reached his hand out to shake theirs. Brown said he didn't have much education, but he could tell they were "top-notch" for the company. Stickler, who was always cordial with Thompson's clients if he bumped into them outside the courtroom, gladly accepted the praise. Then Brown told them he was good at his job too. When Stickler asked what he did for a living, Brown explained that he worked for God. "And I'm standing for the people," he added before he walked away.

Days after the hearing, fears about the water became more urgent in Rawl when people learned that Donetta Blankenship, who lived two houses down from Larry Brown, had been hospitalized. Donetta, who had a shy, smiling disposition, had no relation to Don Blankenship, but because of the similarity of their names she sometimes received glossy brochures for casinos or the Greenbrier resort addressed to him. Donetta's home was crowded with piles of folded clothes that she sold at roadside markets. Most days, she went out yard-saling, as she called it. She had moved to Rawl in 2001, and she had been increasingly worried about breathing problems and stomachaches that her son, thirteen, and daughter, twelve, had been having for months.

She herself had started feeling tired and sick to her stomach three months earlier, in February, but ignored it. Then, earlier in April, her husband and children started asking her with growing concern why her skin looked so yellow. She laughed it off at first—"Honey, when you look *yella*, that means you're about to die," she told her daughter, Amy. Finally, she agreed to go to the hospital, where she learned that her liver enzymes were thirty times higher than they should be; it appeared that her liver was failing, and she was, in fact, dying.

Within days, Donetta responded to medication, and after nearly a week, her enzyme levels had dropped in half. A liver biopsy came back normal, leaving her doctors puzzled. Thompson believed the slurry was to blame, and he worried about all the other illnesses that had been growing silently in the communities. Who might become sick next? When he visited Donetta at the hospital, she told him the doctors couldn't figure out what had caused her liver to nearly fail. Thompson was adamant: "I know what it is. It's the water."

On May 17, Judge Thornsbury held a second hearing, and the Jackson Kelly attorneys once again showed why they were the coal industry's hired guns. Their first witness was a mining engineer and geologist named Ron Mullennex, a genial man who Thompson had heard was also a skilled banjo player specializing in the old-time music that predates bluegrass in Appalachia. Mullennex began his testimony with a lesson on how the aquifers that hold and transmit groundwater had formed in the region as the mountains themselves had come into being. Erosion over millions of years had created the valleys, which then exerted less downward pressure, freeing up water-bearing layers of rock underground, he lectured. It was unlikely that coal slurry had "attacked" any of the wells in the communities, Mullennex said. Arsenic, lead, and other metals all existed naturally in the ground. He explained that Rawl Sales injected slurry in the mid-1980s only as a backup measure when it didn't have space in the impoundment it was building. The slurry went down the injection hole just like rain running down a spout, falling by gravity onto the mine floor. There was little pressure to force the slurry to spread out beyond where gravity would carry it. The old abandoned mines in the Pond Creek seam extended beneath much of the four communities. But Mullennex said most wells in the communities were "up dip" from the injection points, so the slurry would have flowed away from them. It was a strikingly simple argument—everyone knows water doesn't flow uphill.

Mullennex said the wells were tapping an aquifer below the river where water acquired dissolved metals through the rocks over time.

McLusky asked if the water was picking up metals all the time as it trickled down through these fractures.

"Right. It's being exposed to what's naturally there in the rock," Mullennex said.

After McLusky finished, Thompson opened his cross-examination by asking Mullennex to provide him with maps of the Alma and Pond Creek seams, because Thompson had yet to receive them from Jackson Kelly. He asked Mullennex if he had reviewed any injection well permits, and when Mullennex said he hadn't, Thompson said, "That's because they don't exist, isn't it?"

Thompson asked whether the slurry pumped underground could have migrated farther, suggesting that the wells of the roughly 250 homes in the four communities could have affected the flow of water underground. He challenged Mullennex's claim that it would be impossible for water to travel uphill; the slope of the Pond Creek seam was actually quite gentle, Thompson said. But he appeared less certain than McLusky about the area's geology, about hydrology and coal mining generally. He didn't fully grasp technical terms like "dip" that geologists use to describe the direction that water flows underground. And he cut Mullennex short several times, before the geologist could answer. Mullennex insisted that slurry injected into mines was well contained. The residents were pumping water from "really effectively a separate aquifer." As he traded theories with Massey's expert, Thompson realized he was on rocky ground. He risked losing an argument he didn't yet fully understand.

Massey's other expert, Ronald Gots, a physician, pharmacologist, and toxicologist specializing in environmental medicine, dismissed any connection between the area's well water and health problems. Gots, who had a long face and thick head of dark hair, had gotten his MD from the University of Pennsylvania and had published roughly eighty-five professional papers, including some on defending toxic tort lawsuits. One of his books was titled *Toxic Risks: Science, Regulation and Perception.*

"The EPA standards are not as some people think: the safe line between safe and dangerous," he explained from the stand. "There is a regulatory number that's arrived at with a great deal of conservative numbers built into that number. So the fact that one exceeds a regulatory standard by some amount, unless it's a five-hundred-fold or hundred-fold or thousand-fold, does not necessarily by any means mean that there is a health risk associated with that water. In the case of arsenic, we were actually below the regulatory standard."

Gots had reviewed all the studies on the area's wells, including Ben Stout's, and he didn't see any problem with their arsenic or lead levels. The lead standard had been exceeded by only a small amount, he said, adding that the standard itself had been lowered by the EPA only a few years ago. He didn't clarify that the government changed the standard because of concern that the prior level wasn't protective enough.

Stickler asked if the water had "any immediate or irreparable health problems associated with it." Gots said it didn't.

"I'm not saying that some of the water might not taste bad . . . But it was not—there was nothing in here that was a health hazard."

When Thompson cross-examined Gots, the toxicologist wouldn't back down. He seemed to discount the risks of exposure entirely, and the protective purposes of the EPA's standards. With growing frustration, Thompson pulled out a word his mother had taught him years ago in their kitchen when she added a dash of something to the pot—"skosh"—to try to highlight the absurdity of the testimony.

"It's your opinion in this court that a skosh above EPA standards, you could drink it for the rest of your life and you're not going to have lifetime exposure and no health effect?"

"Absolutely," Gots said.

After asking if that was the case for other metals, Thompson said, "And what about the toxic soup effect? I would imagine it's going to be your testimony that arsenic, beryllium, manganese, the whole metal suite poured into a jar is not going to have any higher health effect than if you were to ingest any one of those, is that right?"

"Of course not," Gots said. "They're entirely different. They act differently . . . They don't interact."

Thompson asked Gots if he had seen the water.

"No," Gots said.

"Have you smelled this water?"

"No."

"Have you tasted this water?"

"No."

"Would you be fine to drink this water?"

"I didn't say that," Gots said. "This water may be unpleasant."

Stickler was making a case that there was no need for Massey to provide water to the residents. But he had another goal. He didn't want the judge to certify a class. One of the requirements for granting class-action status is that questions of law or fact are common across all of the plaintiffs. If everyone's water was different, as Gots testified, the judge might be less likely to say they should all be handled as a class.

Trying each resident's claim individually would increase the workload for both sides by orders of magnitude, giving Massey a clear advantage: Jackson Kelly had an army of attorneys and associates in Charleston. The state's oldest and largest law firm, it traced its origins back to 1822, well before West Virginia was granted statehood in 1863, and its coal-related work dated back to the 1870s, according to the firm's own account of its history. Law firms tend to have personalities, and Jackson Kelly was considered by many plaintiffs' lawyers to be as arrogant and cut-throat as any powerful defense firm in the nation. Known for aggressive tactics, the firm would later be accused of withholding medical evidence on behalf of coal companies in cases where miners were seeking black lung benefits. One attorney at the firm would later be suspended for a year from practicing law for having done so.

Thompson, meanwhile, was an upstart: he'd been in Mingo County less than three years and was mostly working out of an old hotel with help from Van Bunch in Chattanooga and a paralegal from Bunch's firm in Phoenix. And yet Thompson thought he had presented the better case that day: the four communities needed bottled water, and Massey should be required to provide it. He didn't believe the judge would be persuaded by the testimony of either Mullennex, who had sounded knowledgeable but in the end said the contaminants in the water were all naturally occurring, or Gots, whose lack of concern about exposures to lead and arsenic had seemed almost willfully callous to Thompson. He and Bunch had a nickname for Gots: they called him Dr. Doom.

The pair fully expected the judge to side with them as they went back to the Mountaineer to pack up. Bunch had flown in for the hearing, and they planned to discuss the case in depth over the weekend at Bunch's cabin on land he owned in a forested stretch of national parkland about a hundred miles north of Chattanooga. They left in Thompson's Ford Explorer, which Bunch had nicknamed "the Exploder," a nod to the model's reputation for safety problems, including spontaneously bursting into flames. The five-hour drive to the "cabin"—a lodge-like house set in the woods with a wraparound deck—was the most time the two lawyers had spent alone together. They discussed their lives and how they'd ended up working together in Mingo County. Like Thompson, Bunch had never expected to find himself representing hundreds of people in the hollows of southern West Virginia. By the time they reached eastern Tennessee, the entire western sky was lit orange, which seemed auspicious. As they drove toward the sunset, Bunch was just as enthusiastic as Thompson about the case. "That was a great day in sports history," he declared, referring to the hearing. Thompson laughed and repeated the line, which he tended to do when someone had perfectly summed up a moment.

PART II

HEART OF THE BILLION DOLLAR COAL FIELD

AUGUST 2005–AUGUST 2007

CHAPTER 7

When Thompson had made his first trip to Rawl in early 2004, more than half the electricity in the United States came from burning coal. The prior year, the nation's mining companies took 1.1 billion tons of the black rock out of the ground. The vast majority of those tons were shipped to power plants. The rest—higher-quality coal derived mostly from underground mines in West Virginia—was sold to steel companies or exported. The US had at least a 250-year supply of coal, by government estimates. In 2003, coal generated a record 1.97 trillion kilowatt hours: more power than petroleum, natural gas, nuclear, wind, solar, and hydroelectric combined. In 1950, the number had been just 154.5 billion kilowatt hours. Coal had fueled the industrial revolution and powered factories, locomotives, and steamships well into the twentieth century; now it lit cities, computers, and cell phones.

Thompson had become a student of Massey, and from corporate filings, he pieced together an outline of its operations. The company dominated the West Virginia coalfields and also had mines in Kentucky and Virginia. It employed 4,428 workers at thirty underground mines and thirteen surface mines. In 2003, it had sold 41 million tons of coal and had $1.3 billion in revenue, making it the nation's fourth-largest coal company.

The company was structured like a set of Russian nesting dolls, with nineteen resource groups, or subsidiaries. It was often hard to tell which business unit was responsible for safety violations or environmental problems at a particular operation, and Thompson knew the lack of clarity was intentional. It was part of the industry's long-standing strategy of shielding the parent company by creating quasi-independent entities. Massey was headquartered in Richmond, Virginia, in a four-story corner office building, where its top executives worked—except for one. Don Blankenship oversaw the entire enterprise from a tan double-wide in Belfry, Kentucky. The building, which looked like a small modular home, was a thirty-minute commute from Sprigg in his black BMW and a few miles south of the commercial stretch of Route 119 outside Williamson, with its Walmart, fast-food restaurants, and a dusty parking lot where people sold items from their homes for a few dollars.

Blankenship ran the Massey coal empire out of a modest office with two secretaries, including one who printed his emails and stacked them on his desk, which had no computer. He had no cell phone, but he kept people's numbers in his head, an associate said. Along one wall, as reporters invariably noted, he kept a Zenith television with a bullet hole in it; in 1985, when he was president of Rawl Sales, striking miners had shot up his former office on Route 49 one night when the lights were still on but Blankenship had already gone home. The souvenir was a reminder of Blankenship's violent clash with the union—and that he had won. Nearly twenty years later, the union had a minimal presence at Massey. Blankenship, meanwhile, had risen from Rawl Sales to become CEO of Massey and, in the process, had amassed wealth and political clout like few others in the state.

In 2003, Blankenship earned more than $6 million, and the *Charleston Gazette* found he was the highest-paid executive in the state that year. The next year, he waded into West Virginia politics, spending $3 million of his own money to help elect a Republican lawyer, Brent Benjamin, to the West Virginia Supreme Court of Appeals, the state's highest court. Blankenship knew little about Benjamin when he decided to bankroll a Super PAC called And for the Sake of the Kids. He said he wanted to elect a Republican to improve the business climate in a state derided by industry groups as a "judicial hellhole." The Super PAC's ads smeared a Democrat up for reelection on the court, saying he had let a child rapist out of prison. Brent Benjamin won and became the first Republican on the court in more than eighty years.

That Blankenship had worked at Rawl Sales in the 1980s—when people in Rawl and Lick Creek said their water had gone bad—amazed Thompson. It linked one of the nation's most notorious CEOs to the onset of the water problems. And as Thompson had seen from Thelma Parsley's house, Blankenship still lived just down the road from people who could no longer drink their water.

Yet Thompson said he couldn't help but be impressed by the CEO's focus on the business and his apparent commitment to the area. Everywhere he went, people knew Blankenship. They'd worked for him or their brother had. The company's influence—and its logo, a red flame rising from a black *M*—could be seen throughout the coalfields. Massey sponsored Little League ball fields and an annual Christmas Extravaganza where employees handed out gifts to children. Massey donated to local fire departments and provided financial assistance to medical students at Marshall University. The list went on.

As the state's top coal executive, Blankenship was a local celebrity—someone to be admired, hated, or feared, depending on one's feelings about the coal industry and Massey. He had recently built a corporate getaway on a mountaintop in Aflex, Kentucky, which could be seen from Williamson. The property had a private drive protected by an electric gate and a security guard carrying a sidearm. The four-story house, with its red roof—like an echo of the Massey logo—was sometimes derisively referred to as Blankenship's castle. It was a mile from Ernie and Carmelita's house, straight across the Tug Fork, and they could see it perched on the hilltop from their kitchen window. At the same time, Blankenship could often be spotted strolling down Second Avenue or having breakfast at a diner called Track's End. "He's not a CEO that lives in an ivory tower by any means," Thompson would later say when he tried to reconcile Blankenship's apparent contradictions. "He's here. He drives the roads. He's a total part of the community. He goes to the bars. He goes to the coffee shops. He's in a tool trailer down the road from Walmart. He's a complex man, that's for sure."

People in other West Virginia communities well beyond Rawl blamed Massey and Blankenship for a host of environmental problems. Coal dust from trucks covered their streets and homes. Activists said the company's mountaintop removal mines contaminated local water, put toxic chemicals into the air, and caused flash floods. Thompson had gone with some activists to witness the practice, which involves blowing up mountains on the scale of a bombing run or meteor strike to recover thin coal seams that would be too costly to mine underground. He felt a series of explosions shake the air and ground, saw plumes of dirt and boulders burst from a deforested mountain that had been turned into a moonscape. The shaping of millions of years was undone in moments. Massey had detonated more of West Virginia than any other coal company. The company's enormous dump trucks, with tires that stood eleven feet tall, pushed rock and dirt into valleys, burying headwaters and allowing heavy loads of minerals and metals to flow into waterways, killing aquatic life. Halfhearted efforts to return the sites to the required "approximate original contour," as required by federal law, were always an aesthetic failure beside the contours of actual mountains and only memorialized the devastation.

In the coalfields, environmental activism had been as much a part of the culture as mining since the 1960s. Often, the clearest voices against mountaintop removal mining were women like Judy Bonds, a coal miner's daughter and former manager of a Pizza Hut who was awarded the Goldman Environmental Prize in 2003, or Maria Gunnoe, whose home in Boone County was nearly washed away by rains flooding down from a mountaintop removal mine and who later received the same prize. Thompson sometimes called on young activists when he needed help taking water samples or knocking on clients' doors. He knew many activists had been harassed and threatened by Massey miners, who felt their livelihoods were under attack. But he also knew that Judy Bonds's mantra, "Fight harder," had become a rallying cry for people around the state trying to halt the assault on their homes and communities, especially by Massey.

While these environmental fights were playing out, Thompson became involved in two more lawsuits against Massey. In Raleigh County, an hour south of Charleston, he represented families whose children attended Marsh Fork Elementary School. State regulators had permitted Massey to build a coal silo 235 feet from the school, which sat beneath an impoundment that could hold up to 2.8 billion gallons of coal slurry. Some parents believed coal dust had caused headaches, asthma, and possibly cancers in students and teachers. Thompson wanted Massey to pay for a medical monitoring program, and he was seeking punitive damages, arguing that the company had created a public nuisance. Meanwhile Massey wanted to build a second coal silo. Blankenship had a sign put up at the school touting the company's commitment to the community, and the situation had divided residents.

Another case took Thompson into Logan County, a forty-five-minute drive northeast of Williamson, where nearly two hundred people who had lived or worked in Chauncey, a community of half a dozen streets at the foot of a hill, had developed a variety of cancers. Thompson blamed soil contamination. Old aerial photos showed a pit where mining refuse had been dumped for years—and where an elementary school and a baseball field now stood. The EPA had found heavy metals and pesticides in the soil there, but a state health consultation led by Barbara Smith, the same state epidemiologist who had initially found no health hazard when she investigated the water in Lick Creek and Rawl, concluded there was "no apparent public health hazard" in Chauncey, as long as the soil wasn't disturbed. Thompson sued a land company, the school district, and Massey, which had operated a mine in nearby Omar. He believed the situation was dire: kids were still attending the school and playing on the playground and baseball field. "It's so intense and sad," Thompson said. "They still play goddamn Little League on a coal ash dump."

As he researched the case, Thompson discovered that the heirs of some of the earliest investors in West Virginia's coal industry were still profiting from the mining at Omar while people in Chauncey were getting sick. Through depositions, he pieced together a tale that led back to 1915, when James O. Cole and Clinton Crane, two aging lumber magnates from Cincinnati, had created a real estate trust so their heirs could profit from the ninety thousand acres of timberland they owned in southern West Virginia; the name of their land man and lawyer, C. W. Campbell, showed up on deeds throughout the coalfields. Campbell had bought up enough land and mineral rights on behalf of the businessmen to ensure the future impoverishment of an entire region, Thompson said. Remarkably, the Cole & Crane Real Estate Trust still distributed $18 million a year in royalty payments to about sixty of their living heirs.

Thompson alleged that when Massey acquired a company in Chauncey called West Virginia Coal & Coke Co. in 1954, it also inherited liability for contamination on the land. The details of the deal were essential to Thompson's case—but they had been obscured by time and a tangle of legal entities. Thompson had tracked down the minutes of the meeting on December 12, 1954, in which E. Morgan Massey, the grandson of A. T. Massey, consummated the acquisition of the mining business in an old hotel in Logan County during a snowstorm.

Thompson found several men who remembered the snowy day but not how the deal was structured. The judge wouldn't permit Thompson to depose Morgan Massey, who still lived in Richmond, and he was skeptical that Thompson could seek damages from the coal company. Even so, the judge described the case as a tour through the early days of coal mining and "a primer on the care exercised by many of the entities involved in resource development to avoid liability."

Now Thompson had cases against Massey in three counties: Mingo, Raleigh, and Logan. Activists around West Virginia were going to the courts to stop Massey's mountaintop removal mines, but Thompson was trying to do something more difficult. In Rawl, for example, he needed to prove not just that the company's slurry had gotten into the wells but that it had harmed people's health. To Massey executives, Thompson was a greedy plaintiffs' lawyer filing frivolous lawsuits. "Anytime there is a problem and coal is mentioned for possible blame, Thompson is there to take the case," Shane Harvey, Massey's general counsel, later told a reporter.

But the more Thompson immersed himself in Massey's practices and its history, the more he began to see that the company regularly defied the limits of environmental and safety regulations, engaging in practices that even other coal companies avoided. And often in its defense, he believed, it offered outright lies.

In the beginning, Massey didn't do any of its own mining; it was founded as a small coal brokerage in 1920 by A. T. Massey, a tall, striking man who wore a pearl lapel pin and often withdrew company funds for trips to the race track. In 1934, his son Evan Massey sent him a letter at the posh Sinton Hotel in Cincinnati, castigating him for "spending money like a drunken sailor" instead of selling coal contracts.

The company's second generation barely kept it afloat through the Great Depression. But E. Morgan Massey was a shrewd dealmaker, and when he took over he greatly expanded the company's mining operations. The company needed his expertise. After World War II, oil and gas dominated coal's traditional markets: home heating, railroads, power plants. Mines shut and coal production fell sharply.

During the 1960s and 1970s, coal markets improved, but companies came up against the constraints of new federal regulations for clean air, clean water, and the reclamation of land damaged by surface mining, in addition to new health and safety protections for miners. These all cut into profits and reshaped the coal business by contributing to a wave of conglomeration. By the early 1980s, Massey was part of Fluor Corporation, a construction behemoth. The sale brought millions of dollars to the Massey family, and E. Morgan Massey kept running the business with Fluor's financial backing. To generate profits, he drew up a twenty-seven-page blueprint called the Massey Doctrine.

Distributed internally in the fall of 1982, the document was marked "CONFIDENTIAL." It was partly a personal manifesto. "The value system is that of E. Morgan Massey, which involves to a great extent the belief that duty comes before self, but in a hedonistic society self comes before society at large," he wrote. In his hierarchy of priorities, customers were at the top, followed by shareholders, employees, and society.

Morgan Massey's goal was to insulate the company from inevitable downturns in the coal markets. He reorganized the company's priorities based on the profitability of coal reserves. That meant controlling thicker coal seams that yielded more coal per unit of labor. Going forward, the company would only own and operate its own mines in reserves that would be profitable in any coal market. For the middle category of reserves—those that might still break even when coal prices fell—the company would mine the coal through a contractor or independent producer, cutting the risk to Massey if the mine could no longer operate at a profit. As for the worst coal reserves, Massey would simply buy the coal cheaply and resell it, with no stake in the mines. When the price for coal was high, all three types of reserves would be profitable, and when prices sank, only the best reserves, those that Massey mined itself, would be profitable.

Morgan Massey wanted to employ as few workers as possible to maximize productivity. He also wanted to organize labor into small teams at the company "for identity, communications and good morale." He advised naming mines in a way that had local community significance, rather than numbering them as most companies did. Though he didn't say it in his doctrine, some of his recommendations were lifted from a guidebook for staying union free. He said he wanted managers to follow an open-door policy in which any employee could resolve problems with managers directly.

To carry out this plan, Morgan Massey created "resource groups," which were geographic units of mines and preparation plants operated semiautonomously, each with its own engineers and a lean managerial staff, reporting back to centrally located managers who handled corporate planning, financial control, and legal administration in Richmond.

It might have sounded like dry corporate-speak, but the Massey Doctrine emphasized measuring coal reserves and labor to maximize profitability in a way that other coal companies hadn't done before. The plan would have far-reaching consequences not only for Massey but for the entire industry, for communities throughout the region, and for a broad swath of mountaintops and streams.

Morgan Massey's policies pushed more financial burdens and safety risks onto smaller operators and contractors, leaving them with the crumbs of the profits. They paid less to workers, had older mining equipment, and invested less in safety measures. Independent operators often mined the more difficult seams on a shoestring. These small mines tended to be more hazardous. The doctrine also effectively necessitated that managers fight off the mine workers' union, and favor a low-cost mining process like mountaintop removal.

The Massey Doctrine was first reported on by *Charleston Gazette* reporter Paul J. Nyden, who chronicled its effects. By 1992, more than 42 percent of coal was mined in Central Appalachia by contractors, including 475 companies hired by Massey since 1977. So many small operators had gone bankrupt by then that they collectively owed the state workers' compensation fund an estimated $200 million. Massey and its peers had saved millions and put the burden on the state.

When he conceived his doctrine, Morgan Massey didn't know that a young manager was about to carry out his plan far better than he ever could. Earlier that year, in 1982, a thirty-two-year-old accountant named Don Blankenship had joined Rawl Sales & Processing as controller. Ten years later, when Morgan Massey retired, Blankenship became president and chairman of the company, the first person to run the business outside the Massey family.

By August 2005, Massey's lawyers had given Thompson more than three thousand pages of Rawl Sales documents and made a former engineer, O. Eugene Kitts, who was known in the coal industry as "Gene

Kitts," available for a deposition at their offices in Charleston. Thompson deposed Kitts for nearly two and a half hours. A savvy civil engineer who wore thin-framed glasses, Kitts came across as a meticulous, well-intentioned professional who believed that coal companies were safeguarding the environment rather than scarring it. A surprising number of prominent coal industry veterans had worked at Rawl Sales early in their careers under Blankenship. Kitts, who was born in Matewan, had been an environmental engineer there from 1981 through 1985 and then again from 1987 to 1991.

Kitts said he thought the company started building the Rawl impoundment in 1984, which matched Mullennex's earlier testimony.

"How long did it take to complete?" Thompson asked.

"That's a difficult question," Kitts said. "Technically they're still building it."

When it came to the basics of coal processing, Thompson was still like a student trying to bluff his way through an exam—even though an October trial date was just a few months away. As Kitts explained, an active impoundment was always a work in progress, because the company would periodically build up the earthen dam in order to be able to keep pumping slurry behind it.

It was Thompson's first deposition of a current or former Rawl Sales employee, and his lack of experience showed in other ways. He was learning the names of the major coal seams in the area: in descending order from the surface, the three most heavily mined seams were the Cedar Grove, the Alma, and the Pond Creek. He asked Kitts if the state's Department of Environmental Protection (DEP) had granted Rawl Sales a permit to inject slurry in the 1980s.

"DEP was not formed until the early nineties," Kitts said.

"I wasn't aware of that," said Thompson. Perhaps he'd been looking for permits at the wrong agency.

Kitts was hazy about the extent of Rawl Sales' slurry injection and the permitting process. He recalled two, or possibly three, injection holes that were drilled during his years at Rawl Sales. He said there could have been more, but he didn't know how many. When he joined Rawl Sales in 1981, the company was already injecting slurry. He thought it had largely filled the old Alma seam workings by then and moved on to the Pond Creek seam.

Sometime in the 1960s, West Virginia stopped letting companies dump coal waste directly into streams. After the prep plant had been built in 1975 or 1976, Kitts said, workers used a machine called a filter press to vacuum the water out of the slurry, creating big disks known as filter cake, and then trucks would take that solid material a short distance away and dump it into a fill. Thompson learned from Kitts that the injection operation was fairly simple: a pump at the prep plant sent the slurry through miles of pipe to the injection well, little more than a concrete well casing with a few feet of steel pipe sticking out of the ground. Slurry ran through the pipe hole into an underground void. A chain or strap kept the slurry line attached to the steel pipe, to keep someone from pulling the line out and letting slurry run onto the ground, or having the pipe rip loose from a surge.

Kitts confirmed two stories Thompson had heard from Don Dillon, the former Massey electrician who lived in Rawl. The first was that in the 1980s slurry had once broken through a mine seal—a wall of solid concrete blocks—and gotten into the active section of a mine under Rawl, forcing miners to evacuate. The second story was that York Smith, the former superintendent of the prep plant, had gotten injured in a slurry line accident. "He was the one that was responsible for getting holes drilled and pipelines run to them and choosing the route and that sort of thing," Kitts said.

Then Thompson came to the heart of the issue and asked who ordered the slurry injection. Kitts said that after 1984, the operation came under the control of Rawl Sales' head office, and the general manager at the prep plant reported directly to the president of Rawl Sales.

"The president of Rawl at that time would have been who in '84?" Thompson asked.

"That would have been Don Blankenship," said Kitts.

It was the first time anyone had said on the record that Blankenship had direct knowledge of the slurry injection at Rawl Sales. But Kitts proved to be even more helpful. He had brought with him a set of documents that listed the daily slurry injection volumes and rates for July 1985. Thompson reviewed the numbers with Kitts: the company had pumped 13,453,257 gallons that month. Thompson was surprised that the company would have pumped so much in a single month in 1985, a year after the impoundment had supposedly been started. The average pumping rate was listed as "500 GPM," which Kitts explained was gallons per minute. Kitts said there would be work maps that showed the injection holes, but he had no idea where such maps were stored.

Thompson noted that the average daily injection volume was 584,924.22 gallons.

"That's what it says," Kitts said. "Someone was being very precise, weren't they?"

Thompson couldn't help but think of Blankenship's reputation for being a numbers-obsessed micromanager. He wanted to know when Rawl Sales had started injecting and when it had stopped, but Kitts couldn't provide those answers. Nor could he say how much the company might have injected in total.

"I wouldn't even have a guess," Kitts said.

Three weeks passed after Kitts's deposition, and Judge Thornsbury had yet to rule on Thompson's emergency motion for temporary water. Thompson was fed up with waiting, and he decided to vent his frustration by putting Massey on the defensive. On August 24, he filed a motion at the courthouse on Second Avenue seeking permission to subpoena Don Blankenship for a deposition within thirty days.

Then he went back to his room at the Mountaineer, where he'd been following reports about a tropical storm named Katrina. Thompson watched the storm for another day and then decided to drive home to New Orleans. By the time he left Williamson, Katrina had grown into a Category 3 hurricane. He and Kathleen hadn't been worried—they both thought the storm would jog east at the last minute, as recent storms had. But when Thompson reached New Orleans, the nearly four-hundred-mile-wide storm had intensified and was bearing down on the Louisiana coast, headed for a direct hit at the mouth of the Mississippi River. Kathleen and thirteen-year-old Kelsey had brought plants and lawn furniture into the family's boarded-up house. Now they and Thompson raced to collect their pets: four dogs and a cat. In two cars, they made it out of the city before the bridges were shut. Then they drove four hundred miles north to a Comfort Inn in Memphis.

In the hotel room, with the dogs piled around them on the bed, Thompson and his wife and daughter were initially relieved when the storm made landfall southeast of New Orleans. But then the levees broke, and they watched with horror as floodwaters covered more than 80 percent of the city, stranding thousands in the poorest neighborhoods.

Thompson called his neighbors and learned that a tree had damaged his roof, but their neighborhood, in one of the highest points of the city, had been spared from flooding. A dozen blocks away, the water had been chest high. He and Kathleen decided to drive to her parents' house in Gallipolis and plot their next move.

After a few days in Gallipolis, Thompson told Kathleen he needed to take care of his cases, and she decided to stay put with Kelsey for a while.

"It's really not worth arguing about," she said. "You need to go do your work, and I need to do mine."

Thompson had to travel back to the devastated city first to retrieve some files. He brought along Kathleen's brother, who was a contractor, and some other workers, and they set about repairing Thompson's house and others in the neighborhood. Relief operations were still unfolding when Thompson left New Orleans again, this time headed for Williamson and on his own.

Kathleen had never told Thompson to spend less time in West Virginia. Even before he'd taken the Rawl case, she didn't like him being away for weeks at a time for his consulting businesses, but she had grown used to it. He never failed to make it back home for Thanksgiving, and they would always celebrate their wedding anniversary on the following Saturday. But years later, when his days away began to outnumber those at home, Thompson's deepest regret would be that he had missed so much time with his family.

CHAPTER 8

All fall, Thompson was whipsawed by victories and setbacks. In early September, Judge Thornsbury handed down an order that fell short of requiring Massey to deliver bottled water but nevertheless gave Thompson hope. The judge agreed that the area's water wasn't drinkable, and he added that it might not be safe for bathing and other uses either. But in the judge's view, Thompson had failed to demonstrate an emergency. The county had been sending a truck with a water tank, called a water buffalo, to the communities during the warmer months, and the judge relied on assurances from county officials that a water line would be built soon. There was evidence that the area's water supply had been degraded, the judge felt, but a jury should assign responsibility.

After more than a year, Judge Thornsbury wrote, neither Thompson nor Jackson Kelly had produced evidence that Rawl Sales had a state permit to inject slurry underground. He ordered the company to stop any injection still taking place, which Thompson also considered a victory. Then the judge canceled the October trial date and didn't immediately set a new one. Thompson was disappointed by the delay, but he tried to stay focused on the positive aspects of the rulings. The judge was taking the people's claims seriously, and, as Thompson had hoped, he apparently hadn't been persuaded by Massey's experts.

The Simpkins trial, to determine whether Arch Coal's subsidiary had contaminated James Simpkins's property, was held in Judge Thornsbury's courtroom in September 2005 and lasted only a few days. A jury returned a verdict in Simpkins's favor and found that Arch Coal had been negligent in mining his land. Simpkins, who happened to be a longtime friend of Don Blankenship, was pleased with Thompson. "He was into it heavy, and he did a good job for me," Simpkins said. "As an attorney goes, he's not bad."

It was Thompson's second victory in Mingo County—and his first jury verdict ever. But he couldn't savor it for long. The verdict came on a Friday. On Monday, Judge Thornsbury ruled that the Rawl case wouldn't be handled as a class action, handing a major win to Massey. The ruling meant that Thompson and Bunch would have to try the claims of each client individually—with a $145 filing fee paid to the court for each complaint—instead of trying the claims of a few class representatives. The judge would decide by the end of the year that the lawyers could argue common issues across the case. But Thompson still had to get water testing data and medical records for everyone. His workload had just expanded exponentially.

Thompson filed 171 individual civil actions in the first big wave of residents to join the case. He worked day and night in his room in the Mountaineer to meet a deadline set by the judge. But in his haste he made a costly mistake: his filings mentioned the Clean Water Act as a cause of action. Jackson Kelly seized on the inclusion of the federal law and immediately sought to have the case removed to federal court. To do so cost Jackson Kelly nearly $50,000 in federal court filing fees, according to Thompson, who was annoyed whenever he had to spend $145 for each complaint he filed in Williamson. Ultimately Thompson and Bunch convinced a federal judge to deny Jackson Kelly's motion, and the case remained in Mingo County. Thompson was grateful to Bunch for minimizing the misstep to his partners in Phoenix. "He soft-pedaled my giant fuckup," Thompson said.

In late October, county officials announced that workers would soon break ground on a water line from Williamson to the four communities. After lobbying at the state capitol by Ernie and Carmelita, B.I., and others, and the attention garnered by Thompson's lawsuit, state lawmakers had at long last secured enough money from federal and state infrastructure programs for the Lick Creek Water Line Extension project, with some twelve miles of water line, a ninety-four-thousand-gallon storage tank, and twenty-eight fire hydrants.

In a clearing on Route 49 near Lick Creek, a handful of residents and a local newspaper reporter turned out when several contractors delivered bids to the county's three commissioners. Wearing a white long-sleeve top, her hair pulled back by a black scrunchie, Carmelita watched the photo op for the local politicians. She'd been waiting almost twenty years for clean water. Even now, her well water smelled as bad as it ever had. Every month, she used five gallons of bleach in her laundry to mute the stench on her clothes. "They still stink so bad from the water that I hate to be around people," she told the reporter. Even so, there was hope in her voice. "This is a big step," Carmelita said. "I believe it may finally happen."

Once again, Thompson had little time to celebrate. He soon learned that his daughter, Kelsey, had become ill back in New Orleans and had to be hospitalized. He dropped all of his work and flew home. Visiting her every day, he wondered at the toll the case was taking on his family. He stayed in New Orleans through Thanksgiving, before returning to West Virginia.

"Kevin literally postponed all of his cases for a month when I went into the hospital and was like, sorry, guys, I can't do it, I got to be here," Kelsey recalled later. "He worked from home and stayed with me for as long as he could."

While he was in New Orleans, Thompson got an unexpected break in the case from West Virginia—his biggest to date. To help him dig into Rawl Sales' past, he had called Jack Spadaro, a mining engineer with extensive contacts with federal and state regulators, who lived in Hamlin, about an hour west of Charleston. Spadaro knew more than anyone about the regulations pertaining to slurry impoundments: he had written many of them during his twenty-eight years at the federal Mine Safety and Health Administration. His career in government was bookended by two of the worst impoundment disasters in the history of the coal industry. He had seen firsthand the devastation caused by the 1972 coal slurry dam collapse on Buffalo Creek, which released a wall of slurry up to twenty feet high that swept away houses and cars, killed 125 people, and left 4,000 homeless. And nearly three decades later, he had written a report on Massey's historic impoundment failure in Martin County, Kentucky, in 2000. He found that Massey officials had known they needed to make repairs to the impoundment but hadn't. The company had said that up to eighty feet of earth separated the impoundment from an abandoned mine below it; in fact, there were only twenty feet, making a collapse all but inevitable. Spadaro believed Massey was criminally negligent, but several George W. Bush appointees at MSHA curtailed his investigation and forced him out of the agency. Spadaro said the interference was unprecedented: "I had never seen anything so corrupt and lawless in my entire career."

Spadaro was a big man with curly hair, a beard, and thick eyebrows, and he tended to dress in tweedy sport coats. He was more like a character out of Dickens than a typical mining engineer from the coalfields. He had grown up poor in Mount Hope, West Virginia, the son of a janitor. He was well-read in high school and had considered studying literature. Then an English teacher suggested he could get a scholarship if he studied to be a mining engineer, and he eventually did at West Virginia University. Spadaro now lived in the woods south of Charleston in a house he built on a hill, so he could see the sun rise and set. He lived by a line from Albert Camus he'd learned as a teen: even if you know that the fight you're in is hopeless and you're going to lose, you're still obligated to fight on anyway. "That was a pretty good thing to learn when you're fifteen," Spadaro said. After he blew the whistle on the Martin County investigation, *60 Minutes* aired a segment on him titled "Who Is Jack Spadaro?" Correspondent Bob Simon answered the question: "He's a man who's devoted his life to the safety of miners and the safety of people who live near mines."

Thompson went on to hire Spadaro for nearly every environmental case he had. The two didn't always get along—Spadaro didn't like disorder, and he got annoyed whenever Thompson didn't pay him on time; he once referred to Thompson's office as a "portable Animal House." But Spadaro also said that he loved Thompson, because he genuinely tried to help people, taking cases no other lawyers would touch because they were so difficult. "I have screamed at Kevin. I have cursed him. I have told him I'll never ever do anything for you," Spadaro said. "He says, 'Okay, you were right.' But I really respect him and admire him for what he's doing."

Spadaro had gone to the offices of the West Virginia DEP in Charleston, where, like Scott Simonton, he was unable to find slurry injection permits for Rawl Sales. Days later, Spadaro got a call from a contact at the agency telling him there were some boxes in a storage closet he should see. When Spadaro returned, the official showed him a stack of documents that, Spadaro believed, had been slated to be thrown out while the agency was in the process of digitizing old files.

"They don't want you to find these," Spadaro recalled the official telling him.

Spadaro photocopied maps and internal Rawl Sales memos, many of them dating to the 1980s. The cache included monthly slurry injection reports that Rawl Sales engineers provided to state environmental regulators from the summer of 1984 through 1987, with daily volumes recorded down to the hundredth of a gallon. The company had pumped more than 20 million gallons of slurry into the mountains in most months, and over time the rate increased to 600 gallons per minute and then 750 gallons per minute. It was hard evidence that the company had injected hundreds of millions of gallons of slurry into the mountains around Rawl. Spadaro totaled injection volumes from 1977 to 1987 and came up with 1.14 billion gallons. He calculated the extent of the slurry in the abandoned mines near the four communities: 1,020 acres, or more than 750 football fields.

Spadaro's document haul included state records showing that other coal companies had injected slurry into more than four hundred sites in West Virginia since the 1960s. The pervasiveness of the practice was a revelation to activists trying to ban it. But the fact that other companies had pumped slurry underground didn't absolve Massey of the consequences of its own actions.

Even as he was shocked by the figures, Thompson was ecstatic. "That was another great day in sports history," he said.

The start of 2006 proved to be deadly for West Virginia coal miners. On January 2, twelve miners were killed following an explosion at International Coal Group's Sago Mine in Upshur County. Seventeen days later, two Massey miners died of carbon monoxide poisoning at the Aracoma Alma Mine No. 1 in Logan County after coal dust on a conveyor belt caught fire and they couldn't find their way out. The accidents were a reminder to Thompson of the heavy price the industry continued to exact from miners, their families, and their communities.

Then, in early February, Thompson learned that the water line construction would be delayed. The first round of bids had all come in too high. Hurricane Katrina cleanup had driven up costs for construction materials nationwide. New bids wouldn't be opened until mid-March, and then construction wouldn't be completed for months. Exasperated,

Thompson filed a brief asking Judge Thornsbury to require Massey to provide water immediately. It was now two years since he had first seen the jars of discolored water in Larry Brown's church.

Thompson's filing read like a letter from a remote outpost where survival is no longer assured: "Beyond question, Rawl Sales injected hundreds of millions of gallons of slurry into abandoned mines. Deadly hydrogen sulfide gas seeps into Rawl homes from slurry-tainted wells. Winter is hard upon us and the water buffaloes are gone," he wrote. Using the name residents had adopted for themselves, Thompson added, "All the while the people of the Forgotten Communities will drink and bathe in water that presents an imminent danger to the health and safety of the public." He concluded: "To think that a sophisticated coal company could inject over a billion gallons of toxic slurry into abandoned mine works overlaying an aquifer, in a confined area like we have here, and believe that there will be no impact on the hydro-geologic balance is to defy common sense."

Thompson put a finer point on it when he was talking to Bunch and others. "It's one thing to inject shitloads of slurry into a single coal seam," he said. "It's something else entirely to inject triple shitloads for years and years into every coal seam in the area."

Judge Thornsbury didn't immediately rule on the motion. And he had yet to set a new trial date. The delay gave Thompson more time to put his case together, and a window to see his wife and daughter in New Orleans. But Larry Brown and others feared it meant the judge was going against them. In their minds, the fight for clean water was the latest battle in a generations-old struggle—in which, time and again, the people had failed to win justice.

CHAPTER 9

Thompson had driven through Mingo County hundreds of times—in the heart of an Appalachian winter, and on summer days when the kudzu blanketed the steep hills and the green blur of the area's wildness crowded into the narrow lanes. It was a place of rare beauty to him, but sometimes it seemed haunted, even cursed. In the winter months, before the leaves appeared, he could see the skeletons of old company houses, their black-eyed windows peering out from underneath dense vines. The traces of the past glimpsed from county roads made time appear to stand still.

The roads that branched off to the homes of his clients led past weathered trailers, porches wrapped in tarps, and smoke rising from cluttered yards. A train track ran at eye level beside a gauntlet of coal camp houses before diving back into the hills. There were old cemeteries, Baptist churches, neat brick homes set back from the road, a dairy bar and pizzeria, an auto-repair shop, the spectacular ruin of a house caved in on itself and left to rot. Then nothing again for miles but the road and the hills until the next mining complex pitched its green conveyors against the sky. A sign outside Williamson welcomed visitors, without a trace of irony, to the "Heart of the Billion Dollar Coal Field," but it was a place where many people had always lived at the fraying edge of poverty.

Another constant in Mingo County was its history of violence. From the legendary Hatfield-McCoy feud in the 1870s and 1880s to the Matewan Massacre and Mine Wars of the early 1920s to a brutal fifteen-month-long strike in the 1980s at Rawl Sales, the Tug Valley had been witness to a remarkable amount of bloodshed. Much of the violence that gave the county its nickname "Bloody Mingo" had occurred close to where Thompson's clients now lived. The stretch of Route 49 was steeped in a history of fighting over land and over labor—and now, with Thompson's lawsuit, over damage to the environment and people's health.

To encourage civic pride and boost tourism, the Tug Valley Chamber of Commerce made the most of a cottage industry of feud books and movies, selling feud-branded coal carvings out of the Coal House and promoting the Hatfield-McCoy Trails, the Hatfield McCoy Marathon, and the Hatfield McCoy Heritage Days festival. Every year, as close to the May 19 anniversary as possible, the Matewan Drama Group, formed by residents to preserve the local history, reenacted the Matewan Massacre, the shoot-out between Baldwin-Felts detectives on one side and the city's sheriff and miners on the other. Children in Matewan took class trips to listen to the recordings about the Mine Wars that played at stations along the city's floodwall and at the old bank building, where they could reach their fingers into the marks left by bullets more than eighty years earlier. Even Don Blankenship, who had gone to high school in Matewan, was a student of the region's history. He paid for a replica of the Matewan train depot, as it existed in 1920, to be built a block away from its original site and serve as a museum. He knew the original depot had been built too close to the tracks and that a corner of its roof had to be shaved off to let trains pass, so he had workers replicate that detail too.

For decades there had been no reason for many parts of the county to change and few resources for them to be able to. Beginning in the 1880s, coal operators had built dozens of communities in the coalfields as company towns, and although the homes had been updated, starting in the 1950s with indoor plumbing and then with more modern conveniences, many who lived in those houses in the early 2000s still had ties to the coal industry. Programs from the Johnson administration's War on Poverty in the mid-1960s had mostly come and gone, after being in some cases co-opted by local politicians for their own purposes. Mining had declined, but no other industry had come to replace it. Even though some of the old infrastructure had rusted in place, coal still exerted more influence than any other force in the county.

Without realizing it, Thompson often drove by the former site of the famous Mingo Oak, a beloved tree that had once stood more than eight feet in diameter. When it was felled in 1938, the tree was nearly six hundred years old and thought to be the biggest and oldest white oak in the world. It was an ancient from a forgotten time when oaks, walnuts, yellow poplars, and sycamores grew to enormous dimensions. As it happened, the Cole & Crane Real Estate Trust—the same company Thompson would later investigate—owned the land surrounding the tree, and it was believed that fumes from a burning waste dump of the Island Creek Coal Company had killed the tree before it was cut down.

Long before it was touched by industry, the land that would become Mingo County had been visited by the Adena, prehistoric people who left behind burial mounds, like Cotiga Mound near the Tug Fork, which was built beginning around 200 BC. When it was excavated twenty centuries later, stone tools and copper bracelets were found with cremated remains. The region's steep terrain and hard-to-navigate river made it inhospitable to settlement by Native Americans, historians say, but it became a hunting ground for them. The sweep of virgin forest teemed with deer, bear, turkey, elk, buffalo, and panther.

By the mid-1700s, it marked the edge of the frontier for white pioneers, drawing trappers and settlers seeking a place to build a rough existence farming, harvesting timber, and distilling whiskey beyond the reach of tax collectors. Sycamores eleven to fourteen feet wide and hollowed out with age sometimes served as shelters for hunters and explorers.

Fur and ginseng were the first commodities to be exported from the territory. Bearskins sold by hunters in Appalachia for one to four dollars apiece were used to make hats for Napoleon's grenadiers. In 1847, one of the region's first coal mines opened in Peach Orchard, Kentucky, but without a railroad the company struggled to transport coal. The massive trees dwarfed the men who came to cut them down. By the 1880s, the giants were mostly gone, and game, including the eastern elk, cougar, and buffalo that had roamed freely, had disappeared as a result of overhunting. Occupying land that had already been in their families for several generations, people living along the Tug Fork made their living by farming or timbering, floating logs they cut to sawmills.

A white historical marker on Route 49 near the entrance to Rawl pinpoints the day—September 22, 1892—that ended that way of life and transformed the entire region.

That was the day the Norfolk and Western railroad completed its Ohio extension, a section of track that connected lines that extended west to Ohio and east to Virginia. The sign says five thousand men worked on the project over two years and "changed the line's character from that of a southern agrarian road into a major Atlantic-Midwest trunk route and mighty 'Pocahontas Coal Carrier.'" Just a few months before completion, in July of 1892, the president of the railroad, Frederick J. Kimball, had complained in a letter to bankers in London about a great loop in the river, known as Hatfield Bend, between what would become Sprigg and Matewan, calling it "the worst place on the Ohio Extension." "There has been so much lawlessness and shooting that we have found it almost impossible to get good men to work," he wrote. Eventually the railroad avoided the bend by crossing the Tug Fork and tunneling eight hundred feet through a mountain before crossing back into West Virginia.

The boundaries of what would become Mingo County hadn't yet been drawn, but the magic dust of capital had already been sprinkled along the railroad's course. A state geological survey had identified all the minable coal seams in the hills, and investors had spent millions buying up land and mineral rights along the planned extension. More than a year before the railroad's arrival, in August 1891, the first coal mining company had been incorporated in the Tug Valley. Coal investors started building Williamson, and fifteen miles to the east, Matewan soon followed.

Even the widely misunderstood Hatfield-McCoy feud was heavily influenced by the industrialization of the Tug Fork Valley that set the stage for violence that has often been attributed to the bloodlust of vicious outlaws. A truer version of events is rooted in the social and economic pressures of the time and far more interesting.

A hundred years before Thompson's clients began to struggle with their water, a violent killing led to another desperate night along the Tug Fork.

On August 9, 1882, three boys from the McCoy family stabbed and shot Ellison Hatfield at an Election Day gathering on the Kentucky side of the Tug Fork where whiskey had been flowing all day. It's not clear what caused the fight. Ellison's brother William Anderson Hatfield, who was known as Anderson or "Anse," insisted that the McCoy boys be brought with him across the river into West Virginia while he and his other brothers Elias and Valentine waited to see if Ellison would survive. On the night of the tenth, Ellison died in Warm Hollow, a few hundred yards from the river bottom where the town of Matewan would later be built. The three McCoy boys had been tied up in a schoolhouse in the hollow that night. The Hatfields kept vigil, while the boys' mother pleaded for them to be freed. The next morning, Anderson and about twenty other men took the boys and crossed back over to a flat river-bank on the Kentucky side of the Tug Fork, tied them to some bushes, and executed them, shooting off the top of one boy's head.

A month later, Kentucky officials indicted Anse Hatfield and twenty others for the murder of the three McCoys. For five years, nothing came of the indictments. The lull has made some historians and local experts question whether there was any Hatfield-McCoy feud as it's commonly understood. It's possible that communities on both sides of the river viewed the murders of the three boys as retributive justice and were content to let the matter rest.

Then in 1887, a handful of Kentucky businessmen became interested in buying up Anse Hatfield's lands. One young businessman from Pikeville, Kentucky, named Perry Cline had lost five thousand acres to Hatfield in a court ruling years earlier. Cline was among those calling most loudly for the indictments to be revived. It was only in 1888 that the Hatfield-McCoy feud began to appear in newspapers, written in the florid style of the time by reporters who frequently got the story from the Kentucky side.

Anse Hatfield formed a group to fend off attempts to arrest him and the other indicted men. He sent a threatening letter to Cline in August 1887: "If you come into this county to take or bother any of the Hatfields, we will follow you to hell or take your hide, and if any of the Hatfields are killed or bothered in any way, we will charge it up to you, and your hide will pay the penalty." He concluded with a sterner warning: "We have a habit of making one-horse lawyers keep their boots on and we have plenty of good strong rope left, and our hangman tied a knot for you and laid it quietly away until we see what you do. We have no particular pleasure in hanging dogs, but we know you and have counted the miles and marked the tree."

Newspaper articles portrayed Hatfield and his supporters—who included some McCoys who had worked for his timber operations—as lawless and violent. In at least one case, his allies lived up to the description. On New Year's Day 1888, with a bounty now on their heads, several men who backed Hatfield set fire to a McCoy house and shot and killed two members of the family, while their father, Randolph "Ole Ran'l" McCoy, fled into the woods with others.

On January 19, 1888, Hatfield and his supporters met a posse of bounty hunters hired by Perry Cline at Grapevine Creek. Hatfield and other men from his side of the river had fought for the Confederacy in the Civil War, as had Randolph McCoy, while many on the Kentucky side of the Tug Fork had sided with the Union. The mix of veterans exchanged a fusillade of bullets across the creek. It was the only true battle of the feud. One man on Hatfield's side was killed; a McCoy on the other side was injured. What had been a dispute between the Hatfield and McCoy families in a remote region of subsistence farming and timber operations had grown into a conflict driven by people seeking an economic advantage on the cusp of the Tug Valley's industrialization.

A few weeks after the battle, Hatfield began selling land along the Tug Fork to a coal agent for investors from Philadelphia: five thousand acres for seven thousand dollars. At the time, one of Hatfield's bitter enemies, the Pike County prosecutor, boasted to a newspaper that the land was really worth fifteen thousand dollars. Two years later, it was valued at seventy-five thousand dollars. Hatfield bought cheaper land twenty miles north in a place called Main Island Creek, and he barricaded himself and his family in a house on a hill. His withdrawal was another sign of the end of preindustrial life in the Tug Valley. It was in the economic interest of Cline and other investors to portray Hatfield and the region's other mountaineers as backward men bent on killing each other. The fiction helped conceal their own intentions to profit from the land at the expense of the people who had called the place home, and it was a strategy that fed into lasting stereotypes of Appalachia. In fact, coal operators soon followed Hatfield north as more mines and coal camps sprang up across the southern mountains. By 1915, Main Island Creek Coal Company had opened mines at Omar—the same operations near Chauncey that were later sold to West Virginia Coal & Coke, and then to Massey.

Anse Hatfield had been a timber entrepreneur. He looked the part of the outlaw mountaineer, with his wiry beard extending down to his chest and black eyes beneath the brim of his felt hat. He posed for a photographer with his Winchester across his lap and the rest of his family lined up beside him with their own guns. Yet in at least one portrait, he wears a black waistcoat and silk tie and could almost be mistaken for a merchant. Even the origins of his nickname "Devil Anse" are obscured by the feud legend. Some say he got the name after he killed a mountain lion as a boy, or while fighting in the Civil War, or that he gave it to himself. Others believe that no one ever called him "Devil Anse" until a New York newspaper reporter coined the sensational name in 1888—and that it came into wide use only after the hostilities had ended. A handful of scholars have drawn a more complex portrait of Hatfield. "Despite his illiteracy, he was a shrewd, ambitious, aggressive, protocapitalist who counted on contracts, lawyers, and courts to protect his interests," concluded Altina Waller, a professor emerita in history at the University of Connecticut, who has put the feud in the context of Tug Valley's rapid industrialization.

If the railroad extension had been placed farther north, along the Guyandotte River as had been considered, the Tug Valley would have been spared much of the violence to come. The world may never have heard the name Devil Anse; the Hatfields and McCoys wouldn't have entered the American lexicon as enduring symbols of the backwardness of Appalachia. Perhaps the most telling fact about the feud's link to coal development is that with the sale of Devil Anse's five thousand acres, the fighting largely ended. A few months after the deal, surveyors for the Norfolk and Western planted their three-legged sight levels on the banks of the Tug Fork. They measured the land with a new precision. The first locomotive was more than three years away. But when the railroad men looked through their sights, they saw the future approaching.

The economic opportunity from mining coal must have seemed limitless to local business owners and out-of-state investors. The path to profits was simple: acquire the mineral rights to land with coal and hire workers to dig that coal at the lowest cost possible. Mingo County was created in 1895 through the influence of coal investors, who could use the new county to consolidate their power. The Norfolk and Western opened one of the biggest rail yards in the United States on the eastern edge of Williamson. By 1910, the Tug Fork between Williamson and Matewan was lined with mines and company houses. Locomotives thundered through the valley, hauling away trainloads of coal and trailing clouds of steam.

While out-of-state companies exploited southern West Virginia for its resources, the region developed the traits of other parts of the world dominated by extractive industries: low economic diversification, a high rate of poverty, and relatively weak government institutions. Social scientists often refer to regions that supply minerals as being peripheral to the wealthy nations that dominate them. Corruption tends to flourish in such places, and it did in Mingo County, which was considered, even in the first few decades of the twentieth century, to be one of the most corrupt places in America, where widespread and blatant vote-buying and ballot-stuffing in elections was a sign of how disenfranchised most people were. In 1908, the county was first called "Bleeding Mingo" in a series of local newspaper articles about its corrupt elections. In 1916, the Mingo County circuit court judge James Damron said he wanted to clean up the voter rolls and remove "illegal voters, dead men, mules and tombstones." He was shot a year later while leaving his office in downtown Williamson, though he recovered. An investigation by the governor's office determined the shooting was either a political vendetta or in response to the judge's womanizing. He was shot again years later, only to recover a second time.

As it turned out, the coal in Mingo County was inferior to the neighboring coalfields of Logan and McDowell Counties. The repercussions from this were surprisingly complex and long-lasting. Mingo County's inferior coal meant that major companies like U.S. Steel invested less in mines there, creating an opportunity for smaller companies, and ultimately rival political factions, to compete with each other. In Logan and McDowell, big corporations controlled the local politicians, and the mine workers' union didn't have a chance to gain a foothold there at the turn of the twentieth century. In Mingo County, however, some mayors and sheriffs supported union organizing, setting the stage for violent clashes between miners and the smaller coal operators in the towns along the Tug Fork.

"Technically Mingo County is part of the southern West Virginia powerhouse, but the bookends are Logan and McDowell. That's where the real coal money was made," said Rebecca Bailey, an associate professor of history at Northern Kentucky University, who has chronicled the causes of the Tug Valley's second wave of violence. "Mingo County was a periphery of a periphery," said Bailey. "There's less to fight over, but people fight that much more viciously."

CHAPTER 10

For the first miners who arrived in the Tug Valley—Don Dillon's family had moved in 1903 from a farm in Virginia into the fledgling community of Merrimac before settling in Rawl—the work was dangerous, and miners soon found themselves living and working in a system that kept them and their families impoverished and under the tight control of the companies and their mine guards.

By 1920, there were 784,000 coal miners across the country. In the prior twenty years, nearly 50,000 had died in accidents, mostly explosions. When organizers from the United Mine Workers of America (UMWA) arrived in Mingo County in the spring of 1920, many of the county's 3,378 miners were prepared to fight for better pay and safety. Nearly three-quarters of the miners were native-born whites, but they also included Hungarian and Italian immigrants and Black migrants. On April 16, 1920, miners posted a declaration at the portal of a mine owned by the Burnwell Coal and Coke Company, demanding the same raise that the federal government had approved for unionized miners in the northern part of the state. "We shall have this 27 per cent raise," the message read. "We want this 27 per cent raise which the Government has granted us."

The posting was a beacon. Hundreds of miners living along the river attended meetings in Matewan to take the union oath. Many miners had been lured to the region by advertisements promising good-paying work, only to find that they and their families were required to live in segregated company-owned towns; to be policed by armed company guards; and to be paid in company scrip with deductions for their equipment, right down to the carbide that burned in their headlamps. On April 22, five hundred men showed up at the Baptist church in Matewan. More than half joined the union. The following day, more than seven hundred men gathered. But wary coal operators started to fire the unionized miners and evict them from their company houses.

May 19, 1920, was an overcast day in Matewan, and the sky threatened rain. Just before noon, Albert and Lee Felts and eleven other agents from the Baldwin-Felts Agency—a detective agency in McDowell County hired by coal operators to undermine the union organizing through violence and by spying on union supporters—got off a train as it pulled into the Matewan station. They drove to the Stone Mountain Coal Company a quarter of a mile away and began forcing the company's miners and their families out of their houses as a drizzle began to fall.

The town was full of miners that Wednesday afternoon. Some gathered to watch the evictions. As tensions grew, teachers at the Matewan elementary school sent children home early. The agents planned to take the 5:15 p.m. train back to McDowell County. While they waited at the train depot, Matewan's police chief Sid Hatfield walked up to Albert Felts and asked him to talk to the mayor, C. C. Testerman. Hatfield, a slim man with jug ears who some local feud historians said was a second cousin to Devil Anse, had his own reputation for violence: he was known as Two-Gun Sid for his habit of carrying a pistol on each hip. The police chief supported the union and didn't like detectives throwing people's clothes and furniture out of their houses. Outside a hardware store, the men began to argue, each claiming he had the authority to arrest the other. Mayor Testerman looked at a warrant that Felts produced and said it was bogus.

Either Felts or Hatfield drew a gun and fired. More shots rang out from miners who may have been waiting for trouble. Most of the detectives were caught in the open and had already packed up their rifles in cases. Albert Felts collapsed. Mayor Testerman held his stomach where he had been shot. Two miners who had opened fire from windows and doorways were killed. In the chaos, at least two other agents returned fire, including Albert Felts's brother Lee, who was then shot and killed. One agent ran to the river, swam across to the Kentucky side, and escaped; two others, wounded, climbed aboard a train that immediately pulled away; another hid in a coal shed; and yet another was gunned down on the porch of a house. A detective who had been shot staggered against a wall and asked for water. According to one story, a miner walked up, spat tobacco juice on him, and said, "That ought to be enough to carry you to hell."

Mayor Testerman was put on a train to Welch, where he died that night. The bodies of Albert Felts, his brother Lee, and five other detectives lay on the ground in their bloodstained clothes, uncovered, until they were taken to Williamson by the county sheriff. By the time the job was over, the arms of the men who loaded the bodies onto the train were covered in blood.

Accounts varied about what happened in the hours after the shoot-out. In one, the night was full of macabre revelry. People in the town danced in an orgy of death, as "a howling, jeering, shrieking mob" poured into the streets, and some people shook hands with the corpses and asked how they liked Matewan. Others said the town passed the night in shock, anxious that Thomas Felts, whose two brothers had been killed, would seek revenge. The violence brought a lasting sense of shame to some residents and spurred some to move away.

Less than forty years had passed since the deathwatch over Ellison Hatfield a few hundred yards away in Warm Hollow. Both nights in the valley involved a burst of violence and an attempt to achieve justice by local citizens rising up against outside forces with greater economic power. Devil Anse had tried to fend off wealthier businessmen from Pikeville. By 1920, the valley reflected the modern industrial world, and the fight was between miners and the companies that profited from their labor. The shoot-out crystalized this charged struggle, and it became known as the Matewan Massacre. It would prove to be the opening salvo in a two-year conflict that would at times turn the stretch of Route 49 between Williamson and Matewan into a battle zone that far surpassed the violence of the Hatfield-McCoy feud.

Coal companies responded to the killings in Matewan by evicting entire communities of miners, and the union provided tents for striking miners and their families. As the winter of 1920 approached, there were 1,700 people living in 500 tents in 9 clusters along the Tug Fork. These settlements became known as tent colonies, and the one at Lick Creek was among the largest, housing about 35 families. A correspondent for the *New York Times* found the tents by the river arranged in rows like streets. A weathered American flag flew above the camp.

There were piles of debris and men hammering together wooden flooring for tents. Black and white children flocked to the center of the camp when a reporter handed out several pounds of candy, but their faces were joyless. "The little children seemed incapable of enthusiasm," the reporter wrote. Even though it was a rare treat, "there were not the screams of delight that might have been expected. They were too subdued for that."

In March, Sid Hatfield and fifteen others charged in the Matewan Massacre were acquitted. To many, the swaggering Two-Gun Sid remained a hero. But tensions simmered among hundreds of families still living in tents, and more violence was to come.

The worst fighting along the Tug Fork between Williamson and Matewan broke out on May 12, 1921, nearly a year after the shoot-out, and lasted for three days. Striking miners from the cover of hillsides on both banks of the river aimed their guns into the mining towns where nonunion replacement miners and company officials and their families had taken up residence. The campaign was highly organized. Striking miners blew up a power plant and a coal tipple, and they cut telegraph and telephone lines, signaling each other by blowing into cow horns, according to Charles Keeney, an assistant professor of history at Southern West Virginia Community and Technical College, whose great-grandfather Frank Keeney had led the organizing campaign for the mine workers' union.

The shooting began at Merrimac and poured into Rawl, Sprigg, and Matewan in West Virginia, and McCarr in Kentucky. A state prohibition officer was shot and killed in a store he owned in Sprigg and two others there were injured. State police and deputy sheriffs rushed to the scene from Williamson but failed to halt the gunfire from the hills. A sergeant with the state police described the scene when a train with passengers pulled into Sprigg. "Bullets were peppering down from the mountains when the train got in," he told a reporter. "Women and children screamed and cried in terror, while virtually every passenger on the train fell prone to the floors of the coaches for protection." When another train pulled into Merrimac at noon, men concealed in the mountains on the Kentucky side opened fire. The shooting at Sprigg was "a continual roar." Women and children hid in cellars and dug-out spaces beneath houses. As night fell, people hiding in their homes turned off the lights to avoid becoming targets for the marksmen.

As the shooting continued into a second day, officials from the mine workers' union and the Williamson coal operators' association each said the other had provoked the violence. On the third day, state police brokered a truce by sending a physician across the lines with a piece of white muslin tied to a stick as miners in the hills held their fire. That night the guns fell silent, as though a deep fatigue had settled over the valley.

Governor Ephraim F. Morgan placed Mingo County under martial law on May 19, declaring a "state of war, riot, and insurrection." By the end of the month, the county jail in Williamson was full of union miners. The governor and at least two other state officials discussed relocating the families from the tent colonies to what was described as a "concentration camp" a good distance from the Tug Fork, which was providing an easy escape route into Kentucky for strikers at Lick Creek and elsewhere.

Still, the violence didn't end. In early June, the state police raided the Lick Creek tent colony and arrested forty-two heavily armed men for violating a martial law proclamation. Ten days later, miners fired on a state official and militia commander as he drove past the camp. A state trooper strafed the tents with a submachine gun and called for reinforcements from Williamson. Soon state police and seventy militia members surrounded the colony. One miner was shot and killed; the camp's mayor was shot through the cheek and a leg; a state trooper was shot in his shoulder and neck. The union said state troopers slashed at the canvas tents, kicked over furniture, and rounded up families at gunpoint, taking forty-seven miners into custody.

The Matewan Massacre and the raid of the Lick Creek tent colony were bookends to the year of violence. The next month, the US Senate's Committee on Education and Labor held eight days of hearings on the conflict. According to an account given to the committee by a lawyer for the coal operators, twenty-seven men, mostly state policemen and nonunion miners, had been killed that May in what became known as the Three Days Battle. By summer's end, two more names were added to the list of the dead: Sid Hatfield, who'd been indicted for conspiring to blow up a coal tipple, was shot and killed walking up the steps of the McDowell County Courthouse along with a friend of his from Matewan, Ed Chambers. C. E. Lively and two other Baldwin-Felts detectives had shot them and eventually pleaded self-defense, though Hatfield's and Chambers's wives testified that their husbands had been unarmed.

To avenge the death of their hero Sid Hatfield, nearly ten thousand union miners prepared to march from Marmet, just south of Charleston, to Mingo County. Union leaders and a brigadier general sent from Washington were unable to turn the men back. They marched as far as Logan County, wearing red bandannas around their necks and singing along the way that they would hang Sheriff Don Chafin from a sour apple tree. Chafin was the coal industry's notorious enforcer in Logan County, known for turning back anyone arriving by train who looked like a union organizer, and beating and jailing them if they refused to leave. In what became known as the Battle of Blair Mountain, all-out warfare between the "Red Neck Army" and Chafin's men and hundreds of militia members lasted for four days along a twelve-mile front in the rugged mountains of Logan County. The US Army sent troops from the 26th Infantry Division, though by then miners were beginning to return home, hiding their weapons along the way. Some two thousand troops formed a cordon and disarmed miners. Military planes flew over the area. The army said they had only conducted reconnaissance. But Chafin's forces had dropped homemade bombs.

Once again the fighting had scarcely affected coal production. During the last week of August, the operators kept running coal—Logan County mines churned out more than one hundred thousand tons, enough to fill about a thousand rail cars.

After Blair Mountain, some miners were proud that it took federal troops to send them home. But there was little else the miners had won. As the journalist Lon Savage put it in his account of the 1920–1921 mine war: "That was the miners' victory, their only victory: they had compelled the nation to pay attention to them and forced the army to come to West Virginia." Striking miners remained in jail in Williamson. C. E. Lively and the two other detectives were acquitted at the same courthouse in McDowell County where they'd killed Sid Hatfield.

The Senate inquiry into conditions in West Virginia concluded in

October 1921, three and a half months after it had begun, without any recommendations on how to improve the situation for miners. By that time, the union officials testifying in Washington seemed more interested in engaging in national issues and attacking U.S. Steel than in addressing the problems in Mingo County.

The nation's interest in the miners' struggle had worn thin. Many journalists hardly seemed to notice that the strike in Mingo County continued through another winter and into the next year. The strike at the mines along the Tug Fork didn't end until the fall of 1922, when miners and their families were facing a third winter in tents. That October, the union called off the strike and its organizing drive in southern West Virginia. It had spent nearly $8 million and had failed to win recognition at the mines, where coal was still being piled into railcars daily.

The union's failure, after the Matewan Massacre and two-year strike, was a tragedy for people along the Tug Fork. Miners there had typically earned between seven and eight dollars a day in 1920 but were receiving less than half that by the middle of the decade, if they were able to find work at all. John L. Lewis, who became head of the UMWA in 1920 and would go on to become a dominant and controversial force in the labor movement, removed the union's leaders in West Virginia, and they lived the rest of their lives as broken men. As the coal industry struggled nationally, the smaller coal companies in the Tug Valley were bought up by U.S. Steel and other steel giants. The UMWA itself nearly collapsed. It was saved, like other industrial unions, by the passage of the National Industrial Recovery Act of 1933 under President Franklin D. Roosevelt, which paved the way for union organizing, including in the nation's coalfields. By the end of the 1930s, the UMWA amassed more than eight hundred thousand members.

When the fighting ceased in 1922, Williamson was still rough-edged, with rows of coal-blackened houses lining the river. But there were also pockets of elegance. Musicians traveled from hundreds of miles away to play at the Vaughan Hotel for the city's professional class, the doctors, lawyers, and merchants who had taken the side of the coal companies during the strike. Jazz had reached the coalfields. In those moments, when music floated out into the streets, the well-off could forget that the coal camps had recently been consumed by conflict. In 1923, leaders of the Williamson Chamber of Commerce were so optimistic about the city's future that they decided it needed another hotel. Two years later, a five-story building was completed in the center of the city and proudly named the Mountaineer Hotel. In addition to its stylish lobby with a front desk that had pigeonhole boxes to hold room keys, it boasted 116 rooms with private baths, electric elevators, and a great cut-glass chandelier in the main ballroom and claimed to have one of the finest restaurants in the state.

"Outside the hotel one might see, up and down the river, great search-lights on the hill tops, that flood the valley with beautiful brilliance," a mining engineer wrote in the 1920s. "There was a soft blue-white glow over the railroad yards and the black sky overhead contrasted strikingly with the hills whose green covering was thus made visible even at night. It was an impressive and cheering sight, until one realized that the lights were a protective measure against violence."

Thompson watched the annual reenactment of the 1920 shoot-out in Matewan several times and heard local actors standing in Mate Street describe the days of all-out war between striking miners and coal operators. One day it was bright and windy, but it hardly mattered that the weather wasn't right. Sid Hatfield and his allies inched toward a line of Baldwin-Felts detectives. A woman sitting on a folding chair in front of UMWA Local 1440, a gray-block building, sang the union song "Which Side Are You On?" even though it was written in 1931, a full decade after the massacre. "My daddy was a miner, and I'm a miner's son. And I'll stick with the union, 'til every battle's won." Her off-key voice cut through the wind and even though the men were obviously in costume there was a ritual power in their movements as they drew closer. The crowd joined the chorus: "Which side are you on, boys? Which side are you on?" When the detectives got shot and fell to the ground, everyone clapped. Puffs of smoke from the guns in the actors' hands hung in the air, and Thompson could feel the disgust people had for the coal company guards.

Thompson wanted to draw parallels to the past that would make a jury in Mingo County sympathetic to his clients. Surely a jury of their peers would understand, with a depth he could only guess at, what it meant to go up against a coal company just as the people in Rawl, Lick Creek, Merrimac, and Sprigg were doing. Thompson homed in on a story from Don Dillon he believed encapsulated the link to the past—one that would help him make the case that the fight against Massey was part of a hundred-year-old struggle.

Dillon's father and uncle and grandfather had been among the striking miners who had taken part in the most violent battles in 1920–1921 between Williamson and Matewan. One day they helped ambush militiamen getting off a train near Sprigg, opening fire from the Kentucky side of the river, so that the militiamen, who included businessmen from Williamson, had to lie in a marshy area for hours.

"They pinned them down in a frog pond," Dillon said, grinning at the thought of his father shooting at men who supported the coal operators. "Dad used to tell that and die laughing. He was a tough old bird."

Dillon showed Thompson a photograph of his father and uncle standing with a line of other men and women in front of a row of white tents. His father, about sixteen years old, held a Winchester balanced on his right shoulder and looked squarely at the camera. Wearing a soft-brimmed hat and overalls, he had the same self-assured expression Don would inherit. The men, women, and children stood barefoot on sandy ground near the river. Some of the men also carried rifles; one held a fiddle case, another a banjo. Thick trees leaned over the tents, and a few women smiled. Their bright faces and clean gingham dresses suggested this was sometime in the summer of 1920, before the strike had taken its full toll.

After living in a tent for months during the strike, one of Dillon's grandfathers had died of a heart attack. "I never did forget that," Dillon said.

Thompson's righteous anger would surface whenever he talked about putting the former Massey electrician on the stand early in the trial. Thompson planned to hold up the photograph so that Dillon could tell the room who was pictured, why they were standing in front of tents, and why his father was holding a Winchester. "You have a long history of fighting coal companies, don't you?" It was a question he couldn't wait to ask Don Dillon in a Mingo County courtroom.

CHAPTER 11

One afternoon in April of 2006, Thompson was called to the front door of the Smith & Thompson offices in Charleston, where a local sheriff standing in the entryway handed him a lawsuit. Thompson could see from the first page that Massey was suing him for defamation. In the four-page document, Massey's attorney Dan Stickler claimed that Thompson had acted with malice, making defamatory statements about Rawl Sales "with willful and reckless disregard for the truth." The company was seeking compensatory damages, punitive damages, and attorneys' fees. The lawsuit quoted a letter Thompson had written five weeks earlier to John Mark Hubbard, a Mingo County commissioner, seeking additional funding for the water line. Holding the lawsuit in his hands, Thompson was incensed.

When a *West Virginia Record* reporter called him to comment on the lawsuit, he still hadn't cooled down. "The biggest opponent of frivolous lawsuits has filed one against me. To hell with them," he said. "If they want to sue me, to hell with them."

Thompson's first thought was that he'd been double-crossed. There were only two people he could blame: Hubbard or Larry Hamrick, a Mingo County insider whom he had recently hired to provide intelligence about the goings-on at the courthouse and who had urged him to write the letter. The lawsuit quoted it in full:

> Dear Mr. Hubbard,
>
> It has come to my attention that you have been actively involved in securing fresh, safe water for the people of Rawl, Merrimac, Lick Creek and Sprigg. I want to commend you for the help that you have given my clients.
>
> We have collected a massive amount of evidence that proves beyond any doubt the water in [*sic*] Forgotten Communities

is deadly. Our evidence proves that Rawl Sales & Processing knowingly contaminated the water. Our evidence shows that they did it without permits. And, our evidence shows that the people of Rawl are slowly dying.

If there is anything that we can do to help our clients get clean, safe water please let me know. We would be willing to share with you all of our documents, scientific evidence, medical advice and expert reports if you think that it might make [sic] difference.

Sincerely,

Kevin Thompson, Esq.

Given Hamrick's past—he was among the Mingo County politicians indicted for corruption and sent to prison in the 1980s—Thompson figured he was the likelier candidate. The man he had hired to offer him access to Mingo County's political machine had instead pulled him into the gears.

Back in the 1980s, Hamrick had run the county's school board and its anti-poverty agency. He pleaded guilty to charges that included jury tampering and using kickback schemes to steal more than sixty thousand dollars in anti-poverty funds, part of which he used to pay off politicians. Prosecutors said Hamrick threatened several witnesses against him in the 1980s. Tall and broad-shouldered, he had notoriously killed a pit bull by strangling it with his bare hands. He was quoted as saying that once you have your hands around the neck of a pit bull, you don't let go.

By the time Thompson came to Williamson, Hamrick and a contemporary of his named Johnie Owens, who had been convicted of trying to sell his county sheriff position for one hundred thousand dollars, had served their time and were part of the community again. It was another peculiarity of Mingo County that certain forms of corruption had been more or less tolerated since the founding of Williamson and Matewan. Periodically the most egregious offenders would be kicked out of office or jailed. But this pruning never touched the roots, and the problems always grew back.

The year before, Thompson had found time to represent Owens

and some of his neighbors in Ragland, halfway between Rawl and Chauncey, against White Flame Energy, another coal company, for damage to their homes from blasting. At the recommendation of a client, Thompson had hired Hamrick to attend county commission meetings and pull records from the courthouse at fifty dollars an hour. Even though he had been permanently retired from public service—he wasn't even supposed to enter the courthouse under the terms of his release—Hamrick still had access to all the county's political players, including Judge Thornsbury and his allies, who ate lunch at the judge's reserved table at the back of Starters. In Mingo County, it wasn't necessarily a bad thing for Thompson to be seen with Hamrick; it might even lend him some credibility. For an old crook, Hamrick seemed to go about his consulting work for Thompson with a high level of professionalism. "As always, I have enjoyed being of service," Hamrick wrote on his invoices.

It was in early March that Hamrick had suggested that Thompson write to Hubbard and tell him about the water situation. A dapper businessman with a beet-red, scrubbed complexion, Hubbard owned a mine-supply company outside Williamson. Thompson forgot about Hamrick's advice, until he was back in New Orleans. He wrote the short letter, printed it, and mailed it himself to the courthouse on East Second Avenue. It was March 17, St. Patrick's Day. Thompson's assistant, Pam Patai, a native of Jefferson Parish outside New Orleans who had worked for him since 1993, would have normally handled his correspondence, but she had a date and Thompson had told her to leave early. As soon as he mailed the letter, Thompson didn't give it another thought.

Within days, Hamrick called again and asked if Thompson could send him an article from the March issue of *National Geographic* that he'd been hearing about but couldn't get ahold of. The article, "The High Cost of Cheap Coal," was about the fight over mountaintop removal mining and referred to the Rawl lawsuit. A photograph showed one of Thompson's clients, Kenny Stroud, standing with one of his sons watching their bathroom sink fill with mud-brown water. "Kenneth Stroud blames the toxic soup flowing from the tap in his home in Rawl for maladies affecting his sons and him. Stroud and some 350 other area residents are suing Massey Energy, claiming that by storing coal sludge in old mine shafts it fouled well water, a charge the company denies," the caption read. The article didn't mention Thompson, but it gave the case some national exposure.

Thompson forgot about this request too, until Hamrick called again. "Kevin, have you sent that article yet?" he asked. Thompson photocopied the article and mailed it to Hamrick's home in Williamson.

Thompson was certain about this sequence of events: he had sent the letter to Hubbard at the courthouse and the article to Hamrick's apartment. Thompson hired a law firm to represent him, but he took the defense into his own hands. He went to a county commission meeting at the courthouse and asked John Mark Hubbard if he had received any letter from him. Sitting on a dais in the cramped room, Hubbard said he hadn't, and he appeared as perplexed about the matter as Thompson.

Thompson got Hubbard to sign an affidavit:

I, John Mark Hubbard, having first been duly sworn state the following:

I am a Mingo County Commissioner. I do not recall receiving a letter at any time from Kevin Thompson, Esquire of Smith & Thompson regarding the Lick Creek Water Project.

In a file room in the courthouse, Thompson found the typed minutes of the commission's recent meetings, which always mentioned correspondence received by the office. There on the page for the March meeting was a mention of Thompson's letter to Hubbard, except that it looked like someone had clumsily taped in a reference to the letter and then photocopied it to make it appear authentic. Thompson believed Hubbard's account and figured that Hamrick had intercepted his letter at the courthouse.

Thompson tried to get the lawsuit against him dismissed by arguing that it was retaliatory and baseless and offended his right to free speech. In a reply, Stickler wrote that Thompson had embarked on "a defamatory tirade against Rawl" and that "Rawl, having established a favorable reputation in the community over the years, could not stand idly by and watch its good name defiled by the wrongful acts of Defendants." He asked for permission to take depositions to investigate Thompson's alleged malice. In a footnote, Stickler acknowledged that

Hubbard had said that he didn't "recall" receiving Thompson's letter, but he assured the judge in Charleston, where the defamation suit had been filed, that the letter had been published to at least one other individual—Larry Hamrick. Stickler's filing included a copy of the letter addressed to Hubbard and dated March 17 and a copy of the envelope addressed to Hamrick and postmarked March 23. There was no explanation for why the envelope had been postmarked nearly a week later. The lawsuit rested entirely on Hamrick's own affidavit, which stated that he had received a copy of Thompson's letter at his home.

Thompson suspected Hamrick had seen an opportunity to make some money and had been a double agent all along. In order to pin down how Stickler had gotten a copy of Thompson's letter, Thompson sent subpoenas to Jackson Kelly's offices, asking for billing records. He also demanded records of any phone calls between Stickler and Hamrick. He never received either.

Ultimately the judge in Charleston decided to stay the defamation case until the Rawl lawsuit was resolved. Thompson regarded the lawsuit as an illegal SLAPP (strategic lawsuit against public participation), intended to silence critics by burdening them with the costs of a legal defense. It wouldn't be the first time Massey had used such a tactic. In 2005, the company had brought defamation suits against the mine workers' union and its president, Cecil Roberts, and a liberal political advocacy group called West Virginia Consumers for Justice. Separately, Blankenship sued the *Charleston Gazette* for defamation, and then Governor Joe Manchin for allegedly violating his own free speech rights by threatening to retaliate against Massey because Blankenship opposed a piece of legislation Manchin supported. A West Virginia website said, "Don Blankenship, Massey Coal's CEO, is suing just about everyone."

Carmelita, who knew Larry Hamrick and all the players at the judge's table at Starters, called the defamation case "a little scare tactic" and told Thompson not to worry. All it meant was that he had gotten Don Blankenship's attention.

While the defamation suit struck Thompson as absurd, it threatened to devastate him financially. Before coming to Mingo County, he had lived a comfortable life. His legal consulting business, Evidence Management, generated between seven and eight hundred thousand dollars a year, and his personal income was in the low six figures. Now his consulting business was failing, partly because of New Orleans's slow recovery after Hurricane Katrina and because he had shifted his focus to West Virginia's coalfields. When he was in Williamson, Thompson didn't bother withdrawing cash at the ATM anymore. Kathleen was paying their bills with help from her mother. Thompson couldn't even spare money to buy gas to drive ninety miles to Charleston, let alone the eight-hundred-mile trip home to New Orleans. By May, he thought he would be marooned at the Mountaineer for the foreseeable future.

Then that month his mother, Vada, died, and the blow brought Thompson down even further. He drove to Point Pleasant to handle the funeral arrangements with his sister, Carlene, using his last functioning credit card to buy plane tickets for Kathleen and Kelsey. His mother had told him that when she died, he should look in a shoebox where she kept money in some socks. When he found the box, it contained sixty dollars. Thompson smiled, because it was like his mother to act as though a stash of dollar bills was a fortune. He took the cash. When it was time to head back to Williamson, he drove his mother's car, a 1992 burgundy Ford Crown Victoria. As he got in, he closed the ashtray to preserve the ends of the last cigarettes she'd smoked.

He used the sixty dollars to fill the gas tank and buy dinner at a Flying J truck stop. He ate as much as he could at the buffet and filled his pockets with fruit on his way out. Then he worried about running out of gas until Williamson came into view.

On June 8, Thompson was back in Judge Thornsbury's windowless courtroom with the green carpeting and maple-colored benches. It was the first hearing in the case since May of the prior year, and Stickler maintained once again that Massey shouldn't have to supply water to the community. Earlier that spring, a fifteen-thousand-dollar grant from the governor's office to distribute pallets of bottled water to families had run out, but Stickler argued that the fifty-thousand-gallon water truck supplied by the county would provide drinking water until November, when it got too cold. Moreover, the county was promising to build a water line from Williamson. "There is no irreparable harm to these folks," Stickler said. "It's inconvenient, admittedly. There is public water on its way, but, more importantly, right now there is water available to them."

To convince the judge of the severity of the problem, Thompson called Ernie Brown to the stand and held up a jar of water from the Browns' house.

"This is a water sample you took this morning, right?"

"Yes," Ernie said.

"Would Your Honor like to smell it?" Thompson asked the judge.

"I can once you get it admitted," the judge replied.

Stickler interrupted to ask what the relevancy was and said, "There's testimony already that water will have a natural odor if there are any kind of bacteria in it that can create that."

Thompson addressed Ernie. "Mr. Brown, have you consistently done an experiment with Pepto-Bismol and water from your home?" he asked.

"Yes, I have," Ernie said.

The judge permitted Thompson to re-create Ernie's experiment in the courtroom. Thompson held up a bottle of Crystal Geyser Alpine Spring Water mixed with Pepto-Bismol: it was pink. Another batch that Van Bunch had mixed using Ernie and Carmelita's water was black. And a third with water Ernie had filled at his house forty-five minutes earlier was gray. The implication was that some chemical reaction was taking place with the couple's well water that didn't occur with clean drinking water.

Larry Brown followed his brother to the witness stand and told the judge that the water truck from the county was empty. Most people didn't use it because it sometimes had a foul, swampy odor. Larry said he didn't trust it himself.

On cross-examination, Stickler asked Larry how much money he got in disability payments, and Larry said less than a thousand dollars a month.

"And your water cost is?" Stickler asked.

"Water cost is approximately three dollars and sixty cents per case over at Walmart," Larry answered.

Thompson pointed out what the weekly cost would be to Massey to supply water for all the residents. "We're talking about twenty-two hundred dollars," he told the judge.

Stickler said he was sympathetic to the residents. He said that he had grown up with "bad water" himself in Lincoln County and had to haul city water to a cistern, and he recalled that the judge had disclosed that he'd grown up in the head of a hollow, drinking well water. But a jury would have to decide what caused their water problems, Stickler said, and Massey shouldn't have to provide replacement water. "Regardless of how sympathetic we are to these folks, there are still standards that have to be met, burdens that have to be overcome by the plaintiffs," he said. "We are still faced with a situation with conflicting expert testimony . . . They have a burden on injunctive relief they've got to overcome, and that is, is there irreparable harm threatened? And the answer is no."

When it came to setting a date for trial, Stickler said he didn't want to schedule a trial within the year because he had 399 depositions of Thompson's clients to conduct, and he planned to do them all. The first phase of the trial would only cover whether Massey was liable for the bad water, and Bunch argued that Stickler knew that 399 people weren't going to testify.

But Stickler persisted. "That's an interesting theory, Your Honor, except for one thing," he said. "We need to know where the wells are located, how deep they are, how long it began, when did it begin that they had these problems. We get that through deposition and discovery, because it's going to bear on the overall issue."

Before he rose to leave, Judge Thornsbury set a trial date for November 28, a little more than five months away. But he didn't indicate how he planned to rule on the water motion.

Bunch had decided to run the Hatfield McCoy Marathon two days after the hearing. Thompson welcomed the extended visit from Uncle Van, as he called him. The two lawyers ate a spaghetti dinner at the Brass Tree restaurant in the Sycamore Inn and watched local actors perform a skit about Devil Anse and Ole Ran'l McCoy to entertain the runners. David Hatfield, a great-nephew of Sid Hatfield and the marathon's organizer, welcomed Bunch's suggestion that Thompson serve as a safety volunteer during the race.

The next morning, Thompson dropped Bunch at the starting line and then borrowed a bicycle from the only other permanent resident at the Mountaineer, a retired opera singer named Jay. Thompson rode the course along the Tug Fork, watching as spectators handed out cups of water, watermelon, grapes, bananas, rags soaked in ice water, and even fried chicken. Ernie and Carmelita had set up a cheering section for Bunch. A banner read, "Go, Van Bunch, Go."

It was a warm morning, and when the first runners finally came through downtown Matewan before heading back to a small road on the Kentucky side of the Tug Fork, they looked drained from the hills. On the bridge near the Rawl Sales offices, Thompson saw a man fall to the ground as though he had been cut down by a sniper. He biked over and walked the man to the shade of a tree and then waved for a medic to attend to him. It was Thompson's first rescue of the day. Later, he found two more people doubled over by the side of the road and gave them water. Finally he went looking for Bunch, riding hard toward the finish line on East Second Avenue.

Thompson arrived just in time to see Bunch—in a tie-dye T-shirt, iPod wires dangling from his ears—crossing the finish line, where he was engulfed by a contingent from Rawl. Judge Thornsbury was standing nearby in slacks and a polo shirt, watching behind his tinted glasses. When he spotted the two lawyers, he stared for a few seconds, as Bunch dripped sweat.

"You ran that whole way?" the judge said.

"Yeah, pretty good time too," Bunch replied. He was the forty-sixth person across the finish line.

The judge shook his head, as though he was wondering why a grown man would do such a thing. When the race coordinator walked over and congratulated Thompson, the judge asked, "What did he do?"

"He saved three people," Thompson recalled the coordinator saying.

"Really?" the judge said, smiling.

To Thompson, the chance encounter felt like good karma. The judge had seen that Thompson, and even Bunch, a lawyer from Tennessee, were becoming a part of the community.

After the race, the partners went back to the hotel. Bunch showered and then left for home, and Thompson collapsed and took a nap. He woke to shouting. Out the window, he saw a state trooper holding a young man up against the side of the Coal House. Then he watched as a heavyset police officer ran up and took over. When the trooper was out of sight, the police officer started beating the man until the owner of the Mountaineer, Mark Mitchell—in a chef's coat and checkered pants—ran into the alley, shouting at the officer to stop.

Thompson couldn't get the bizarre scene out of his mind. He called the West Virginia State Police headquarters and spoke to the colonel in charge, who said he had known one of Thompson's grandfathers and thanked Thompson for letting him know about the incident and the trooper's innocence. The trooper had been terrified that he would be wrongly accused of beating the man, the colonel said.

Afterward, Thompson tried to make light of the incident by joking that he and Bunch now had to save people from police corruption as well as from contaminated water. But the violence stayed with him, and Williamson felt less safe.

In July, while Thompson was broke in Williamson, Blankenship was vacationing on the French Riviera. The Massey CEO was there with his old friend Elliott "Spike" Maynard, now a justice on the West Virginia Supreme Court of Appeals, the state's highest court. The men had grown up in one of the poorest counties in the United States, and they were now tourists in the kingdom of Monaco, a sovereign city-state lined with palm trees and luxury cars where 30 percent of the population were millionaires. Blankenship played blackjack at the Casino de Monte-Carlo. With its endless gold-framed mirrors and crystal chandeliers, the opulent casino was like a jewel box containing centuries of inherited wealth. Their mere presence in such a place meant both men had already beaten the odds.

But that month, Thompson and his clients also got a long-awaited victory. Judge Thornsbury ordered Massey to provide replacement water immediately. The judge noted the $2,200 cost per week to supply 250 families with bottled water and that Massey had earned $5.6 million in the first quarter of 2006. There was substantial evidence, the judge wrote, that could lead a jury to conclude that Massey was responsible for contaminated water in the area. "The Court is not passing judgment," he wrote, but added: "the evidence tends to implicate the defendants."

Massey had to provide a case of bottled water per person for about eighty families within seventy-two hours, and continue to do so each week until the water line reached their homes. The judge ordered Larry Brown to coordinate the water distribution and send a list of families receiving water to Thompson every week, so he could then share it with Jackson Kelly.

Three days later, however, no water arrived. Jackson Kelly had appealed the order. Larry had to turn away people who showed up at his church. But the judge held firm, and two weeks later, the first truck drove up Dick Williamson Branch Road. It was a county-owned truck, with prisoners from the jail to unload the water and a convicted felon in the front passenger seat. Thompson complained that it was inappropriate for the county to be providing the service for Massey, and soon the company hired its own trucks.

Boxes of bottled water filled the basement of Larry's church, and distributing and tracking it became a full-time job. He was thrilled to be able to hand out water to people. But he knew Massey would complain if a single bottle went astray. The Rawl Sales property ended at the top of the hollow near Larry's house, and the company had security guards watching the water delivery and cameras aimed toward the church, all of which Thompson viewed as unnecessary intimidation.

Perhaps it was only a coincidence, but just before the judge's order, workers started digging trenches along Route 49 to lay the water line. The cost of the project was now about $4.3 million, and it wasn't expected to be finished until the following year. Massey would have to deliver water well into 2007.

That summer, Larry provided his own affidavit in Massey's defamation suit against Thompson. He said he had asked Thompson to do anything he could to help the community get clean drinking water. Thompson's statement that the water was making people sick wasn't defamatory. "I firmly believe that the water is deadly and is killing the people in the community," Larry said. In his view, he added, without Thompson's lawsuit, construction on the water line would have never begun.

CHAPTER 12

On August 16, a year after he had deposed Gene Kitts, Thompson sat across from a second former Rawl Sales executive. Ben Hatfield had grown up in Williamson, and he had also launched his career at Rawl Sales in the 1980s under Blankenship. As a Hatfield, he had deep roots in the Tug Valley. In 1882, it was Ben Hatfield's great-grandfather, John Wallace Hatfield, who found the three McCoy boys who had been killed on the riverbank across from Matewan and brought their bodies on a sled to their parents.

Hatfield was now CEO of International Coal Group, or ICG, and Gene Kitts was a vice president at the company. Seven months earlier when the company's Sago Mine had exploded, Hatfield had been visibly shaken when he stood before news cameras, pointing out the location on a mine map where thirteen miners had become trapped. Only one would survive. The mine was criticized for having serious safety problems when ICG had bought it less than two months before the accident. A serious-minded coal executive, Hatfield didn't have Blankenship's imposing aura. People around Williamson described Hatfield as good-hearted and a gentleman but he hadn't escaped blame for the deaths of the Sago miners.

Two decades after he had worked as chief engineer for Rawl Sales, Hatfield remembered the names of all the coal seams in the Tug Valley. He recalled several injection holes, including the one at the head of Lick Creek, and he said Blankenship had been involved in "consensus decisions" about where to place injection holes, along with the company's engineers and prep plant personnel.

"Underground injection was a commonly used practice in that day by many coal companies, so it wasn't at all unusual or thought to be problematic," Hatfield said. "The major risk in the Sprouse Creek situation was the ongoing exposure to environmental spills, which was a serious concern."

Hatfield said that sometimes a slurry line would break apart in the hills or fail where the pipe was spliced at the injection site. The worst case occurred in June 1984, he said, when the slurry had spilled into Lick Creek. Blankenship had become president of Rawl Sales a month earlier. He and Hatfield drove out to see what had happened. A state environmental inspector had issued a violation for the spill. Workers put straw bales in the creek to soak up the sludge and used backhoes and excavators to cart it away.

"We were shocked and frustrated at how much of the slurry had leaked out before the system was shut off," Hatfield said. After the spill, the company made improvements, including installing alarms to shut off the system if a pipe burst. Yet Hatfield said he wasn't aware of well water complaints from residents. "It's my recollection that there was no connection recognized or anticipated between the wells and the underground injection," Hatfield said.

The mess in the creek, Hatfield said, made Blankenship and him "all the more determined to get the impoundment moving quickly."

The impoundment, Thompson confirmed, should have ended the need to inject slurry.

"Yes, normally that would be the case," Hatfield said. "The purpose of the impoundment is to eliminate the requirement to do underground injection."

Thompson was left with a question that would explain why hundreds of millions of gallons of slurry had been injected near the communities: Why had it taken at least three years after the spill in 1984 to build the impoundment?

Since Jackson Kelly had asserted its right to depose every plaintiff at the June hearing, Thompson had been walking two blocks to the Sycamore Inn every morning to sit with as many as four people a day as they were questioned about their well water and their health. Thompson started referring to the process as "The Depo War." He continued to visit people in their homes and collect medical records, receipts for plumbing fixtures, work histories, and property deeds—all of which he had no effective system for organizing. Yet the evidence of lives disrupted was mounting. No matter what Massey did to derail him, Thompson felt there was a toll of suffering that couldn't be denied.

He had also been keeping a rough spreadsheet of his clients' health concerns. By the time he had spoken to 390 people, he did some calculations and found that 180 people, or nearly half, had regular bouts of diarrhea; 177 had experienced skin rashes; 160 had suffered from kidney or urinary tract infections. The percentage suffering from migraines (56 percent), memory problems (39 percent), muscle tremors (33 percent), and heart disease (23 percent) also seemed extraordinarily high to Thompson. Fifteen people, or nearly 4 percent, had had their gallbladders removed. Twenty-six people, or almost 7 percent, had had a form of cancer.

Thompson wasn't the only one finding widespread health problems. Patricia Feeney, an OVEC organizer, had interviewed many residents about their health problems, and a local family physician, Dr. Diane Shafer, told Feeney, "There is no question about illnesses caused by poor water quality." Shafer had found high incidences of Alzheimer's disease, blood pressure problems, cancers apparently not related to smoking, kidney stones, kidney failure, dementia, birth defects, thyroid issues, and gastrointestinal problems. Feeney asked B.I. what the community was doing while it waited for the municipal water line. "We're dying," he replied.

The depositions were handled by Dan Stickler, another Jackson Kelly attorney named Al Sebok, and several Jackson Kelly associates. They asked many of the same questions: When did you first believe your water had gone bad? How deep is your well? How is it maintained? What health problems do you blame on the water? Many of Thompson's clients found the process invasive. They were asked to talk about intimate health issues. As Thompson described it, the average person living in the community had suffered from "consistent, explosive, continuous diarrhea for years on end." Now people had to describe these experiences with a court reporter putting everything on the record.

On August 29, Thompson sat next to Carmelita Brown while Al Sebok deposed her. Sebok had been with Jackson Kelly since 1985 and was said to have a photographic memory for legal citations. But he lacked the easy manner that made Stickler such an effective trial lawyer. Sebok was oppressively exacting. Everything about him irritated Thompson.

Much of the deposition focused on what living with the water had been like for Carmelita, Ernie, and their two children. Sebok asked Carmelita to recount her health issues. She told him she hadn't been feeling well that day. She had a headache and suspected that she might be having a new problem with her kidneys. Then she went on to list the long-term problems she had endured.

"Kidney stones, kidney problems, cysts, diarrhea every day, every morning," Carmelita said. "I was up at five o'clock this morning with it . . . I'm losing my sight. I'm losing my hearing. I'm losing my sense of smell. I break out with rashes at times. I have female problems, and my hair's falling out."

"Anything else?" Sebok asked.

"Not as I can think of," she said.

Prompted by Sebok, Carmelita described what the kidney stones had done to her body. The last time she visited her doctor, he had found three small stones. "They'll grow and set up infection in my body," she said. "The last time, it set up septicemia in every part of my body. It was even in my bone marrow." She hadn't seen her doctor in two years because she was afraid of what he might find. "When I start throwing up, and I start fevers and chills and hurting in my back . . . ," she said, "I can feel them moving around in there, and when I urinate, I have a burning sensation."

"My kidney is bothering me right now," she added. "I'd say it was maybe a kidney infection from the stones, and that's the reason I'm drinking plenty of water."

Sebok repeated her health problems and came to diarrhea. Carmelita explained that she hadn't had a solid bowel movement in ten or twelve years.

"Sometime, then, in the mid-nineties?" Sebok asked.

"Possibly."

"Has there been anything you would consider embarrassing things happening with diarrhea?" Sebok asked.

"Not too often, but I try to stay close to home," Carmelita said.

Thompson sat beside Carmelita through the deposition. Hers stood out as the hardest to get through. The probing infuriated him, especially when she had to describe her "female problems." She had cysts "in my female parts," she said. "I hemorrhage every time me and my husband have intimate relations."

"And when did that start?" Sebok asked.

Sebok asked more than two dozen follow-up questions: where the bleeding was coming from, how long it lasted, whether it was more of a problem when she was having her period, whether pain was associated with the bleeding, and how often Carmelita and Ernie had sex. Carmelita answered each question. Later, she added, "I want to be able to have an intimate relationship with my husband without crying every time we—" before breaking off. When they moved on to the next subject—her hair coming out in handfuls after she showered—it was a relief.

Sebok asked Carmelita what she wanted to be reimbursed for, and her voice filled with emotion.

"Well, let's see," she began. "The filters that I'm buying. The filter that I had to pay for that I didn't normally have to have, the potassium. The water that I had to buy to drink, to cook with, sometimes to take a bath with. My heating and cooling unit, my refrigerators, my faucets that's falling off, my plumbing. Painting trying to get the smell out of my house. All the little things I had to buy for to try to do away with the smell so people wouldn't think my house stunk. My medicals, the aggravation I've been through, my health back, my mom and dad back, my nerves back, my kidneys, my life with my husband back. I'd like to be able to have my grandbabies and not send them home dirty."

The grueling questioning brought the emotional weight of the case down on Thompson. He started drinking whiskey in the evenings at the Mountaineer, dreaming of the day that Blankenship would have to endure the same probing as his clients.

With the water line victory, more people wanted to join the lawsuit, despite their misgivings about suing Massey.

"This is a train going down the track and we keep adding passengers on with no evidence at all," Stickler complained to the judge at a hearing in late August.

As the list of plaintiffs grew, "the train" became the dominant metaphor for the case. Even Thompson started using it. There was little else the two lawyers agreed on.

In his defense, Thompson said people kept telling him they wanted to join the lawsuit.

"I don't know how to stop them," he told the judge.

"It's America. You don't stop them," the judge replied.

Since June, the number of plaintiffs had swelled to 560, and the deposition process had been painfully slow. Only 100 people had been deposed so far, leaving 460 to go. Stickler complained that he hadn't received any reports from Thompson's experts, and Jackson Kelly also wanted its doctors to conduct medical exams of people. Thompson suggested that if they followed an ambitious schedule, everything could be completed by August 2007.

Judge Thornsbury did some quick math from the bench. Litigating hundreds of personal injury claims could take up to 1,300 days, he estimated—and he would be 112 years old by then.

"I'm an optimist, but I don't think I'm going to live that long," the judge said.

"Well, I hope you do, Your Honor, and if you stay away from the water in Rawl, you might," Thompson said.

"I appreciate that," the judge said. He soon set a new date for roughly a year away, on October 16, 2007.

Meanwhile, Thompson was astonished at Massey's pettiness. As Larry Brown had feared, Jackson Kelly complained that he was distributing water to people who weren't on the approved list. When Judge Thornsbury rejected Stickler's motion, he appealed the ruling to the West Virginia Supreme Court of Appeals, whose five members included Blankenship's friend Spike Maynard and the justice Blankenship helped elect, Brent Benjamin. Someone at Massey didn't want to deliver those cases of bottled water, no matter how insignificant the cost.

The state's highest court also ruled that Massey had to continue delivering water until the line was built. It had taken more than two years of litigation, but Thompson had finally defeated Jackson Kelly on the issue. He had won clean drinking water for the Forgotten Communities.

CHAPTER 13

At one level, all complex litigation is a war of paper, and Thompson was losing this one. By September, he couldn't keep up with Jackson Kelly's requests for information on his growing list of clients. In room 309, there were nineteen boxes containing an estimated thirty thousand pages of medical records that he needed to hand over once he had sifted through them himself. More and more paper arrived every week, like a tide that never receded.

Just before Labor Day, Stuart Smith and his partner Mike Stag in New Orleans agreed to invest seven hundred thousand dollars in the Rawl case, and they wired the first tranche of seventy-five thousand dollars into an account for Thompson. It was a lifeline, but he knew he risked giving up some of his independence by tying himself further to the demanding Smith. It always happened the same way: Smith would call from somewhere around the globe—a bazaar in Morocco; his yacht in the Greek isles—and ask Thompson to help him with a case. At Smith's request, Thompson had already made several trips to the Martha Oil Field in Kentucky to measure radioactivity on a farm. If Thompson asked for some context, Smith would reply, "Jesus Christ, Kevin. I gave you the number. Just handle it." Thompson wasn't about to take any orders when it came to Rawl.

The first person Thompson hired to work with him at the Mountaineer was Stephen Wussow, a twenty-five-year-old aspiring journalist who had been working for an environmental group called Appalachian Voices. Wussow went to the hotel expecting a normal job interview, but he found that room 309 was where Thompson slept and worked. It was one of the larger guest rooms in the hotel, with a white minifridge and a microwave and space for a table and two chairs. Heavy teal-colored curtains kept the room, with its wood paneling and sixties decor, as dim as a cave.

Thompson listened as the scruffy, dark-haired young man described growing up in the highlands of Papua New Guinea with his missionary parents. After the family moved back to North Carolina, Wussow went to Appalachian State University and graduated with a degree in political science and sociology. He had worked on an organic farm in Mexico and trekked through Spain. Thompson had heard enough; he said Wussow should work for him and help take on Massey. "Think of it as a Peace Corps stint," Thompson said. "We're going to trial in a year." He offered to pay Wussow fifteen dollars an hour and said he could put anything he ordered at the hotel café on the firm's tab. "There's free coffee and burritos," Thompson said. "Just keep track of your hours."

Thompson gave his room to Wussow and took a smaller one next door, because he'd be traveling back and forth to New Orleans while Wussow was at the hotel full-time. Then Thompson worked out a deal with Mark Mitchell to rent room 409—three narrow, connected rooms one floor up—as an office. One of Wussow's first jobs was interviewing the hundreds of clients about their health and water, to create a database for the entire case. Thompson knew his office would always be outmanned by Jackson Kelly; his only hope was to develop a technology advantage. He told Wussow to write a computer program that would churn out responses to questions about clients posed by Jackson Kelly as quickly as Massey's lawyers could submit them. The responses were part of the pretrial discovery process, which also included depositions and the exchange of documents, and with so many clients to keep track of Thompson was struggling to meet deadlines. Wussow didn't know how to code, but he said he would figure it out.

The two developed a routine. In the morning, they rolled out of their rooms, got coffee downstairs, and headed back up to room 409 to sort through paperwork, including poring over thousands of pages of Rawl Sales documents Jackson Kelly was providing through discovery, and then begin fielding calls from clients. When Thompson wasn't attending depositions, he would drive out with Wussow to Rawl to talk to Larry Brown about the water distribution, or videotape the water sampling at clients' homes being done by Scott Simonton and Massey's experts. In the evening, they took a break for dinner or worked out in the hotel's basement, where Thompson kept a rowing machine next to Mark Mitchell's bench press and weights. An alarm on Thompson's watch reminded him to call Kelsey in New Orleans every night just before 9 p.m. to say good night.

Thompson realized it was time for another change. He was still technically part of Smith & Thompson, but he decided to dissolve the partnership with Marty Smith in Charleston to create a new one where his own cases would be the sole focus. He called a young associate he respected at the firm, Dave Barney, and made a straightforward pitch: "Hey, do you want to start a law firm?" They'd have no real office and operate out of the hotel on a shoestring for now, but it was an opportunity to create something from scratch together. Thompson hoped that Barney could handle some Rawl depositions and help bring in money from other cases. A reliable attorney with thinning brown hair parted in the middle, Barney was content to play a secondary role. He had grown up in a tiny coalfield community called Lanark, outside Beckley. His grandfathers had been union miners and lived in coal camps. The Rawl fight seemed like a worthy cause to him too.

"You grow up in coal country, you certainly understand that the coal companies are only out to help themselves," Barney said. "They're out to make a dollar. And whether a miner's hurt, whether they poison water, they don't care. It's the almighty dollar. And that's the way it's always been."

The lawyers formed Thompson Barney at the beginning of 2007. Barney started driving his bronze-colored Chevy Impala down to Williamson for days at a time. He would represent hundreds of Rawl clients in depositions at the Sycamore Inn, sometimes from 8:30 a.m. to 5 p.m. Barney, who was thrifty himself, kept the firm's bills paid, including those of court reporters who now demanded that when they produced transcripts of depositions they be paid up front because Thompson had fallen so far behind. Barney was the kind of responsible person Thompson attracted to himself to keep the guardrails up.

By early spring, Wussow, who worked alone in the hotel while Thompson was traveling, got a database program up and running with help from a friend of Thompson's who was a coder. The program allowed Thompson to churn out thousands of pages at a time with client information inserted into paragraphs to meet Jackson Kelly's discovery requests. Thompson dubbed it "the Breeder Reactor." He thought it was more sophisticated than anything any other law firm in the country was using at the time. He gave Wussow all the credit. "Steve applied his big brain and came up with the Breeder Reactor," he said. It was asymmetrical warfare. Now Thompson could print ten thousand pages in a single run and bury Jackson Kelly's lawyers in floods of paper.

In March 2007, the water line from Williamson reached every home in Rawl, Lick Creek, Merrimac, and Sprigg. Having city water immediately changed life in ways both profound and ordinary. For more than a decade, people had longed, lobbied, and prayed for clean water to drink and bathe in. Once it flowed into their homes, old habits had to be unlearned. Ernie Brown kept reaching for a jug of water to make his morning coffee, forgetting that the water from the kitchen sink was safe to use. Carmelita opened the lid of her washing machine to make sure the water hadn't turned black. The couple was no longer embarrassed to invite friends over; their house no longer smelled like rotten eggs. When they showered, they could smell the shampoo, and their skin didn't itch. Once again, Carmelita's skin felt smooth after a bath. "I praise God and I thank Him every day," she said.

Larry Brown had diligently kept handwritten water distribution records over thirty-two weeks. The last report he faxed to Thompson's office at the Mountaineer listed 122 people who had picked up their final bottles of water. The church basement was empty for the first time since the prior summer. At the top of the page, Larry wrote, "Last of the Water."

Three months later, Thompson upped the ante on the Depo War when he deposed twelve current and former executives with Massey and Rawl Sales, a grueling series of interviews that gave him access to the inner workings of the companies and the prep plant, with its constant churn of coal and slurry.

As Thompson learned more, his fascination with the technical details these engineers offered—his increasing mastery of the vernacular of mining—often took a backseat to his indignation. At times, it seemed like there were two Massey cultures: the brute-force mining side that got the coal out of the ground and the investor-facing side that held meetings in air-conditioned offices in Richmond. Both, in Thompson's view, had a shocking lack of concern about the potential environmental risks of their activities. He could see that government regulators should have exercised more oversight. But nothing Thompson learned altered his belief that the slurry injection at Rawl Sales had been carried out in a deceptive manner. The company apparently hadn't told anyone who studied the area's wells in the 1990s and early 2000s about the history of injection. Back in the spring of 2005, the company hadn't owned up to the extent of the injection in Judge Thornsbury's courtroom. That history had only begun to emerge with the depositions of former employees like Gene Kitts and Ben Hatfield, and they had said they were unaware of risks to local drinking water.

What had happened at Rawl Sales when people started complaining about their water? Thompson deposed Gary Hatfield, the mining and environmental engineer who had originally fielded complaints from Carmelita and Maude Rice. When water complaints came in, Hatfield said he found the resident's home on a map, looked at the distance to the nearest mine, and sent the information off to an insurance company. That's just the way things were done, he said. Yet there also seemed to be concern about losing credibility with state regulators. In a 1993 memo, Hatfield had listed a handful of residents who had complained about their water, and he wrote that the company had strenuously argued to the state over the prior two years that it hadn't affected people's water in Lick Creek. He asked: "If we pay for damages now, how will we look in the eyes of the DEP?"

Shouldn't Hatfield, or someone at Massey, have hired experts to study the effects of the slurry injection from the 1970s and 1980s on the area's water quality? Thompson asked.

"Hindsight is always twenty-twenty," Hatfield said.

Yet another Hatfield at Massey provided Thompson with an additional key piece of information. Steve Hatfield said it had cost $5 million to build an impoundment at another subsidiary, while the cost to inject slurry over five years was under $2 million. Slurry injection was the cheaper way to store slurry, Thompson would argue.

An old surveyor named Don Crum gave Thompson the most complete picture to date of the slurry injection at Rawl Sales. He said the filter press system had fallen out of favor early on because in the winter the slurry would turn into a jellylike substance that was difficult to place in a fill. More importantly, Crum had brought a box of old notebooks that were a bright shade of yellow orange, like goldenrod. The surveyor's notebooks, called field transit notes, ran from 1975 through 1985. Crum had identified thirty-six sets of boreholes (typically an injection hole paired with an air-relief hole). Suddenly the days when Massey claimed it had only pumped slurry into the head of Lick Creek and Sprouse Creek seemed like a lifetime ago.

Using drafting software, Crum had placed the holes on four maps that showed the old workings of four coal seams underneath and around the four communities. On his own initiative, he had included geographic features like creeks, rivers, and towns. Thompson could see where the injections had occurred in relation to the four communities, the prep plant, and other landmarks. Crum cautioned that not every borehole that had been surveyed had subsequently been drilled. But he recalled nine actual injection holes into the Pond Creek seam. And he confirmed that Rawl Sales had injected slurry into all four coal seams.

Crum said surveyors needed to keep three or four holes ahead of the current injection hole, in case it filled suddenly. Sometimes holes failed if the drill rig wasn't exactly vertical or if a mine roof had already caved in and filled the void. Occasionally the drill bit ran into a solid block of coal. The earliest injection hole Crum had found was surveyed in March 1979, giving Thompson a potential rough starting date for slurry injection at the prep plant, which had begun operating in 1977. Crum had reviewed notebooks only through 1985, to cover his tenure at Rawl Sales. He said there were more volumes in the company's mine map vault in Sidney, Kentucky.

"Is the mine vault a massive underground facility guarded by machine-gun-toting dudes from a Bond movie?" Thompson asked.

Crum described a more humble concrete-and-steel structure built to code. A few weeks later, the judge granted Thompson access, and after traveling to the site in Sidney, he was brought to a room that contained drawers full of decades-old mine maps, including some that had originally been hand-drawn. But, as Thompson would later recall when the issue of the company's maps came up again, there was nothing in that room that shed new light on slurry injection at Rawl Sales. Only later would questions arise about whether Jackson Kelly had turned over every map in its possession.

• • •

By now Thompson had already pieced together a damning paper trail from a cache of Rawl Sales documents provided by Jackson Kelly. As it turned out, state regulators had voiced concerns about the company's slurry injection as early as the late 1970s, and in the 1980s they had even tried to halt it.

In April 1983, a state inspector named Charles Morris found slurry leaking from a storage pond near the processing plant into Sprouse Creek. Morris signed five complaints against the company for negligently operating a preparation plant and discharging waste, noting that the company water-discharge permit had expired in 1981. Thompson discovered that Morris issued an arrest warrant against Rawl Sales & Processing. But little happened. The Mingo County prosecutor gave the company thirty days to send its permit renewal application to the state. Rawl Sales pleaded guilty to one count of negligent stream pollution but said the other instances were an act of God. It paid a small fine.

A year later, in March 1984—just before Blankenship took over as president of Rawl Sales—Morris visited the prep plant again and found the company pumping slurry into the abandoned Pond Creek No. 1 Mine without a permit. "After examining the mine maps of the slurry injection area, it is not known at this time if water wells along Lick Creek would be adversely affected by the slurry," Morris wrote to his superiors at the Department of Natural Resources (DNR). He recommended that the company's water-discharge permit be revoked or suspended indefinitely.

"In my opinion, Sprouse Creek Prep Plant cannot operate at its present capacity and not cause water pollution," Morris concluded.

Revoking the permit would shut down the prep plant. No more coal would flow in or out of the big green building. A flurry of letters back and forth between Rawl Sales and state regulators expressed the urgency of the situation. On April 3, 1984, the DNR's water resources division told Macs Hall, acting head of Sprouse Creek Processing—a subsidiary of Rawl Sales, which was itself a subsidiary—that the company was in violation of its water-discharge permit, which had just been issued in February.

On April 13, Hall replied, listing steps taken to clean up problems around the plant, in what Thompson started calling "the only true solution" memo. The company had stopped using the filter press system, and Hall argued that slurry injection was the best option environmentally. "The only true solution to this problem is underground disposal of the slurry," he wrote.

On April 17, a higher-ranking water resources division official told Hall that Sprouse Creek could inject slurry for six months, until its impoundment was built. But the company had to record the daily injection volumes and rates. It couldn't exceed a rate of 600 gallons per minute. It had to submit monthly monitoring reports. The company had to drill a monitoring hole and measure the height of water in the mine on a regular basis, so regulators could tell how full the coal seam was getting. Finally, the company had to report the progress on its impoundment construction.

From April 23 to April 29, the company injected 46,037 gallons of slurry, according to Gene Kitts's first monitoring report to the state. In May, it injected 283,086 gallons. Then sometime on the night of June 8, the slurry line broke above Lick Creek, and slurry ran down the length of the creek, and the company dredged the creek and used straw bales to try to absorb the slurry, according to a state notice of violation. On July 3, Kitts told regulators in a letter that the company had started construction on the impoundment. It would be ready to receive slurry later that year.

Meanwhile, a state official wrote a letter that same July to the Environmental Protection Agency's regional office in Philadelphia, to inform the federal agency about Rawl Sales' unauthorized use of an abandoned mine for slurry injection.

Thompson also now had evidence that a group of residents had put federal regulators on notice about the spill in Lick Creek. Among the files Jack Spadaro had found at the state Department of Environmental Protection was a letter written by Sarah Mollett, who lived more than a mile up Lick Creek from B.I. in a peaceful spot beside a rushing creek. In her July letter to the Department of the Interior, Mollett wrote:

> A week has passed and our stream is still black and there is from four to five inches of black mining waste on the creek bank. . . .
> The pets—cats, dogs, horses, etc. along with the wild animals are drinking this polluted water. We only hope that they don't all fall dead. The teenagers used to catch minnows and crawdads

for fish bait, but none can live in the black sludge. The children have always played in the creek until now.

We look to you for help in finding a solution to this problem. . . .

The letter had fifty-two signatures. Thompson recognized all the names. They had all become his clients.

On July 30, the regional administrator for the EPA wrote to Mollett, saying that state regulators had issued a violation for the spill. The company would be allowed to inject slurry for several months while its impoundment was being built.

The next day, Rawl Sales pleaded no contest to a charge of stream pollution in Mingo County. A magistrate judge found the company guilty and fined it five hundred dollars plus court costs. It was a slap on the wrist, and the company kept injecting.

Thompson now had a window into the first months when Blankenship was running Rawl Sales. In July 1984, Rawl Sales pumped 14.1 million gallons into the voids of the Pond Creek seam. In August, the number rose to 21.3 million gallons. In September, a strike by the UMWA at Rawl Sales temporarily shut the prep plant.

When the state's order allowing Rawl Sales to inject slurry for six months expired on October 17, a testy exchange of letters was sent between the company and the state.

On January 25, 1985, Erkan Esmer, an engineering consultant for Rawl Sales, notified state regulators by letter that monitoring tests showed there was no pollution of the groundwater and the slurry injection was clearly preventing aboveground pollution. He copied Governor Arch Moore Jr., who had taken office earlier that month. Esmer said the company was in a catch-22 situation. The prep plant needed to operate, because it generated rock along with slurry, and the rock was needed to build the dam of the impoundment. "Therefore, we have a vicious circle in which the only solution is to pump slurry underground to operate the facility in an environmentally acceptable fashion," Esmer wrote. He asked for a six-month extension. "Without this order there will either be pollution or several hundred jobs will be lost."

The state allowed the company to keep injecting slurry for another six months, but a regulator disputed Esmer's characterization of the situation and said his agency wouldn't be threatened with politics: the state, he wrote, had tried to expedite "a legal cleanup of the mess the company has created."

The state division in charge of approving water-discharge permits had tried to keep Rawl Sales on a short leash. Kitts and Ben Hatfield had said that slurry injection was a common practice in the 1980s with little oversight—claims that now rang hollow.

Rawl Sales blew past the six-month extension granted in early 1985. A curious thing happened in its monthly monitoring reports too. The company stopped mentioning the impoundment altogether, as though its construction was no longer a priority. It dropped references to monitoring required by the state. It simply went on pumping slurry.

Thompson found more. State regulators cited Rawl Sales in 1986, 1987, 1988, and 1989 for surface spills of slurry. The most serious violation occurred in November 1987 and was one of the few incidents that showed Blankenship's detailed knowledge of the injection process. This was the time that slurry broke through a sealed portion of the mine, forcing miners to evacuate. In a November 21 memo, Gene Kitts wrote to Blankenship to propose drilling a new borehole to replace the one that had "malfunctioned." They hired a contractor, but the contractor failed to hit an empty mine.

Thompson also found the results of the water tests that Rawl Sales had done on Carmelita and Ernie Brown's well in 1987. The well tested high for iron, manganese, and aluminum. Rawl Sales didn't test for arsenic, lead, or other heavy metals. The company had never provided the results to the Browns or to any state agency, as far as Thompson could tell. If not for his digging, these records also would have been lost forever. Instead he added them to his growing list of trial exhibits.

Thompson got the chance to depose Erkan Esmer—the engineering consultant who had told regulators that Rawl Sales needed to keep injecting slurry before it could build the impoundment—at the Charleston offices of Esmer's attorney on August 23, 2007. Bob McLusky, the Jackson Kelly attorney, attended on behalf of Massey. It wasn't long before Thompson realized that Doc Esmer, as he was known in the coal industry, had no loyalty to the company. He also had an irreverent streak. When Thompson gave his opening spiel, telling Esmer to ask for clarification if there was any ambiguity in his questions, Esmer replied, "Lawyers are always ambiguous. What else is new?"

Originally from Turkey, Esmer had been working for coal companies since he started his consulting business in 1970, and he had designed 206 impoundments for mining companies from Virginia to Utah. Sid Young, Blankenship's predecessor as president of Rawl Sales, had hired Esmer in the early 1980s when the company's slurry ponds were leaking and the filter press system wasn't working.

Esmer said it was his view in 1984 that the company needed to inject slurry for three or four months to give the prep plant enough time to produce the rock, known as coarse refuse, needed to build up the initial dam for the impoundment. Sid Young had approved a plan to speed up the process by strip-mining coal nearby to produce additional coarse refuse. The mining would cost fifty-five thousand dollars.

"And I did not want to pump underground because lots of problems could occur because of that," Esmer volunteered.

The statement, offered matter-of-factly, piqued Thompson's interest. "What kinds of problems could occur if you pumped underground?" he asked.

At the time, Esmer explained, several coal seams around the prep plant had been mined out and there were "cracks all over." Injecting slurry was unpredictable at best, Esmer said. An injection hole might last two weeks or three years.

"Well, in underground, when you start pumping slurry, you never know where it goes to," Esmer said. The engineer explained that if it was injected under pressure, slurry could rise to higher elevations through subsidence cracks in the rock strata, much like an artesian spring.

It was all damning testimony from an expert with direct knowledge of the environmental problems at Rawl Sales and the risks of injecting slurry. But Thompson wanted to know why it had taken years to build the impoundment when Esmer had told state regulators the company needed only a few months to get started.

"Well, we had a falling-out with Don Blankenship," Esmer said.

Blankenship had taken control of Rawl Sales in the middle
design and construction of the impoundment. Suddenly, there
problem with Esmer's plan to strip-mine coal to speed up constru
of the impoundment.

"I think Don thought that fifty-five thousand dollars was too m
to spend and complained about that," Esmer said.

Esmer had gone to the Rawl Sales offices on Route 49 to talk
Blankenship about it and Blankenship kept him waiting forty-fiv
minutes. "So I went in and wasn't very nice to him. Then I told him
will quit and I will write him a letter," Esmer said.

Could it be that Rawl Sales had injected hundreds of millions of
gallons of slurry because Blankenship, in what was possibly the first
major decision of his coal career, vetoed a strip mine to save fifty-
five thousand dollars? They took a smoke break for Esmer, and then
Thompson asked him to explain it again.

"So if you can, what did Don Blankenship, at any meeting you had
with him, what did he indicate to you were his opinions about your
engineering concerns?" Thompson asked.

"He said fifty-five thousand dollars is a lot of money to spend, as
well I am remembering," Esmer said.

Thompson asked if the decision not to spend the money resulted in
the slurry injection continuing beyond the few months Esmer thought
was appropriate. The engineer said yes, it probably did.

"Was there any reason the slurry injection needed to continue until
1987?" Thompson asked.

"I don't think so," Esmer said.

Did he think injecting more than a billion gallons of slurry into the
Pond Creek and Alma seams from 1977 to 1987 had affected the area's
groundwater?

Esmer said yes.

PART III

THE QUANTIFICATION OF INTUITION

JULY 2007–OCTOBER 2008

CHAPTER 14

No matter how many millions Don Blankenship earned, he liked people to know he'd grown up poor in Mingo County. He said he never forgot living with a mother who struggled to put food on the table and using an outhouse because he didn't have indoor plumbing. "I know what it is to be poor, I know what it is to be rich," he once remarked in a speech to supporters in 2018. He seemed to say he was no different from anyone else who had grown up in the coalfields in the 1950s. But there was a boast buried in every recollection. Few if any people from such humble beginnings in West Virginia had ever achieved his level of wealth and influence.

Donald Leon Blankenship was born on March 14, 1950, in Stopover, Kentucky, a place surrounded by low green hills, a spacious sky, and not much else. He had three older siblings—Anthony, Beulah, and George—and his first home was a camper that his mother, Nancy McCoy, bought with part of a thousand-dollar divorce settlement. She used the rest to buy a Gulf station and grocery store in Delorme, West Virginia, seven miles northwest and halfway to Matewan, and eventually moved the family into the apartment above it. With children to feed, Nancy McCoy kept the business, with its neat window display and "Drink *Coca-Cola*" signs out front, open nearly a hundred hours a week year-round. On Christmas Day, she took off the morning and reopened by noon.

Because the cinder-block building didn't have plumbing, the family used an outhouse and drew water from a well. Before he was old enough to pump gas or work the register, Blankenship helped fetch the water for drinking, cooking, and washing. He followed his brothers across the railroad tracks behind the gas station—the same line that passed by Rawl and Matewan and followed the winding Tug Fork— and then they hiked up a green slope and took turns working the pump. Don would struggle to carry home a bucket of the cold water. One summer day, he tried to step over the railroad tracks but slipped and burned his leg on a steel rail that had been baking in the sun. It was one of his earliest memories, and he remembered never complaining about the burn or about having to carry the water. Even as a boy, he took pride in being tough and never backing down.

Blankenship was a McCoy living on land that was once part of Devil Anse Hatfield's thousands of acres of timber holdings. The other side of his family went back generations in the Tug Valley. Obediah Blankenship was one of the area's original settlers on Peter Creek, not far from Delorme. But the Norfolk and Western's current black-diesel locomotives held more fascination for young Don than the history of the area or family lore. Far sleeker than the steam-powered engines that rattled the hills in the 1890s, these modern engines still hauled coal out of the valley in trains a mile long. At night, the trains slowed through the knot of houses in Delorme, their wheels clattering past his bedroom window, before carrying coal east to Norfolk, Virginia, or as far west as Cincinnati, Ohio.

Blankenship liked people to know that Delorme was a tough place then. "It probably led the nation in shootings at the time," he boasted of his hometown, which had about four hundred residents when he was growing up. With a two-room schoolhouse and a Pentecostal church, the community was calm and Mayberry-like during the week, but on Friday nights it became a hot spot, when miners from dry counties in Kentucky and Virginia drove in. Delorme had half a dozen beer joints with neon signs. There were Stump's, Cruz's, Daniel's, Prater's, and Gooslin's, names Blankenship could list off the top of his head years later. Another one called the Bloody Bucket was owned by a man who died suspiciously in a fire. Once, when Blankenship was eight, he had to dive around the corner of a building after he heard gunshots. At night, he and a friend would climb onto the slanted roof of the town's barbershop, where they had a ringside view of the fights that regularly broke out on the street. "You could lay on it with only your head sticking over the edge so you felt like you weren't going to get shot," he said.

Blankenship's mother set his moral compass early on, offering correctives to the vice and violence and other human failings that Blankenship later said were on display in Delorme. If someone was falling-over drunk, she said, "You don't ever want to be staggering down the road. Look how foolish they look." If someone came into the store asking for heartburn medicine, she chalked it up to alcohol. In the 1950s, she pointed out the dangers of cigarettes. As a store owner, she opposed stealing: "You don't need to steal to get through the world." She didn't like cursing: "If you're smart enough, you can find a way to express yourself without it." As a result, Blankenship never smoked or cursed and, he said, he never stole anything.

Nancy McCoy had hardened herself to survive, but she could be compassionate, even to strangers. One day, two Kentucky state policemen chased a car across the bridge into Delorme, and the car crashed into a building, Blankenship said. The police opened fire, drawing a crowd into the street, including Blankenship and his mother. One of the men was killed; the other lay in the street bleeding. Blankenship's mother pulled up her dress and tore off part of her slip to make a tourniquet. "She tied his arm off even though nobody else would touch him, because they were afraid to," Blankenship recalled.

The deeper lesson was that his mother did what she thought was right, regardless of what anyone else thought. The same became true of her son: he always viewed himself as being in the right, even when others saw him as being insensitive, even blind, to the suffering of others.

The key to Blankenship's success came down to a singular talent he learned he possessed in the third grade. (His school had a total of thirty-six students; toilet paper was strictly rationed, and children would challenge each other to touch the potbelly coal stove in winter.) That year, his teachers discovered he was able to do college-level math. His ability to manipulate numbers was a gift he hardly understood himself. "I didn't realize it until my kids were in the seventh or eighth grade, and I picked up their math book and it was teaching what they called new math," he said. "That 19 times 19 was not 9 times 9 put down the 1 and carry the 8. It was 20 times 19, which is 380, minus 19, which is 361. I knew that when I was born almost. I don't understand why."

Blankenship spent much of his youth pumping gas for coal miners, playing baseball in a coalfield league, and memorizing the stats of players, including his hero, Willie Mays. At Magnolia High School, in Matewan, Blankenship was quiet but popular. His lean face was clean-shaven, with a mole visible above the left corner of his mouth. In the 1968 *Messenger*, his high school yearbook, President "Donnie Blankenship" is listed with the other senior class officers. In one photograph, he wears a suit and tie next to three girls in bobs and sweaters. In another picture, he poses at a lectern, leaning over a sheaf of papers with an awkward but genuine smile.

It was a turbulent year. Major cities around the country were rocked by riots after the assassination of Martin Luther King Jr. in April. The nation grieved again in June when Robert F. Kennedy was shot and killed. Psychedelics were bending the collective consciousness. The Beatles' "Hey Jude" was the year's top single, *2001: A Space Odyssey* was the most profitable film, and opposition to the Vietnam War was growing. But those were distant events for people living in Matewan. In 1968, Blankenship's classmates felt the shock of the Farmington Mine disaster more than they did the cultural changes sweeping the country. On November 20, a massive explosion at Consolidation Coal Company's No. 9 mine killed seventy-eight miners, some of whose bodies were never recovered. The explosion was felt 12 miles away, and flames shot up 150 feet into the air. The fire burned for more than a week, before the mine was sealed with concrete. The accident spurred the passage of stronger mine-safety laws and the creation of the Mine Safety and Health Administration.

For its size, Mingo County sent a large number of young men to fight in Vietnam. Blankenship saw one of his brothers go to war and come back a different person. George Blankenship was six feet five inches tall, weighed two hundred pounds, and had a thirty-inch waist. "He was the fastest guy in the 101st Airborne and carried a machine gun," Blankenship said. He proudly recounted that George fought in the Battle of Hamburger Hill in May 1969 and was awarded two Bronze Stars, one with a *V* for valor. It was one of the bloodiest assaults of the war, on a numbered hill with no strategic significance. News reports of the bloodshed helped shift public opinion against the war.

After George's return to Delorme, a group of men were holding a cockfight behind one of the bars, and one of the gamecocks ran away to avoid getting torn apart. The bird's owner caught it and shoved it alive into a potbelly stove. "My brother was just sitting there at the bar and walked over and took him by the back of the neck and put his head next to the fire," Blankenship said. "He said, 'If you ever throw another chicken in that fire in my presence, I'll throw you in it.' And that told me how much he had changed."

Many of Blankenship's classmates later said they knew there was something special about him. "He was just one of those people that you didn't forget," said Wilma Steele, who was three grades below him. "He was so self-controlled. Motivated as far as grades. Behavior above reproach. Very humble acting. I don't ever remember hearing a smart word out of him." The only negative story she ever heard about Blankenship during high school was that, to show off, he drove one night on the wrong side of the road with his headlights off. In high school, he wrecked an old-model car in the rain, was thrown from the passenger door, and skidded two hundred feet on the highway while his car slid on its roof beside him. He said he got up and walked away. Others said he later liked to drive fast in his brother's dark-blue Camaro.

One night on a date, a girlfriend asked Blankenship if he knew who his real father was. That was how he learned that he had a different father from his siblings. His mother's ex-husband had never let on that Blankenship wasn't his son or that his mother had had an affair while he was off fighting in Korea. "At that time, jobs were scarce and it was tough back in this part of the world," Blankenship said, explaining the infidelity of a woman who was so unforgiving of the transgressions of others. "So I ended up being an illegitimate child, if you will." Blankenship discussed the matter only once with his mother. One day, she handed him a slip of newsprint that contained a short obituary. "That was your dad," she said. He read that his father had been a truck driver and had owned his own trucking company. In his later years, he became a pastor. That was all Blankenship would ever know. "I could tell she was bothered by it, so I didn't have any conversation," he said.

After Blankenship graduated with the second-highest grades in his class, he enrolled at Marshall University to study accounting. In college, he started growing a mustache to cover the mole above his upper lip. The mole bled when he nicked it shaving, and he didn't have enough money to have it removed. He doubled up on courses and worked in coal mines during the summers, vacations, and holidays. He shot coal, which involved drilling a hole into the coal face, setting an explosive charge, and then getting out of the way. It was dangerous work. If he wasn't careful, the heavy butterfly drill could easily spin out of control and knock out his teeth. He worked one job beside a man who had lost an arm in the mines. When Blankenship was twenty and working for Eastern Associated Coal Corporation, he learned that the miner who worked the same job on the shift before him had been killed. He said his own fear kept him safe. "I was so scared of explosives and what it was all about, I wasn't very likely to get killed," he said.

Later, when he ran Massey, he would say he had an appreciation for the work miners did and their safety concerns. He calculated that he had worked the equivalent of two years underground. "I understood what it was all about," he said.

Blankenship got his accounting degree in 1972, after three years at Marshall, and he had to sit for his CPA exam only once. At the time, there were few opportunities for CPAs or math savants in the coalfields, and he decided to leave Mingo County, as many of his friends had, in order to make his way in the corporate world. He got his first job after he responded to an ad in a Cincinnati newspaper.

Central Soya, a soybean company in Chattanooga, Tennessee, was looking for what it called a "green accountant"—someone to literally count beans. He drove to Chattanooga and walked into a room with about forty other people sitting at desks who had seen the same ad. A woman passed out a job application with fifty math questions on it. Blankenship answered forty-nine before the timer went off. Soon the woman called him into another room and said, "This is not possible. You got forty-nine out of fifty, and you answered them all right and there's not a single mark on the paper. Only answers. Did you have the answers?"

"I do the math in my head," he said.

Central Soya flew him to their headquarters in Fort Wayne, Indiana—his first time on an airplane—for an interview. His mother bought him a clip-on tie for the trip. He got the job.

Back in Chattanooga, Blankenship found it difficult to make friends after growing up in a town of four hundred people. Within a year, he quit and drove back to Mingo County, where he knew he could find temporary work in a coal mine. When he grew restless again, Blankenship took another accounting job in Macon, Georgia, with Keebler, the maker of "Uncommonly Good" cookies. The company sent him to Chicago and then to Denver, where he fell in love and got married. His wife, Mary, was from Wray, a community on the Colorado plains about two hundred miles east of Denver. They had a son they named John and a daughter, Jennifer. Blankenship studied Keebler's marketing campaigns in print and on TV. He struck up a friendship with the artist who had drawn the Keebler elves for years.

But in 1977, after four years, Blankenship was ready to move on and started fielding calls from headhunters. Massey Energy called, but he turned it down—he was trying to build a career in the food industry. He soon accepted a position with Flowers Industries, of Thomasville, Georgia, which operated bakeries throughout the southeast.

By this time, Blankenship was applying his obsessive habit of cost analysis to his personal life. While he and Mary were preparing to relocate to Georgia, she bought $400 worth of wicker furniture. The store was going to charge $600 to ship it. That seemed crazy to Blankenship. Not far from the furniture store, he spotted a blue 1965 Chevrolet pickup in a farmer's yard with a "For Sale" sign. He told Mary to wait in the car. Blankenship bought the truck for $400. "It seems like everything costs $400 around here," he joked to the farmer. He paid a mechanic about $40 to flush the radiator and change the hoses, the oil, and the fan belt. Blankenship then drove the truck all the way to Georgia with the furniture strapped down, through one of the worst ice storms the South had seen in thirty years. But he had saved $160.

Blankenship saw himself becoming a CEO. He turned down an opportunity to become controller at Flowers, but then he had a chance to become president of the company's bakery in South Carolina. The only condition was that he'd have to shave his mustache. By now, though, it was part of his identity, and he had no intention of shaving it. "I told them, 'Well, I'm not going to cut my mustache, so you'll need to find somebody else if the promotion depends on my mustache,'" he said later.

He quit for the third time.

After a decade living around the country, Blankenship moved his family back to Mingo County in early 1982. His mother had severe arthritis, and he wanted to help take care of her. Soon Sid Young, the president of Rawl Sales, called with a job offer. Young's father had been superintendent at the company, and Young had practically grown up there. Now he needed an accountant and he was confident that Blankenship, whom he had known in high school, would be perfect for the job.

Blankenship accepted and became the highest-paid controller at Massey and the only one who was a CPA. Within two years, Blankenship would have Sid Young's job running Rawl Sales. He'd also moved his family onto the property in Sprigg where Young had grown up.

"It changed my entire life to come back here," Blankenship said later. "I oftentimes wish I hadn't, because I think I would have been CEO of a much less difficult company in a lot less difficult industry." Then he added matter-of-factly, "It was obvious that I was going to be a CEO." Plus, they let him keep his mustache. "I figured they weren't worried about hair getting in coal like they were in bread."

Blankenship didn't need a map to find his way along Route 49 or any of the other roads that threaded their way along the creeks and hollows. The Tug Valley was his world. "It was like predestination," he said. "I wanted to be here."

CHAPTER 15

In the spring of 1982, when Blankenship arrived at Rawl Sales, the operation included a small network of mines and a preparation plant that washed the coal so it could be shipped by rail. His office was in a two-story building set back from Route 49 near the river, in an area between Sprigg and Matewan called Lobata. Across the road, standing out from the area's green hills and scattering of homes, was the Rawl Sales coal loadout facility: two white coal silos, a train track, and a green conveyor belt leading up a tipple where coal was dumped into trains.

Massey was hiring CPAs at the behest of Fluor Corp., a global construction business based in Los Angeles. The new parent company wanted Massey to root out corruption, and Blankenship soon found practices he didn't like. Some managers were loaning heavy equipment to friends, among other kickback schemes, according to Blankenship. "I cleaned up so much corruption," he said. "I said, 'What you do away from what I'm managing I can't do anything about, but you're not going to do that here.'" An executive tried to get Blankenship fired, saying he was "unsupervisable." But E. Morgan Massey recognized Blankenship's abilities and said he would remain at the company. Two years later, Sid Young was sent to Richmond, where he stayed only a few months because he wasn't cut out for administrative work—or as he put it, "I couldn't get tassels on my boots." Meanwhile, Blankenship became president of Rawl Sales.

Blankenship still had traces of his boyish diffidence. But he was training his mind on the business of coal mining as no other executive had ever done at Massey, or anywhere else in the industry. He found inefficiencies at every stage of the company's operations—in how the coal was mined, transported to the preparation plant, washed, put on trains or trucks, and shipped out. He made changes that he considered little more than common sense. At the prep plant, where machines crushed coal to different-size pieces and stripped out ash and other contaminants, he changed out equipment that had been breaking down ten times a day. Soon the plant could run three shifts without a single minute of lost time. He cut labor costs. The company had been trucking coal from one of its mines to the prep plant, but Blankenship discovered it would be cheaper to send the coal by belt line, traveling half the distance through the hills. The belt line was built. Truck drivers were let go or sent to other jobs within the company.

The prep plant was designed to process about 1.8 million tons of coal per year. After Blankenship's improvements, it washed and shipped 6 million tons in one year. Rawl Sales went from losing $19 million a year to earning a profit of $25 million one year. The increases in volume and profit caught the eye of Morgan Massey. Even the Fluor board of directors, who paid little attention to Massey beyond its top-line numbers, couldn't help but notice the manager turning losses into profits. Morgan Massey brought Blankenship along to meetings with Fluor's board of directors and let him handle the technical questions.

Blankenship was applying himself at a company that already kept its costs low by following the Massey Doctrine. Still Blankenship looked at the entire business, down to purchasing and budgeting. He knew from his own experience about the jobs miners did underground. He started thinking in terms of coal production per foot of advance: What was the total cost of moving equipment one foot deeper into the coal seam? One mine might have a loose top that required extra roof bolts—four- to six-foot-long steel rods like rebar driven into a mine's shale or sandstone roof and secured with a fast-setting resin, or glue. So he would factor in the cost of roof bolts when assessing a mine's potential profitability.

Instead of relying on the subjective opinions of managers about how long jobs like installing roof bolts or loading coal took inside a mine, Blankenship sent consultants underground to run time studies on how long each job should take. Then he set exacting standards for workers to meet for numerous routine tasks. The process imposed a machinelike precision across the company's mines, and left little room for local decision-making. Blankenship gave this mathematics of coal mining a grandiose name: "the quantification of intuition."

But it was an odd pairing—his gift for abstraction and the messy, dangerous activity of coal mining, where actual lives were at risk—and soon his data-driven managerial style ran into opposition from miners. In 1984, after Morgan Massey refused to sign on to a national agreement with the mine workers' union, the union went on strike in October and Blankenship faced a pivotal decision. Most coal was still trucked to the processing plant—up to a thousand loads every day, from mines in West Virginia and Kentucky—and it was easy for the union to disrupt the process. A single lost day of production threatened the ability of Rawl Sales to fill orders for customers. Blankenship decided that any time the union struck, the company would run coal anyway—a tactic that had seldom been tried in West Virginia in the decades since the UMWA had consolidated its power in the 1930s.

Over the next fifteen months, Blankenship hired replacement workers and brought in armed security guards who wore helmets, carried riot shields, and videotaped strikers. Striking miners accused the company of provoking them, so their reactions could be filmed and used against them in court, where Spike Maynard, Blankenship's friend, was the county's judge. Maynard fined the union two hundred thousand dollars for misconduct, but the fine was overturned by the state Supreme Court.

The entry to the Sprouse Creek prep plant was protected by machine-gun nests and barbed-wire fences. Several hundred striking miners held sit-ins and church services near the plant entrance, and they blocked Route 49 with pickups and cars. They spread twisted nails called jack rocks across roads to puncture the tires of managers' cars and coal trucks. When cars slowed, the striking miners broke windshields with bats. Blankenship later said the strikers had broken up to a hundred windows and flattened as many tires in a day. It was around this time that someone fired eleven bullets into Blankenship's office on Route 49 one night and one round lodged in the Zenith TV in his office. In May 1985, a nonunion coal truck driver, Hayes West, thirty-five, was killed by snipers as he reached a gap at the top of Coeburn Mountain on Route 119 in Kentucky near the West Virginia border. West was shot more than twenty times, and died in the arms of his brother Phillip, another driver. Four union members were later convicted of various federal charges and sentenced to between thirty and forty-five years in prison.

The union was seeking an umbrella contract with all of Massey, arguing that otherwise the company could shut individual mines and reopen them nonunion. Morgan Massey said he couldn't negotiate on behalf of the company's different resource groups. But Richard Trumka, then head of the UMWA, accused the company of playing a "corporate shell game." When filmmakers came to document the strike, Blankenship explained his own reasons for resisting the union. In the footage, Blankenship, looking young for his thirty-five years, hunches over his desk with a calculator and a primitive computer. The muscles of his face barely move as he speaks in a soft monotone, equating the strike to "union terrorism."

"First of all, I grew up in what many people consider to be the toughest town in Mingo County, in Delorme," Blankenship said in *Mine War on Blackberry Creek*, a documentary from 1986. "I know the history of the Matewan Massacre and the Hatfield-McCoy feud, and all that kind of violence. The only thing I can say about that is that it's not conducive to a good business climate."

Blankenship made the case in the twenty-nine-minute film that the company couldn't operate profitably under the terms the union wanted. The math was straightforward, as was the logic of busting the union.

"What you have to accept in a capitalist society generally is that— I always make the comparison that it's like a jungle, where the jungle is the survival of the fittest," Blankenship said. "Unions, communities, people, everybody is going to have to learn to accept that in the United States you have a capitalist society, and that capitalism from a business viewpoint is survival of the most productive . . . In the long term it's going to be the most productive people who benefit."

Former classmates who had grown up with Blankenship said his conservative views hardened during the strike, which turned him into the natural enemy of the UMWA, labor-friendly politicians in eastern Kentucky and West Virginia, and much of the local population. Many were stunned that someone from Mingo County would try to break the union right outside Matewan. In addition to the bullets fired into his office, Blankenship received death threats. He slept in a safe house under guard and sent his wife and children away out of concern for their safety. He drove a bulletproof car with solid tires to the office, and he kept a loaded Israeli machine gun on the passenger seat. He and other managers barely slept for months, he later recalled. One morning as he passed through the picket line, strikers shot at his car and tried to stop it, and he nearly ran them over.

"He's a different person," said Wilma Steele, his former classmate, whose husband was a union miner during the strike. "With that bullet, he just snapped and he became a different person."

At the height of the strike, Massey executives and the leaders of the UMWA and West Virginia governor Arch Moore Jr. negotiated a deal in Washington, DC, without Blankenship's knowledge. A Massey executive called Blankenship and told him not to run any coal the next day with scabs; the company had reached a settlement.

"I said, 'Well, I think we're going to work tomorrow, because we're set up,'" Blankenship recalled. "They said, 'Nope, won't be any trucking tomorrow.' I said, 'Where you guys at?' 'Over in Washington, DC, with the governor and the union. We've got this arrangement made. There's no trucking tomorrow.' I said, 'Well, if you're in Washington, DC, there'll be trucking tomorrow.'"

The coal trucks ran the next day, and the deal with the union fell apart. A Massey official came to Rawl Sales and asked for Blankenship's resignation. But he refused to sign it. "He says, 'Don, you know, we all want people who are determined, but I'm going to have to let you go.' I said, 'I'm not surprised. I'd probably let me go too if I told someone to do something and they didn't do it.' He said, 'Well, I need for you to sign this paperwork.' I said, 'What's it say?' He said, 'You resign.' I said, 'No . . . You can fire me, because when I go out of here I want to tell all these guys that have been in here with me and been shot at and everything else that I got fired. I'm not going to tell them that I quit.' He said, 'Well, if you sign this paper we can arrange some severance for you.' I said, 'I don't know why you care. Why don't you just fire me?' He said, 'There's some people who don't agree.'"

"Some people" likely included Morgan Massey himself, because Blankenship soon learned that he was not to be fired. "I said, 'I guess you better get out of here, because we're going to win this thing.'"

In the end, after fifteen months and no other options, the union capitulated, just as it had in the 1920s.

At times, the 1984–1985 strike had been just as violent as the one in 1920–1921. James Gardner, who was Massey's general counsel and one of Blankenship's closest advisers for many years, estimated that there were perhaps a thousand rounds of ammunition fired in Blankenship's direction and more than a hundred people wounded, including the truck driver who was killed. After all that, the union had been forced to concede, ushering in a period of decline. "That is the ultimate source of the animosity toward Don," said Gardner.

Blankenship had opposed the union because it handcuffed his ability to respond to business conditions, he said, especially in down markets. He believed the company, the workers, and the community were better off without the union. "When we threw off that domination, they disintegrated, and they've hated me ever since," Blankenship said.

In fact, the union had helped bring a new level of financial security to a swath of the county in the 1970s and early 1980s. After the strike, many of those gains would be lost too. To many people in Mingo County, Blankenship's role in defeating the union made him a coal boss, no matter where he'd been born.

The violence along Route 49 was national news, but few noticed that the prep plant back in the hills continued to process coal and produce slurry. Some twenty years later, Thompson believed that not only had Blankenship launched his career by crushing the mine workers' union and cutting labor costs and increasing profits, he had done so while pumping toxic slurry into the mountains.

Blankenship's star continued to rise, and Morgan Massey gave him more authority. In the past, Massey had always granted his managers a relatively free hand to run the company's subsidiaries. But Blankenship kept those beneath him on a short leash. He retained an encyclopedic grasp of operational detail across the company and gave orders, down to minor purchasing and hiring decisions. It was a management style that would later put him in legal jeopardy when Thompson and other lawyers argued that his hands-on involvement made him responsible for the company's failings.

Within the company, Blankenship's staunchest defender was also the person who mattered most: Morgan Massey. "You've met people that can remember any name of anybody they've ever met. Don is a guy that can remember any number he's ever seen," Massey said. "You can call him a micromanager if you want. But you have to understand how he thinks."

Yet sometimes Blankenship had trouble getting subordinates to do what he wanted, which irritated him to no end. In 1990, when Blankenship was named president of Massey Coal Services, Baxter Phillips, a longtime Massey executive in Richmond, suggested that he apply a lighter touch with subordinates. Rather than dressing down managers who disappointed him, he could pass out cans of Dad's Root Beer as a reminder to "Do As Don Says." Blankenship tried it out. But for some managers the humor didn't translate. The cans became another indication that the boss wasn't happy. Managers hoped they wouldn't come to work and find a can or, worse, a six-pack of root beer sitting on their desk.

"I believed in process," Blankenship said. "I believed in guidelines. I believed in budgets. I believed in responsibility and accountability. And I could fire you just as easily as I'm talking to you right now. And say, I'm sorry but we just don't need you anymore. People thought it was cold. But I didn't see any reason to yell at anybody."

Blankenship didn't go in for the usual trappings of the C-suite. He was an atrocious golfer and had no appetite for tennis, preferring instead to play basketball or ride his motorcycle. He worked through weekends, and he liked to be near the operations and talk to workers, something group presidents frequently complained about. "He always said he liked having the operations within a one-hour helicopter ride," said Jeff Wilson, who reported to Blankenship for fifteen years at Massey. "Don would end up on the refuse dump talking to the dozer operator on the second or third shift, and in the morning you'd have a note from him saying, why weren't you paying attention to such and such? Because the dozer operator knew about it."

More than a dozen operating subsidiaries had to send in daily profit and loss reports, each sometimes fifty to sixty pages long. Blankenship read them all. "I'd get a call from Don saying, 'Look at page forty-three. What about the cost of roof bolts at your Peerless mine?'" Wilson said. "I used to say the guy's got twenty megs of RAM. He didn't forget anything."

When Wilson oversaw the construction of a $55 million preparation plant to clean coal from the Upper Big Branch Mine, one of the company's most profitable deep mines, Blankenship used the corporate helicopter daily to check on the plant's progress. "Every morning, you would hear the *wha-wha-wha*—here he comes," Wilson recalled. "He would stay until dark, and he would be right back in the morning."

Wilson said Blankenship gave more than lip service to safety, despite what others thought. Blankenship was credited with industry-leading innovations like putting reflective stripes on miners' clothing and pushing for the development of sensors on heavy equipment underground to prevent miners from getting run over or crushed. While Massey group presidents got reports faxed to their homes in the evenings that listed the mid-shift production at their mines, the reports also included any safety problems. "With coal mines, workers' compensation and things like that, it's extremely expensive not to be safe. Just from a pure accounting standpoint, I can't imagine why Don would not want a place to be safe." Wilson added, "He wanted safety; he wanted production. He wanted it all, and he wanted it to be perfect."

But some miners told a different story. They said the pressure to "stay in the coal" was constant. And when there was a choice to be made between cleaning something up or advancing into the coal seam, there was no question about which took precedence. Clay Mullins, who worked at Upper Big Branch through the 1990s and early 2000s, said the pressure there was as intense as anywhere in the company. "They was just mining coal all the time," said Mullins, whose brother Rex would later die in the mine. "They didn't want to do maintenance. Just enough to keep it running." He remembered Blankenship's visits too. "He told the foreman what he wanted done. Then the foremen would tell the men, and the men would do it," said Mullins. "He had his hand in everything they did. He controlled them all."

The Upper Big Branch Mine, located in Whitesville, next to the Marsh Fork Elementary School, was hugely important to Massey. It was part of Blankenship's strategy to acquire reserves to dominate the market for steelmaking coal. When struggling steel companies needed to sell their reserves, Blankenship bought them cheaply. By the late 1990s, Massey was the biggest coal producer in Central Appalachia, and it controlled more reserves of steelmaking coal in North America than any other company. The coal seam at the Upper Big Branch Mine possessed some of the highest-quality coal found anywhere. Unlike the room-and-pillar mines around Rawl, the company used a longwall machine that sheared away the coal in thousand-foot-wide swaths, a far more profitable method.

Years later, a massive accident at the mine with fatal consequences would lead to the greatest crisis of Blankenship's career and draw national attention to the company's recklessness. Scenes from the mine would play on millions of televisions across the country, and the president of the United States would travel to Whitesville to mourn the lives of miners lost. But when the mine was operating in the late 1990s, few could have predicted that it would end in disaster. It was just another Massey operation where Blankenship tried to maximize the tons coming out every day.

In December 2000, Massey Energy Co. started trading as an independent corporation on the New York Stock Exchange, after Fluor spun off the coal business. Blankenship was named chairman and CEO. The company's board of directors expanded to include company officials, a university chancellor, and the former director of the National Security Agency, Admiral Bobby Ray Inman. It was two months after the impoundment failure in Martin County, Kentucky. The board was there to provide oversight and to check on company practices that might now present a risk to shareholders, in addition to communities and the environment. But Blankenship was chairman, and by many accounts, from the start the board acceded to his management style and grasp of the company's operations. Under his leadership, Massey mined more coal and revenue rose steadily. But the company had trouble turning a profit. In the early 2000s, it had several years of losses due to low coal prices and the high cost of mining in West Virginia, where most thick coal seams had already been mined. The losses only put greater pressure on mining coal more cheaply.

With Massey now public, Blankenship became the face of a company that leveled mountains, poisoned streams, contaminated the air, and used miners as expendable parts to extract as much coal as possible from West Virginia. In his view, he'd been villainized by people with an agenda.

"You become a target for people to benefit from disliking you," Blankenship said, explaining the animosity and rage directed toward him. "They benefit through lawsuits, they benefit politically. They benefit because their story sells. So everybody benefits by being 'anti' a guy who is operating a 'dirty' industry successfully using nonunion labor while he's taking off the tops of mountains.

"Some people don't think I'm human," Blankenship said.

CHAPTER 16

"**D**on Blankenship runs his company very hands on."

It was July 17, 2007, and Thompson was back in Judge Thornsbury's courtroom, listing reasons why he should be allowed to depose Blankenship. The October trial date was approaching fast. Three houses owned by Rawl Sales in Sprigg, including Blankenship's, were on Matewan water, Thompson said. He wanted to know why Blankenship had made the switch. Most importantly, the ultimate decision to inject slurry in the 1980s rather than build the impoundment rested with Blankenship, he told the judge.

"They should have put the impoundment up in 1978, Your Honor, when the law said you've got to start doing things right," Thompson said. "He's the one who made those decisions. He made them solely. He's the one who figured it out. He's the one who said, 'Yep, now the cat's out of the bag with the slurry spill in Lick Creek and now we've got to get the impoundment going.' I don't think you're going to find a case in this country where a CEO started his career out at the very place where a toxic tort springs forth decades later, and then that CEO—at the time everyone else is complaining about the quality of their water—that CEO decides he's going to get water from public water and the line stops at his house."

Thompson accused Massey and Jackson Kelly of concealing the extent of the slurry injection from him and the judge. "Your Honor, we've now found out through these depositions that they weren't forthcoming to you and I about what seams were injected in. Now we know it's not just Pond Creek, it's not just Alma, now they've admitted it's Winifred, it's Upper Cedar Grove." And Blankenship's house sat on top of those seams. "Every other well we've got around there was turning bad at that time. My guess is his well was turning bad too, and I want to talk to him about it. I don't think I'm out of bounds here . . . I think my people deserve this."

Thompson sat down. His impassioned speech apparently had an effect on the judge, who had previously said he didn't see why Blankenship should sit for a deposition when other managers were available. Now Thornsbury said he would consider the matter, and Thompson began to feel more confident that soon he'd be face-to-face with Blankenship.

Back at room 409, Thompson expanded his staff to get ready for trial. A college friend of Wussow's showed up one evening when Thompson and Wussow were on the hotel roof drinking beers and watching the sun set. Eric Mathis had grown up in a trailer park in North Carolina and gone on to study political philosophy, economic theory, and Appalachian history. He had read all the Appalachian scholars in an attempt to become one himself. He had already run off to Latin America, worked in community gardening, and marched for women's rights. Preternaturally smart, Mathis could talk like an academic, but in jeans and a baggy T-shirt, he looked like a young coal miner. He told Thompson he wanted to build a sustainability movement in a place like Williamson. When he saw what Thompson was up to, he said, "Plug me in, man." Thompson hired him.

Another hire who came on for trial preparation, Melissa Ellsworth, a petite twenty-two-year-old with shoulder-length brown hair and a quiet confidence, was heading into her senior year at the School of the Museum of Fine Arts in Boston. A talented video producer, she had first come to Williamson as a volunteer with OVEC. After years of preparing trial graphics, Thompson saw the value of hiring an artist. He wanted her to shoot footage of the prep plant during a court-sanctioned tour of the plant he was going to take on August 14. The footage could show the messy industrial process of cleaning coal inside the prep plant and convey to a jury the scale of the impoundment and how the slurry lines had been laid through the mountains. He wanted to find a broken slurry pipeline too.

The night before the site visit, Thompson gathered Bunch, Simonton, Wussow, Mathis, and Ellsworth in room 409 to plot their invasion of Rawl Sales. On a trip to Walmart, "Uncle Van" had bought Ellsworth a pair of steel-toe boots, but he declined to buy a machete that Wussow wanted to get. Thompson laid out his strategy around an aerial photograph of the prep plant and neighboring hills. When the tour moved outside, he said, they would break into two groups and hike into the hills as fast as they could, leaving Stickler and the other Jackson Kelly lawyers behind. The best places to look for slurry pipes would be near the haul roads the company could have used to carry the pipe, Simonton suggested. Pointing to two promising locations on the photograph, Thompson stood up with such excitement that he banged his knee against the table.

He was still limping the next morning when they got to the prep plant. On her shoulder, Ellsworth carried the video camera Thompson used for depositions. She captured footage wherever they went, beginning with their safety training in the prep plant office, where a bumper sticker said "Earth first. We'll mine the rest later."

The calendar on the wall was several months out of date; the prep plant had been shut down that spring. The guts of the big green building, which for years had churned with rivers of coal and slurry, had been silenced by a downturn in the coal markets. Leaders from Rawl Sales walked Thompson's crew through the plant for several hours. When the tour moved outside, Ellsworth, trailing everyone as they walked across a steel catwalk, got footage of the circular holding tank under them called "the thickener." Now rusty and stagnant, it was the color of pumpkin soup in the sun.

It had been a warm morning, and the heat was rising in the hills. Their guide warned everyone to watch out for snakes. Now that they were outside, Thompson's plan to outrun Jackson Kelly—so thrilling the night before—seemed silly. They'd already been walking around for hours; Thompson still couldn't put his full weight on his leg, and now there was a risk of snakes. But Bunch, Simonton, and Mathis started to hike in one direction, and Thompson, Wussow, and Ellsworth broke in another, Ellsworth still carrying the heavy camera.

Thompson and his team looked out of place hiking next to the company's officials and attorneys. When Bunch got into an argument with Mathis over whether to set a butterfly free from a spiderweb, the Jackson Kelly lawyers looked on with disbelief as Bunch pulled part of the web aside and let the butterfly go. It wasn't the only comical moment. Within minutes, Simonton inadvertently stepped on a log and released a swarm of hornets, which attacked Bunch's head and flew up his shorts. He swatted wildly at them, cursing Simonton. Thompson, limping painfully, cackled at the sight. They hiked for close to an hour. Just when they wondered if they were wasting their time, Wussow climbed up ahead of Thompson and began yelling: "Blown-apart PVC pipe!"

As everyone followed up the hillside, Ellsworth pointed the video camera down at shards of gray PVC pipe half covered by tall grass. Thompson and the others searched the area in the heat, but the vegetation was too thick; they never found an injection hole.

Still, Thompson considered the find a victory. The PVC pipe was hard evidence that Rawl Sales had used an inferior type of pipe, instead of the reinforced kind that Doc Esmer had recommended: under Blankenship the company had taken the cheapest route possible in the short term to dispose of the prep plant's coal slurry, Thompson would argue. "We knew what we had," he said.

In September, Judge Thornsbury moved the trial back again, to May 2008, partly because Jackson Kelly argued that Thompson had been slow to turn over medical records. The delay, while frustrating to Thompson, gave him some breathing room again, and life at the Mountaineer hummed through the fall and winter. More residents were joining "the train" every week. They often called with questions about the case and concerns about their health, and Thompson needed another hand in the office.

Wussow called Nick Getzen, another friend from Appalachian State, and persuaded him to join them at the Mountaineer. Getzen was a math genius who'd been supporting himself by playing poker and bartending. In college, he had been president of a group called Students Actively Volunteering for the Environment, and the idea of fighting Massey appealed to him too. He got a room on the third floor and would invite the others over for goulash or ramen cooked on a hot plate, the aroma filling the hallways. The hotel was still mostly empty, although it was acquiring some polish, especially in the lobby, where bluegrass music played all day and four clocks on a wall showed the times for Seoul, Los Angeles, London, and Dingess, a tiny community twenty-five miles to the north whose claim to fame was a former railroad tunnel that was said to be haunted. Mark Mitchell's partner, Edna Thompson, who was no relation to Thompson, worked at the reception desk when called to check in arriving guests.

Thompson's group worked long hours in the Treehouse, which is what they had started calling the office. Scattered with laptops and anchored by a secure server, it resembled a tech start-up, with a Mingo County flavor. A *Dark Side of the Moon* poster hung on one wall, and mine maps were tacked to another. Dan Stickler's face had been photoshopped onto a picture of Chef Boyardee ravioli. Thompson, in cargo pants and a Mothman T-shirt, leaned back in his office chair on the phone, with a blown-up aerial view of the mountains around Rawl behind him. Strips of paper marked the homes of his clients in four clusters. A speaker played New Orleans funk and bluegrass. A wooden sign that Bunch had found one day on a run along the river now hung above a doorway: "REVIVAL NOW IN PROGRESS."

In early 2008, Thompson believed he and his staff—"the hippies," he liked to call them—were kicking Jackson Kelly's teeth in. Wussow continued to manage the database with myriad details about hundreds of clients' medical problems and property damage. He was now using Google Earth to develop a video that flew over the communities. Thompson was also determined to create an animation that would take the jury on a three-dimensional journey, diving below people's homes and traveling through the abandoned coal mines where the slurry had been pumped. Adding a surreal element to the Treehouse, a husband-and-wife team of documentary filmmakers, Filippo Piscopo and Lorena Luciano, began filming in the office periodically. They had decided to document the lawsuit after reading a 2006 OVEC article online that mentioned the Forgotten Communities.

The couple would make about ten trips to Mingo County from their home in New York. They had made a film about Dario Fo, the Italian playwright and winner of the Nobel Prize in Literature. Now they started trailing Thompson and meeting some of the people who lived along Route 49.

Unlike Blankenship, Thompson was no micromanager. Under his guidance, everyone in the Treehouse took on parts of the case with some autonomy. Getzen, the poker player, had an easy rapport with many clients, and he drove those with neuropsychological claims to Charleston to be examined by Thompson's expert psychiatrist. Thompson believed that the contaminated water had contributed to people's learning disabilities and other psychological issues. A few had been in and out of prison. Others suffered from attention deficit disorder or memory problems.

Ellsworth, who had started dating Wussow, put together binders with photos and medical information and other damages for each client, which Thompson hoped to show a jury. He flipped through the binders for hours sometimes, looking at the faces of his clients and reviewing their health issues. "If you start looking through those books you'll get addicted," he said to Van Bunch once. "You'll just get all sad. That's what those books do to you." For a school project, Ellsworth had created a split-screen video of well water running through garden hoses at Don Dillon's and B.I.'s homes. After a while, red water pours from one hose and black water from the other. "Have you seen anything like that in the United States?" B.I. asks off-screen as the water continued to flow. "That's the reason my children are in the shape they're in, and the reason I'm in the shape I'm in." Thompson wanted to include the video as a trial exhibit.

She also shot stark black-and-white portraits of Thompson's clients. Larry and Brenda stood in front of the church at Rawl; Ernie and Carmelita sat on their porch swing. Thompson wanted to use the photos at trial too.

Mathis, meanwhile, sitting at a desk in room 409 with a pair of headphones on to help him stay focused, spent weeks combing through hundreds of depositions. He pulled out information that Thompson could use to counter one of Jackson Kelly's key arguments for dismissing people's claims: that the statute of limitations in the case had expired, because many people in Rawl and the other communities knew as far back as the 1980s that Rawl Sales had caused their water problems but had done nothing about it.

James Berlin Anderson, a forty-one-year-old truck driver on a surface mine who had recently joined the case, had grown up down the road from Ernie and Carmelita in Rawl and gave the lie to that argument.

"We moved there in '77, and the water was good," Anderson said. But when it changed in the 1980s and started to smell, the family didn't know what had caused it to go bad, Anderson said. They were busy much of the time just trying to survive. His mother kept a garbage can outside "with sheets over the top of it and she would catch rain water to wash our clothes in it. Because it was pitiful. You couldn't do nothing with the water, it stunk so bad," he said.

Anderson, who usually wore a grease-smudged ball cap tipped back on his head, remembered getting boils that everyone called summer sores. He thought they were normal at the time. "Like I said, we was poor. We couldn't go to the doctor for nothing," he said. "They'd swell up like a red knot and stand up pretty high, sore as they could be." His mother put oatmeal poultices on him to draw out the toxins.

As a boy, Anderson had shown a talent for drawing, especially cars. He wanted to be a designer or even an architect someday. In Anderson's binder for the jury, Ellsworth included car sketches that he'd kept all these years. In 1979, when Anderson was twelve, a Ford Motor Company executive had written to him, "We wish to commend you for your renditions of new model cars, particularly in view of your age and experience . . . If you plan a career in designing, the attached material should be of help to you."

Thompson believed that dream had come to an end because Anderson drank contaminated well water in his youth. In the early days, before the water had become too offensive, the family had mixed it with Kool-Aid. Anderson's grades began to suffer before he entered high school, and though his sister had graduated second in her class, he dropped out in the tenth grade. He had never been diagnosed with a learning disorder, but Thompson believed he'd suffered with problems like ADHD, learning disabilities, and memory deficits. For years he worked as a mechanic at a body shop, repairing cars instead of designing them.

Anderson had gotten the better-paying job at a surface mine. But his memory problems were worsening. After spending a few months away from work following an injury, he could no longer remember the route for his truck, so he followed other drivers. "That's the only way I knew how to do it without looking like an idiot to my boss," he said.

Anderson and his wife, Lisa, had Thompson and his crew over for burgers and beers. Thompson developed a deep affection for the unassuming and wisecracking miner. Sometimes Anderson showed off slabs of stone that he had salvaged from mine sites. Each had preserved fossils of ancient plants and could have hung in a museum. When he talked about things that fascinated him, he had a boyish wonder about him. He liked to tell the story of discovering an entire fossilized tree standing upright when a wall of stone cleaved away at a strip job. The tree was so impressive that he and his coworkers, who spent their days tearing up the mountain, treated it with a respect that was close to reverence. They left it in place along with the coal beneath it.

With the addition of people like James Berlin Anderson, Thompson believed he was in good shape for the upcoming May trial. At the same time, he was concerned about the safety of his staff in Williamson, where support for the coal industry ran high.

Bunch sometimes called Williamson "Toon Town," because of its outsize characters, from Blankenship to corrupt former politicos like Larry Hamrick. Thompson joked that living in Williamson and suing Massey was like living in Moscow at the height of the Cold War. But he also thought the threat was real. By now many people in the city were aware that he was an environmental lawyer and that he and his staff were living in the Mountaineer and suing Massey. Thompson had told only a handful of clients the exact location of his office in the hotel. Mark Mitchell helped keep the office's location secret by assigning it a different phone number. Clients coming to meet with Thompson or his staff were told to use the phone at the front desk and dial room 425, which didn't exist. When the phone rang in room 409, someone would ride the ancient elevator down to the lobby to meet the client. Thompson put blackout shades on the windows of the Treehouse and pulled them down at night so people on the street couldn't figure out where the office was. Thompson and the others watched what they said on the streets of Williamson. They became part of the community, even though it felt at times like they were living behind enemy lines.

Thompson had become a regular at Starters, drinking a whiskey or beer over dinner and picking up whatever gossip he could. He was on a first-name basis with the waitresses. There were even several nights when Blankenship showed up and a waitress nervously ushered Thompson to the other end of the bar. If Eric Mathis, the brash intellectual, was with Thompson, he would walk up to Blankenship just to interact with him and try to pierce the persona and see what he was really like. Wearing a loose T-shirt and jeans, Mathis looked like any number of young men in Williamson. He would reach out and shake Blankenship's hand, loudly calling him "Donnie B." Blankenship was polite and always made small talk.

But Thompson kept his distance. Blankenship knew him by name, but the two had never been introduced, and Thompson wanted to keep it that way. In the meantime, he noticed the effect Blankenship had whenever he entered the restaurant. One night, a band was playing quietly. They seemed to be holding back until Blankenship and his party paid their bill and walked out. Thompson felt the tension ease in the room. The band started playing up-tempo, and people danced and talked more freely, it seemed to Thompson. "Voldemort has left the building," he said.

Another time, Thompson was sitting alone a few feet from a woman he recognized as Blankenship's girlfriend, a local lawyer with blond highlights in her teased hair. She and her girlfriends were celebrating a birthday, drinking margaritas, and discussing the men in their lives. One of the women complained about a coal executive she was dating, who would fly his helicopter to her house. "Everybody knows you're just putting that chopper down and getting your jollies off," she said she told him. "It makes me look like a whore." As Thompson recalled, Blankenship's girlfriend said, "I told the same thing to Don, you know. I don't want to see that helicopter near my house." She went on to describe a trip she took to Jamaica with Blankenship, who'd complained he was sick to his stomach and couldn't leave the hotel. Thompson started wondering if Blankenship himself had long-term digestive problems—"Rawl syndrome," as he called it—from previously drinking the water. The Massey CEO's girlfriend didn't know Thompson, but she noticed him sitting there. She reached a hand toward him playfully and said, "Oh, this one's getting an earful!"

CHAPTER 17

The year 2008 would bring a parade of unwelcome publicity for Blankenship. In January, the *New York Times* published photographs of him and his friend Spike Maynard, the state Supreme Court justice, vacationing in the South of France in the summer of 2006. In one photograph that would later be used in political ads against Maynard, he and Blankenship sat next to each other at a restaurant in Nice, grinning broadly with flutes of champagne in front of them. Maynard denied that Blankenship had paid for his flight or other vacation expenses.

During that summer of 2006, Massey had been appealing a $50 million verdict before the state Supreme Court—and the images of the two men traveling together set off a firestorm in West Virginia. Massey had lost the case in state court in 2002, when a jury sided with a bankrupt coal operator named Hugh Caperton, who claimed that Blankenship illegally reneged on a contract in order to drive him out of business. Now people argued that Blankenship spending $3 million to help elect Brent Benjamin to the court in 2004 had been part of a plot to overturn the verdict too. There was a certain logic to the claim: spend $3 million to reverse a $50 million verdict.

To Blankenship, the charge made no sense. He had wanted a more pro-business court, and he hadn't expected favors from Benjamin or Maynard, he said. He was from Mingo County and knew politicians didn't "stay bought." Plus, the verdict, which had already grown to more than $75 million with interest in 2008, would likely be paid by Massey or its insurers. Blankenship personally stood to lose nothing. Maynard agreed to recuse himself from the Caperton case, but Benjamin refused, leading Caperton's lawyer to petition the US Supreme Court. More national headlines followed.

As Thompson watched these battles and others play out, he noticed that Caperton's lawyer, Bruce Stanley, seemed to have a special antagonism toward Blankenship. Stanley, who was from Mingo County himself, was now suing Massey on behalf of the widows of two miners killed in the 2006 fire at the company's Aracoma Alma Mine No. 1. Among the trove of documents Stanley unearthed was one that became known as the "run coal memo." More than any other piece of paper, it cemented Blankenship's national reputation as a ruthless executive who put profits before safety.

Dated October 19, 2005—less than three months before the Aracoma fire—and addressed to all of Massey's underground mine superintendents, the letter read in part, "If any of you have been asked by your group presidents, your supervisors, engineers or anyone else to do anything other than run coal (i.e.—build overcasts, do construction jobs, or whatever), you need to ignore them and run coal," Blankenship wrote. "This memo is necessary only because we seem not to understand that the coal pays the bills."

Someone in Massey's legal department must have seen the liability created by the memo, because a week later Blankenship issued a follow-up. "By now each of you should know that safety and S-1 is our first responsibility. Productivity and P-2 are second. It has been the culture of our Company for a long time," Blankenship wrote, referring to the company's formula for success: "S-1 (Safety) + P-2 (Production) + M-3 (Measurement) = Shareholder Value." "Last week I sent each of you a memo on running coal. Some of you may have interpreted that memo to imply that safety and S-1 are secondary. I would question the membership of anyone who thought that I consider safety to be a secondary responsibility."

On April 3, 2008, Blankenship made it into the national spotlight again for grabbing the camera of an ABC News reporter. Footage showed him in the parking lot of his Belfry office as the reporter scrambled over to him. "If you're going to start taking pictures of me, you're liable to get shot," Blankenship said, before reaching his hand out to cover the lens and blot out the picture. The reporter begged Blankenship to take his hands off the camera, but the CEO twisted the viewfinder and broke the microphone off. ABC aired the footage on *Nightline* and *World News with Charles Gibson*. Blankenship's lawyers defended his actions, noting that he had been a frequent target of harassment. "The notion that I have taken any action to improperly influence the Supreme Court of West Virginia is baseless and absurd," Blankenship added in a written statement. He later said the reporter had ambushed him, following him down Route 119, pulling into the company's parking lot, and shoving a camera in his face.

Thompson had a different take: Blankenship's threat of gun violence wasn't exactly uncommon around Williamson. Nearly all his clients owned guns. Frank Coleman frequently told Melissa Ellsworth to let him know if anyone was bothering her, so he could kill them. Nevertheless, Thompson printed a still from the video that showed a company security guard in front of Blankenship lunging toward the camera. He tacked it on the wall behind his desk next to the aerial photograph of the Rawl area. The encounter was comical on one level. But it was still a threat, and Thompson wanted everyone in the office to know what Blankenship's "enforcer," the security guard, looked like.

The series of embarrassments continued when the state Supreme Court ruled in June that Blankenship's former maid, Deborah May, was entitled to unemployment benefits because the CEO had treated her so badly that she had no choice but to quit. May had been hired in the spring of 2001 to clean Blankenship's house; by 2005, for the same pay, she was cleaning four homes, including the hilltop mansion, and a coach bus she had to stock with snacks. Blankenship denied her requests for a raise. A pay slip showed she worked thirty-three hours of overtime one week. In October 2005, she was under so much strain that she took herself to the hospital because she thought she was having a heart attack. She resigned the next month.

May had submitted a nine-page handwritten summary of her duties and "rather colorful evidence" of "Blankenship's strident behavior," the court noted in its unanimous opinion supporting her. Blankenship had required her to write a letter explaining why there was no ice cream at one of his houses. Once, when she brought back a McDonald's breakfast order that had been filled incorrectly, he "started slinging the food and he grabbed Ms. May's wrist, telling her 'Any time I want you to do exactly what I tell you to do and nothing more and nothing less,'" the court wrote. Another time, when May forgot to leave a coat hanger out for Blankenship, he tore the coat hanger and a rack out of the closet, leaving May a note: "You have or will get a call on why I tore the rack down. I've had 3 dogs stolen in 9 days, mines robbed, people complain incessantly, all of them want more money. None of them do what their [*sic*] asked. I can't hang my coat or my tie on my hope or dreams. Life is reality & if we all do our part it can be good for everyone. If everyone leaves it to a few to do things life isn't good for anyone." Two justices wrote that Blankenship's conduct was an affront to common decency.

All the negative media attention could only help Thompson's case. But as long as Massey's financial performance was strong, Blankenship's position at the company was secure. He had a lock on the company's board of directors, and Massey had had an exceptionally good year in 2007, reaping a record profit of $94 million. Blankenship's total compensation was an estimated $23.7 million that year. And Massey had 2.3 billion tons of coal reserves, more than any other company in Central Appalachia, and more than enough to sustain it over the next decade.

Many nights, Thompson sat at his desk and aimed a telescope at the mountaintop where Blankenship had built the four-story corporate getaway. In the crisp magnification, the cupola looked like a crow's nest, with a 360-degree view of the whole region, the kind that money and power afford. Bunch called it the Dr. Seuss house. To Thompson, it was more of a Gatsby-like folly. He knew Blankenship was there when the long driveway was lit up like a constellation of stars in the otherwise black night. The house was tantalizingly close. "It's what drives me," Thompson said.

With the May 2008 trial date just weeks away, the seven hundred thousand dollars Stuart Smith had invested was almost gone. It had paid for most of Thompson's expenses, including for his staff and tab at the Mountaineer, court filing fees, printer paper and ink, food, and gas. Amid the rush to prepare for trial, Thompson rehearsed his opening as his colleagues sat around the office, trying to commit the words to memory and get the tone just right. "For over a hundred years, the water beneath Lick Creek, Rawl, Merrimac, and Sprigg sustained life for the families who have called those four hollows home," he planned to begin:

> And the evidence will show that thirty years ago, in 1978, that same life-sustaining water began to bring sickness, sorrow, fear, and even death because the Defendant in this action, Massey,

through its subsidiary Rawl Sales & Processing, knowingly, illegally began to contaminate those waters by flushing over a billion gallons of slurry, sludge, and wastewater from their prep plant, into abandoned underground mines—below, above, and all around the wells that the people used for life-giving water. The evidence in this case will show: the water is contaminated, the people are sick, and Massey's to blame.

And then Judge Thornsbury bumped the trial back again, pushing it to the fall of 2008, citing his own scheduling conflict as the reason.

Thompson was stunned. He could only wonder at the judge's motivation this time. He had noticed that the judge had lost a significant amount of weight and started wearing colorful shirts under his sport coats. He was cutting a new figure in Williamson. A few weeks later, Thompson noticed the judge was driving a new white Mercedes too.

Nearly broke and facing another summer with no resolution, Thompson vented his frustration at Jackson Kelly. One of the firm's lawyers had mentioned that he'd seen Stickler in a seersucker suit—an uncharacteristically bold gesture at the staid firm. Thompson left Stickler a voicemail: "Hey, Dan, I just got to tell you I admire your style and sartorial courage for wearing a seersucker suit in downtown Charleston. More men need to do that." He later heard that Stickler had spent the rest of the day on a manhunt, trying to find out who had told Thompson about his suit.

As Thompson's financial problems deepened, the financial risks to Massey from the Rawl lawsuit broke into the news, with help from Thompson, causing a brief panic among investors. Bloomberg reported on July 2 that the company might have to pay $125 million in damages, or more than half its projected net income for 2008, if it lost the case and its insurance companies refused to cover the costs. Massey could face up to $1 billion in punitive damages. The figures came from Thompson, who said he was seeking $28.5 million for medical monitoring and about $95 million in lost earnings, property damage, and pain and suffering and emotional distress. Bunch said that he and Thompson intended to prove "a pattern of disregard for environmental laws." Within hours, Massey's stock price plummeted nearly 20 percent.

With any other company, Thompson thought, the prospect of such a loss would have pushed it toward a settlement. But he was convinced that Blankenship relished the fight. Negative press only seemed to make Massey dig in its heels more.

Thompson tried to keep morale up in the Treehouse. When Williamson suffered a blackout on July 22, he led Wussow, Ellsworth, and Getzen out to buy beer and brought his video camera to document the adventure. They joked that zombies had overtaken Williamson. It was eerily dark on East Second Avenue, but the bars in town were full and people had come outside to party in the darkness. A few cars raced down the street, and passengers leaned from their windows and hooted. Getzen shined the video camera's light on the statue of Chief Logan. The corner office on the fourth floor of the Mountaineer was the only light on in the city, because Thompson had installed an apocalypse-proof backup battery system.

They walked toward the Kentucky border, where the lights of businesses were on. Ellsworth had her arm through Wussow's. Getzen walked by himself a few yards away.

"We're here in the heart of the trillion-dollar coalfields, and we can't light Williamson," Thompson said.

Two days later, a black plume rose into the sky across the river in Kentucky—a transformer in South Williamson, not far from Blankenship's corporate getaway in Aflex, had caught fire. Thompson and Getzen brought the video camera out to the roof of the Mountaineer. "It's been two days since the zombies came to Williamson, took the power out, and attacked the city," Thompson said for the camera. "It looks like they've finally gotten to Blankenship's hideout."

But privately, Thompson was growing worried. He was out of money again and mostly living off what Getzen and the others were contributing toward groceries. On a drive from New Orleans back to Williamson, he had nearly run out of gas. Even though his checking account was tapped out, he could usually still use his debit card to buy gas one or two more times. In London, Kentucky, however, the trick didn't work. With no other choice, he made a sign that said he needed gas to get to Williamson, West Virginia, and he held it up outside a Walmart. Within a few minutes, a woman handed him a twenty-dollar bill and said, "Here you go, honey." He bought gas and several granola bars, and once again was relieved to make it to the Mountaineer's parking garage.

Soon after, Thompson called a meeting with Wussow, Ellsworth, Getzen, and Mathis and told them he couldn't pay them for the foreseeable future. He suggested they go home, but they said they would work without pay. For eleven days, Thompson was flat broke. He canceled depositions that he'd have to travel for because he didn't want to use the remaining gas in his car. Meanwhile Getzen played no-limit Texas hold 'em at a casino outside Charleston, and he contributed some of his winnings—usually a few hundred dollars a night—to buy food and office supplies; Thompson had been reduced to asking visitors to bring printer paper and ink. The camaraderie that had existed in the office all year had worn thin. Getzen and Mathis stayed in town at a house they had begun renting. But Wussow and Ellsworth retreated to her parents' six hours away in Shepherdstown, on the border with Maryland. Thompson felt ready for trial, but he was stranded: far from his wife and daughter in New Orleans, and now far from his work family.

One day as dusk settled over Williamson and Thompson was alone in the office, he looked through his video camera at the city. A train with black tanker cars snaked past some buildings. Red taillights glowed on East Second Avenue in the blue evening light. He panned over to the highway and then to the houses set in the hills. He zoomed in toward the Massey house on the mountaintop, where the driveway lights were already on. For all he knew, Blankenship was there. He brought the house into tight focus again and again. With his last twenty dollars, Thompson had bought a bag of apples, a bag of oranges, and as many granola bars as he could. He'd lived alone for days in the empty hotel. He had shielded Larry Brown and Ernie and Carmelita and everyone else from his worsening financial situation, not wanting to add to their anxiety about the case. The details of the case had taken on an unreality as he retreated into himself.

Finally, a high school friend of Thompson's named Allen Sowards drove down from Point Pleasant and gave him a lift to New Orleans. The night before they left town, Thompson turned the camera on himself one final time. "It's been hard, and I'm going mad, it's true," he said, as the Williamson night pressed against the windows of room 409. The office now had a placard outside the door that said "The John DeLorean Suite." As part of the renovation, every room now bore the name of a celebrity who had stayed at the hotel, from Henry Ford to Conway Twitty. But the office itself was unchanged. On a shelf, an orange sat next to a box of Wheat Thins and a coffee pitcher. "That's my last orange," Thompson said. "It's kind of moldy, so I didn't eat it."

He joined Sowards in the hotel's lobby, with its polished red-and-black checkered floor, and the two sat in leather wingback chairs drinking Miller beers. "Anyone who comes to visit should bring, like, four or five manila folders, some paper," Thompson said laconically. "Paper is key. It's our stock-in-trade. It's our ammunition. . . . And Mr. Wussow is the master of our paper. That man can shit out more paper than two floors of Jackson Kelly paralegals on laxatives. Mr. Wussow is a paper-shitting machine."

Thompson reversed the camera's viewfinder and looked at himself, patting down his hair and letting out a squawk. "I'm Kevin Thompson," he said, and then repeated it twice. "In today's episode, we attack evil coal-doers." The two men might have been the only people in the hotel. The song "Here's Where the Story Ends" by the Sundays, soothing and bittersweet, echoed through the lobby. It was a quarter after midnight, and there was white tulle wrapped around the staircase leading to the mezzanine from a recent wedding. The hotel had largely been restored, and the lobby especially had become a gem of Williamson once again. Its enormous crystal chandelier broke up the light with hundreds of tiny prisms. "There ain't nothing like the Mountaineer," Thompson said.

He and Sowards drove to New Orleans through the next day and night. Thompson was finally home. The following morning, the friends sat in wicker chairs on the balcony of Thompson's house, as a rainstorm whipped an American flag hanging off the balcony and the trees on his street swayed. Neither spoke. Thompson, completely spent, held his dog Blue against his chest.

CHAPTER 18

When Van Bunch learned how dire Thompson's financial situation had become, he agreed to advance enough money to cover the monthly expenses to keep the Treehouse running. Bunch's firm had been paying major expenses, such as expert fees and the cost of acquiring medical records. Now Bunch started paying the salaries of everyone working with Thompson at the hotel. He considered it an advance on Thompson's fee in the case, which would be reconciled when and if there was a jury award or settlement.

In September, after a break of nearly a month, everyone was back at their desks at the Treehouse. It had been three years since Thompson first asked Judge Thornsbury for an order allowing him to depose Blankenship—and he still didn't have an answer. When Thompson was in the judge's courtroom on September 22 for a brief scheduling conference, he didn't mince words.

"I'd like an order for Don Blankenship's deposition on Wednesday," Thompson demanded. And to his shock, Thornsbury responded: "I'm going to let you take his deposition, but I'm going to give you parameters on it."

Two days later, several dozen lawyers representing Massey's insurers crowded into the courtroom, along with Thompson, Bunch, Barney, and Stickler. Under Blankenship, Massey had bought an extraordinary number of insurance policies over the years, and now sorting out the coverage had become a tangled mess. Each insurance company was trying to limit its exposure in the case by making conflicting claims against Massey and one another. Some argued that they shouldn't provide coverage because their policies had pollution exclusion clauses. But Massey's lawyers called those "silly arguments." In their eyes, coal slurry was a necessary by-product of mining coal, not a pollutant.

There was no love lost between Massey and its insurers. One lawyer told the judge that it would be "ludicrous" for the insurance company Old Republic to pay when Massey polluted people's drinking water. "These are concentrations of known human carcinogens and toxins in the water supply," the lawyer said. "This case is about pollution and nothing but pollution."

To quiet the lawyers, Judge Thornsbury threatened to use his gavel. But Thompson found the crossfire interesting. He wanted to know how much Massey's insurance companies were going to be able to pay when he won a verdict or negotiated a settlement. He'd been asking since 2005 how much coverage Massey had. A week earlier, he'd sent a letter to Jackson Kelly offering to settle the case for $211 million—a figure based on his estimates of Massey's insurance coverage. When Thompson saw a slide presented in the courtroom listing Massey's coverage, he jumped up. "There's over $600 million of insurance I've never seen, heard about, got a wisp of. I can't tell you the motive for why they're hiding and not answering discovery," Thompson told the judge. "There could be a billion dollars' worth of coverage, and they're only telling me about $211 million." Thornsbury, already exasperated by the insurance dispute, told Thompson to file a motion.

About two weeks later, the judge set a trial date for February 17, 2009. Nearly all of the more than five hundred adult plaintiffs had been deposed and there were four hundred thousand medical records in the case. "There has to be finality in all things and it's time to try the underlying cases," the judge said.

But there was still one more matter to argue over: setting parameters for Blankenship's deposition. Thompson wanted to ask the CEO about the slurry injection operations, the decision to get a water line extension to his house in Sprigg, and the decision not to spend fifty-five thousand dollars to build the impoundment, which had forced the company to inject slurry for far longer.

When the judge agreed, Thompson asked for a written order. Stickler thought that was too much.

"He's got what he asked for," said Stickler.

"Yes, you've got a pound. Don't ask for a ton," the judge said. "You've got about everything that the law possibly allows you to get. Be satisfied."

• • •

Outside the courtroom, the case was taking a toll. Getzen and another recent addition, Ian Henderson—a tall, Nordic-looking history major also from Appalachian State whose nickname was "Thor"—said they had been followed on Route 49 by a Dodge Charger with tinted windows. Thompson didn't doubt them; Larry Brown said he had been followed too, though he'd described a silver pickup. The Charger would cruise up to the rear bumper menacingly and then retreat. The intimidation bothered Thompson; even a slight contact on the curving road could be deadly. For the time being, he didn't see what he could do beyond telling everyone to be careful and let him know if they saw the car again.

Thompson had more complicated problems to solve. Even if he could show that Massey knew the risks of injecting slurry, that Blankenship ordered the process to continue in the 1980s, that the slurry had contaminated the wells with heavy metals, and that the people were suffering from a frightening array of illnesses, there was still the problem of proving that it was the slurry that had made people sick. Jackson Kelly's experts would argue that the people were sick for reasons that had nothing to do with Massey, such as smoking.

Then the ideal weapon fell into Thompson's lap in the form of a scientific study. As it happened, a scientist with the US Geological Survey named Joseph E. Bunnell had begun in 2006 to study the effects of a sample of coal slurry from Mingo County on human liver cells. Thompson had nothing to do with the origins of the study. Federal scientists were aware of the growing controversy in West Virginia and elsewhere over injecting slurry underground. Some West Virginia lawmakers had been considering the need for new rules on coal slurry storage since at least 2005. Deborah Sammons, B.I.'s wife, and Donetta Blankenship had given moving testimony in November 2006 to a state senate committee at the capitol. Jack Spadaro and Scott Simonton testified as well.

At a follow-up hearing before the same committee in January 2007, Chris Hamilton, an official with the West Virginia Coal Association, had tried to put the brakes on the legislature. From the industry's point of view, he said, the only controversy was in the Rawl area. (In fact, residents of Prenter, south of Charleston, were also complaining about health problems they believed were caused by slurry injection.) The coal association was obviously well versed in the Rawl lawsuit. "Do we think there's an issue with the quality of these wells? We certainly do.

Do we support providing drinking water, fresh drinking water, to this community? We absolutely do," Hamilton told about a dozen state senators. "We think the only issue here is culpability on one system. And that is being litigated, and we would maintain that based on the expert testimony that we have perused that there's no correlation between the active mining operations and the contamination."

Thompson had seen the state's coal industry circling the wagons to prevent the regulation of slurry—and his case was at the center of that fight. There were even broader implications. For decades, the EPA had allowed companies to deposit waste into more than five thousand abandoned mines in at least seventeen states. It wasn't known how many of those sites contained coal slurry or waste from other industrial sites. The Associated Press contacted five Appalachian states to find out how many active coal slurry injection sites the states had. Kentucky had fourteen; Alabama had eleven; Pennsylvania had two; and Ohio had two. West Virginia regulators said they permitted fifteen companies to inject slurry, but the number of injection sites was larger. If Thompson's case was opening a Pandora's box, no wonder the coal industry wanted to shut the lid.

Bunnell hadn't completed his study yet, but when someone in the coal industry inquired about it, he followed protocol and released a preliminary analysis. So far, he had found that coal slurry impeded liver cell growth. Moreover, as the concentration of slurry increased, so did its toxic effects on the line of liver cells he studied. Here was an independent study of the toxicity of coal slurry. Not in a distant country, but from Mingo County. It would certainly be a home run for a jury there. It could also very well help change the rules for storing coal slurry across the state and beyond.

Thompson's excitement about Bunnell's study was short-lived. In October 2008, he was alarmed to learn that Barbara Smith—the same West Virginia health official who'd initially concluded in 2004 that there was no health hazard from the water in the four communities— was weighing in on the state's coal slurry debate and Bunnell's study. Smith had retired, but she'd still been offering her help to the state Department of Environmental Protection; she still wanted to show that there could be other causes of the poor water quality in Rawl, Lick Creek, Merrimac, and Sprigg.

Thompson subpoenaed the state of West Virginia, demanding it turn over relevant emails from Smith. He discovered that Smith had sent a four-page document to the DEP in June 2007 outlining other causes of foul-smelling and discolored water besides coal slurry. "In rare instances it can result from pollution," she wrote. More recently, she had written to Bunnell directly, questioning his entire methodology. "Assessing human health impact from cell culture data is complex," she lectured. "Interpretation of results is challenging and difficult to relate to exposures within the human body . . ."

Smith then wrote to Bunnell's superiors at the US Geological Survey and pointed out several errors in his preliminary results. The errors didn't change the overall trend. Cell growth was still inhibited by exposure to coal slurry. Her tone became increasingly strident in follow-up letters, and finally Bunnell's boss seemed to lose his patience.

"We are perplexed by many of your comments and questions," he wrote back to Smith. "You seem to be attacking standard approaches in toxicology such as the use of cell line cultures and the MTT assay, admittedly without having any hands-on experience with cell cultures as you indicated in your email of 9/14/08." Smith offered another tart response on October 23. "I'll make the same audacious suggestion I did in the previous letter: a toxicologist trained in cell culture work would be an asset to your research team."

Smith had also emailed a friend at a law firm and asked who was handling the water-quality case in Mingo County, meaning which defense firm. She had an opinion she wanted to offer to Massey's lawyers.

Thompson subpoenaed Smith to sit for a deposition. On November 18, he sat across from her in a conference room at the offices of Johnny Jackson & Associates, a court reporting firm in Charleston.

Thompson had thought maybe Smith was fishing for a job as a lobbyist for the coal industry. It seemed to him that Smith was doing Jackson Kelly's work for them. But Smith told Thompson she got involved in the debate over coal slurry regulation because she wanted to offer her thoughts as a concerned citizen, just as she had in the past on other public health issues. In the 1990s, she said, she'd advised the legislature on food inspections. When Thompson pressed her and asked if she had ever been paid by any coal association, by Massey or by Jackson Kelly, Smith said no each time.

Thompson wanted to know why Smith had never seriously considered coal slurry as a potential cause of the degraded water in Lick Creek—either when she issued her first report in 2004 or when she took account of Ben Stout's findings and said in 2005 that the water was indeed a health threat. Shouldn't Smith have tried to figure out what was in coal slurry to determine if it could have caused a health risk?

"I had no reason to determine what slurry was," Smith said. "I looked at the data that we had."

Every time Thompson asked Smith if, as a public health official, she should have been concerned about the potential impact of slurry on drinking water, she said that was beyond the scope of her work. Her job, Smith said, was to find all the available data and issue a report based on that, not conduct water sampling or another investigation.

"Now, I've asked you five times now, and I'll ask again, you understood that slurry had been injected, correct?" Thompson said.

"I understood that slurry was injected into the Pond Creek mine," Smith said. But she explained that the 1995 study of Lick Creek wells by a state geologist had found that only one well had been negatively impacted by that mine.

"Right. Now, no one told you that Massey's lied for twenty years about this, did they?" Thompson asked.

"I was not aware that Massey's lied about this," Smith said.

"Well, they have," Thompson said.

Thompson asked Smith if she would have changed her opinion about the potential impact of coal slurry if someone had given her government documents—the ones that Jack Spadaro had found—that showed that a billion gallons of slurry had been injected into five coal seams.

Smith said she couldn't answer the question. Once again, it was beyond the scope of her investigation. Thompson reminded her that she was being deposed under oath.

"Ma'am, yes or no, as a government official, when you were investigating the complaint of the citizens, didn't you have a duty to find every potential contaminant that could have harmed these people?"

"No, not according to the grant and the conditions of doing this report," Smith said.

He then asked her if, "as a human," she had a responsibility to try to find out every potential contaminant that people were being exposed to.

"Am I a human or am I a government official?" Smith said.

"You're a human, ma'am," Thompson said.

She soon added, "The question that we attempted to answer was, are chemicals from these various sites liable to impact the water."

"You have just drank the Kool-Aid, ma'am," Thompson said. "If a billion gallons of slurry were injected and you weren't told about it, how can you issue a report and stand behind it? Like if, in fact, I show you evidence that over a billion gallons of slurry was injected by Rawl Sales & Processing into seams above, below, and all around these wells, are you still going to stand behind that report?"

"I'm standing behind this report. This was the data that I had that I used," Smith replied.

Thompson kept pressing, until Stickler objected. Stickler said the volume of slurry injected into the ground wasn't important. What mattered was what had gotten into the water. "You're basing it upon a wrong characterization of the evidence," Stickler said. He twice accused Thompson of trying to intimidate Smith.

After four and a half hours, it was nearing 3 p.m., the scheduled end point for the deposition.

"You've been studying this now for years," said Thompson. "Is the water in Rawl safe to drink?"

"There's a wide variety of chemical components from each well," said Smith. "I cannot make a blanket statement."

He said it would take her a full week at trial to make a determination about every single well. Then he offered to give Smith every deposition in the case, every expert report, and every well test and asked her if she wanted that. She said no.

"But if I'm called to testify on it, I will," Smith said.

Thompson believed she would be a powerful witness—for the plaintiffs—because he thought she would come across as a coal industry apologist, rather than an impartial health expert. "You're going to be called to testify," he said.

It was already getting dark when Thompson walked out of Johnny Jackson's offices, and it had begun to snow. On the ninety-minute drive back to Williamson, as Route 119 wove between mountains and high road-cuts, delivering him back into the coalfields, Thompson obsessed over Smith's involvement in the state legislature's study on coal slurry, her apparent willingness to help Stickler and Jackson Kelly defend Massey, and her contacts with scientists at a federal agency, the USGS.

When he pulled into Williamson, he was in mad-Ahab mode. He decided the one thing he could do that night was find the driver of the black Dodge Charger who had been harassing his staff. He drove through the city block by block, looking for the car. In an alley behind the city police and fire station, he thought he had finally found it. Wearing his black overcoat over a black suit and tie in the frigid air, he banged on the locked glass doors of the station. In high school, he and his friends used to break into the gymnasium to shoot hoops by hitting these kinds of doors a certain way. He struck one of the doors and it opened. The noise brought one of the firemen to the hallway.

"Produce for me whoever owns the black Charger," Thompson said.

The fireman said that would be Otis, and he left to get him. Otis, a heavyset man well over six feet tall wearing an EMT shirt, came down the hall between two firemen. He said he owned a black Charger.

"Are you a cop?" Thompson asked, without introducing himself. "Are you a paid informant?"

The big man was deferential. "No, sir."

"Are you working in any way for law enforcement?" Thompson asked.

When Otis said no, Thompson asked if he was an ambulance driver or EMT. Again Otis said no. Thompson was still sizing up the man, and he remembered that one of his grandfathers had told him the most dangerous guy is someone who wants to be a cop and isn't.

"Somebody's following my guys, and it's a black Charger," Thompson said.

"It must have been Don Blankenship," said Otis.

"What did you say?" Thompson said, taking a step backward and registering the shock.

"He's got a GTX, and it's got antennas and sometimes people think it's Don Blankenship and it's me," Otis said.

"Listen," Thompson said. "I don't want to catch you following my guys again."

One of the firemen asked Thompson if he was FBI.

"You don't want to know who I am," Thompson said, turning to leave.

Thompson found Ellsworth, Wussow, and Getzen hanging out in

Wussow's room at the Mountaineer, room 309, and he eagerly started telling them about his encounter at the fire station. Thor, who'd been out buying cigarettes across the street, returned to say he had just seen the black car at a red light. He'd pointed at the car, and he aimed his finger like a gun to demonstrate. The Charger had taken off before the light changed. Thompson thought it was a reckless gesture, and he believed from the direction the car was heading—east toward Lick Creek—that Otis was probably on his way to Blankenship's house.

The group went downstairs and piled into Wussow's white Chevy Lumina. Unlike Getzen or Thor, Wussow had a strong instinct for self-preservation. He liked to keep a low profile in Williamson, perhaps because he'd spent more time there than anyone except for Thompson. They drove past the firehouse out of Williamson, past the Norfolk Southern rail yard. The snow made the road slick, and they bumped along through the woods before coming out along the Tug Fork. Thompson's only plan was to see if they could catch Otis at Blankenship's house in Sprigg.

They stopped to see Frank Coleman, the square-jawed Vietnam vet with fading reddish hair. Coleman wasn't easily intimidated, Thompson knew, and maybe he would let them use his Jeep. Coleman answered the door holding a gun. He hadn't recognized Wussow's car on the video cameras outside his house at the entrance of Dick Williamson Branch Road.

"Kevin?" he asked, squinting at the cold air and looking confused to see them all on his doorstep.

Thompson and the others talked over each other as they told him about the Charger. Coleman could see they were pumped full of adrenaline and practically out of breath. He wouldn't loan them his Jeep but agreed to drive them to Sprigg along Route 49, and when he climbed into the driver seat he put his .40 caliber Glock between his thighs.

It seemed plausible to Thompson that Blankenship was paying someone to harass them. But maybe Thompson was the one seeing conspiracies this time. Drained from the long, contentious Smith deposition and amped up from meeting Otis, Thompson knew he was no longer thinking clearly. He had wanted to protect his young staff from harassment, and here they were on a slick road in one of the darkest corners of West Virginia in the middle of a snowstorm hunting a phantom car. Thompson had joked about what he called Mingo Madness—whenever he heard about someone acting out violently in the county. Now he had been swept up in it, and he had no plan for what to do when they found the driver of the Charger.

Coleman flew over the road, and the car swayed with the curves. Snow swirled in the Jeep's headlights. The Dodge Charger still hadn't materialized out of the darkness. In the backseat, Ellsworth, Getzen, and Thor anxiously talked about what they should do if they found the car. Wussow was half lying in the Jeep's rear compartment.

At Blankenship's house, Coleman slowed down, and seeing the black metal gate open, he pulled onto the property.

"Turn this car around," Wussow said from the back. "Turn this car around."

Ellsworth turned to look at Wussow and told him to be quiet. "Be a man," she said.

Coleman cut the lights and started to roll up the long driveway. The house and the sloping lawn were floodlit through the snow. Thompson looked for the Charger near the detached garage, but the glare from the floodlights obscured his view. Coleman still had his gun on his seat between his legs.

"You know they could shut that gate behind us and we'll be trapped?" Wussow said.

The possibility that they could be caught on Blankenship's property raised the anxiety in the car, and Thompson told Coleman they should leave immediately. Coleman looked at Thompson with a devilish grin, put the car in reverse, and skidded down the driveway and back onto Route 49.

A pair of headlights appeared behind them. "Someone's following us," Coleman said. He sped up on the twisting road and turned onto a dirt road near Merrimac, using his emergency brake to stop and cutting the lights again. They waited until the car passed. Coleman said it was someone he knew, and everyone exhaled.

No one working in the Treehouse ever saw the black Charger again. And Blankenship never knew that the lawyer suing him—and one of that lawyer's clients—had driven onto his property with a loaded gun in their car.

PART IV

EXODUS

JANUARY 2009–AUGUST 2009

CHAPTER 19

At the start of 2009, Thompson was flush with cash again. In December, he had brought Eric Mathis with him to New Orleans to help Stuart Smith prepare for a case. One day, Thompson threatened to blow up Smith's trial preparation if he didn't invest more in the Rawl lawsuit. Standing in Smith's office, Thompson described himself as a terrorist on a bus full of kids and said he was ready to drive it off a bridge. To prove his point, he told Mathis to pack up their laptops. In a scene that Thompson would later recount as yet another absurd moment in the Rawl saga, Mathis marched down the halls of the Smith Stag law firm carrying their equipment and ululating at the top of his lungs. In the end, Smith crushed the unfiltered Dunhill he had been smoking into an ashtray and agreed to a three-hundred-thousand-dollar extension to a line of credit that Thompson could draw from to pay expenses.

After New Year's, Thompson returned to Williamson for his own trial preparation. On January 14, he got an urgent call from Larry Brown: the creek in Rawl behind his church was running black with coal slurry. Thompson raced out to Dick Williamson Branch Road and called the state DEP's spill hotline. The environmental agency sent an inspector, but by the time Thompson and Larry gained access to Rawl Sales' property, workers had moved so much dirt around that it was impossible to find the source of the slurry. It was a small spill, one that Larry had smelled before he'd seen it. A month before the scheduled trial, it was a fresh reminder that people were still dealing with slurry in the mountains.

One week later, Thompson was back in Judge Thornsbury's courtroom to fight off twenty pretrial motions. The benches were again packed with clients, including Larry and Brenda Brown, Ernie and Carmelita, B.I., Bo Scott, and Don Dillon. Jackson Kelly was asking the judge to dismiss parts of the case—if he didn't agree that it should be thrown out entirely.

The judge said he would push some of Thompson's clients to a second trial group in May, rather than dismiss them for missing a medical examination with Massey's experts, but he said he was going to be a stickler for the rules going forward.

"No pun intended," he said to Stickler. The Jackson Kelly lawyer said he took it as a compliment.

Judge Thornsbury was in an unusually chatty mood. "Is someone taking copious notes? Because I'm making rulings fast and furious," he said. He was now the one saying they needed to get the case tried. "There gets to the point that it becomes ridiculous, and you are at that point," he said to the attorneys. Saying he was a glutton for punishment, he invited Al Sebok to argue all twenty of Jackson Kelly's motions in a row. Thompson steeled himself. He'd read Jackson Kelly's legal briefs, and he was champing at the bit to refute them.

In a shrapnel blast of arguments, Sebok took the floor for more than an hour, laying out Jackson Kelly's reasons for why the plaintiffs' claims should be thrown out. He said the judge should dismiss parts of the case because the standard of strict liability hadn't been met: Thompson hadn't proved that Rawl Sales had caused any contamination. He argued that statutes of limitations had run out for 172 people; that Thompson had provided insufficient employment records for many plaintiffs; and that 7 claims, including Larry Brown's and Bo Scott's, should be dismissed under the principle of res judicata, because people had already sued Rawl Sales years earlier, claiming the company had damaged their water.

Thompson's anger rose steadily as Sebok enumerated his arguments in legalese that seemed detached from the reality in the four communities. Sebok argued that many plaintiffs had known back in the 1980s that Rawl Sales was to blame for their water problems but hadn't taken legal action until it was too late under the statute of limitations. Even more infuriating to Thompson was Sebok's argument that the entire case should be thrown out, because under West Virginia law the owners of land don't have an absolute right to the water beneath their homes. To Thompson, that was like arguing that coal companies should be allowed to victimize landowners a second time, after outside investors effectively stole their mineral rights beginning in the 1880s. If West Virginia regulators had been troubled by Rawl Sales' slurry injection in the 1980s, "they would have come in and said something," Sebok said. But Thompson could recite the paper trail showing that regulators had, in fact, been alarmed by the company's slurry disposal and had approved it only on the condition that it would be temporary.

Then Sebok pointed to petitions some Rawl residents had signed in 1993 and 1999 seeking a municipal water line. The latter petition contained a sentence that Sebok argued proved that residents had known then that the company's slurry injection had contaminated their water: "Preparation plants pump sludge underground affecting the water quality." The two-year statute of limitations since that statement had been made in 1999 had run out. Jackson Kelly had a list of nearly eighty plaintiffs it wanted to exclude from the case, Carmelita and Ernie Brown, Maude Rice, and Frank Coleman among them.

Thompson interrupted and said that the statement was "a lie." He told the judge that he believed the statement had been planted there by none other than Larry Hamrick.

"As you know, from the defamation case, Larry Hamrick has done a lot in this courthouse," Thompson said. "I've accused him of stealing mail out of the county commission office . . . Now Larry Hamrick probably put that in there. All right?"

Behind Thompson were several dozen of his clients with concerned looks on their faces. He told the judge that they were prepared to testify that "the typewritten grammatically perfect defense of statute of limitation" wasn't part of the document when they signed it.

Sebok planned to call a woman to testify that she'd seen the statement in the petition in 2003 when she started at the courthouse. But the woman was one of Thompson's clients in the case, and she also worked for the judge part-time. The judge said that if she was going to be called to testify he might have to recuse himself from the case. He told Thompson and Stickler to talk to their clients about the issue and ask if they had any problem with him presiding over the case. Stickler said he would talk to his client, presumably Massey's general counsel or Blankenship himself. Alarm bells went off in Thompson's brain.

"*Whoa, whoa, whoa, whoa, whoa, whoa, whoa, no,*" Thompson said. He worried that Blankenship would welcome any chance for another delay. "They're going to go straight to Don Blankenship, and he's going to say, 'Hey, excellent, this is bumped for a year and a half,'" Thompson said. "This is so dangerous. I don't want to lose you in this courtroom and this jury. I'll do whatever I have to do not to lose you, the courtroom, and the jury, okay?"

These words would come back to haunt Thompson. But at the moment, he feared another delay and believed that the judge was presiding over the case fairly—and that Jackson Kelly had good reasons for wanting him gone. Even with the suspected corruption he'd witnessed from Larry Hamrick and others close to the court, Thompson had never doubted that the judge himself would remain impartial.

The matter was tabled, and at least for a moment, Thompson felt that he had dodged a bullet. Sebok picked up where he had left off. Hitting the statute of limitations argument again, he said the clock should have started when Carmelita Brown had first complained to Rawl Sales about her water in the mid-1980s. He concluded by saying that Thompson had failed to show that Massey as the parent company of Rawl Sales should be held liable for actions that Rawl Sales had taken. "There's no evidence that they've submitted to pierce the corporate veil at that point."

Thompson was confident that he could counter each of Sebok's motions, and he spoke for nearly two hours. In some ways, the hearing was a practice run for the trial, because it required him to run through large parts of his case. He guided the judge through the documents he had combed through. "We found documents that were not provided to us in discovery," he said, "but had been squirreled away by a DEP geologist."

Thompson dismissed Sebok's argument that Carmelita Brown knew in the 1980s that Rawl Sales was responsible for her water problems. The company had never given her any information that would enable her to know for sure, even though Thompson had records of its tests from June to September 1987. "Ernie Brown kicked them off his property because they wouldn't tell him what they found in his water," Thompson said.

Thompson reminded the judge that in the beginning the company's experts had said Rawl Sales had injected into two or possibly three boreholes. By now Thompson was up to forty-three boreholes and counting. He didn't know when or if the company had stopped injecting slurry. He called the case one of the largest in US history for an ongoing course of corporate abandonment of the rules for protecting the environment.

"None of the people could have known this water was harming them because every time they asked someone, every time the government investigated, it was, 'No, Massey's not responsible; we don't think there's anything wrong with your water'; no, no, no, no, no, but you can't blame the government for that because the government never had the benefit of all of the evidence, Your Honor. The evidence was withheld from them."

When Thompson sat down, Jackson Kelly had fifteen minutes left for a rebuttal.

"Judge, I'll keep this brief," Stickler said. "I'm worn out from listening to the hyperbole."

He asked the judge to move all the plaintiffs scheduled for trial in February to May and said he was planning a motion to move the case out of Mingo County. Jackson Kelly had commissioned a survey of 1,600 residents, and 70 percent of the 400 respondents said they believed it was very likely or somewhat likely that Rawl Sales had contaminated local wells and caused health problems for people. "The point of it is we can't get a fair trial down here," Stickler said.

Thompson believed the poll itself was another dirty trick: its real intent was to influence potential jurors or determine how people would vote if they were selected for the jury. "Your Honor, we're playing with fire, I think, trying to taint the jury pool," Thompson said.

The hearing was five hours all told, and when the lawyers had finished, the judge complimented both sides on their arguments and left the courtroom through a side door. As people filed out of the courtroom and the attorneys gathered up their papers, Thompson was smiling. He felt confident he had done enough to beat back Jackson Kelly one more time.

CHAPTER 20

Seeing Don Blankenship walk into the ballroom of the Mountaineer was surreal. In Thompson's mind, the hotel, where he had lived and worked for years, had become his second home, a protected territory from which he'd been waging a guerrilla war against Massey. Now the enemy had arrived, and Thompson was going to depose him.

Reserved and affable, Blankenship defied expectations in person. He wore a navy blue sport coat with a blue-checked shirt open at the collar. He knew Larry Brown and some of the other dozen plaintiffs in attendance by sight, and after attempting small talk with them, he took his seat at a table next to Al Sebok. Blankenship brought his own videographer to the deposition—a move Thompson had never seen before—presumably to intimidate the plaintiffs' lawyer. One camera was aimed at Blankenship, the other at Thompson.

It was February 10, 2009. Thompson had been preparing for this encounter practically since he had first driven to Larry Brown's church five years earlier. Blankenship, who had worked at Rawl Sales from 1982 to 1989, was now the face of the coal industry, worth tens of millions of dollars even though he lived a stone's throw from Thelma Parsley's house in Sprigg. Van Bunch sat at the table beside Thompson, and behind him, Larry Brown, Bo Scott, Ernie and Carmelita Brown, and a handful of other clients sat in a row of chairs. About half a dozen lawyers representing Massey's insurers had dialed in on a conference call line. Stuart Smith and his partner Mike Stag were listening in New Orleans.

As Thompson reviewed his notes, the expression on Blankenship's face shifted. It had been pleasant and open, but a shadow passed over it and his heavy-lidded eyes bored into Thompson. At times the CEO's jaw and mouth worked nervously, as though he were trying to clear peanut butter away from his teeth. If they had been sitting at a poker table, the tic would have been Blankenship's tell, signaling his discomfort.

"Mr. Blankenship, would you please state your full name for the record?" Thompson said.

"Donald Leon Blankenship."

Thompson asked if he planned to testify when the case went to trial.

"I don't know."

"Are you planning to attend the trial?"

"I don't know," Blankenship said, his voice even-toned and unemotional.

"As CEO, are you directing the defense of this case?" Thompson asked.

Sebok objected to the question, saying it was beyond the scope of Judge Thornsbury's boundaries for the questioning.

Blankenship confirmed that he had started working for Rawl Sales as office manager in January 1982. Then Thompson asked him if he knew who Ben Hatfield was, and Blankenship said yes.

"Mr. Blankenship, if you could, speak a little louder," Thompson said. "People are having a hard time hearing you in other cities."

"That's normal," Blankenship said, without elaborating or changing the volume of his voice.

Thompson tried to hand Blankenship a copy of Hatfield's deposition, in which Hatfield described the day in June 1984 when the two men had gone to Lick Creek after the slurry line had broken and sludge had flooded the hollow overnight. Thompson wanted to ask Blankenship about the day, but Sebok intercepted the document.

"Go ahead and look at it, Al," Thompson said. "Take your time."

Sebok said there was only one area Judge Thornsbury had allowed Thompson to get into in the deposition: the decision to construct a water line to Blankenship's house in Sprigg.

Thompson ignored him. "Mr. Blankenship, I would like you to look at—"

"You are going to show it to me first," Sebok said.

"Al, I already showed it to you."

"Well, no. I have instructed him not to answer," Sebok said. "Then let's move on."

"The court ordered that there were two areas of inquiry," Thompson said.

"No, the court didn't order that there were two areas of inquiry," Sebok said.

KRIS MAHER

The two lawyers argued over the discrepancy in Judge Thornsbury's statements from November. Sebok held out a written order that said Thompson could ask Blankenship questions about construction of the water line to his house from Matewan. Thompson read from the transcript of the hearing in which the judge had said there were two areas of inquiry, including Blankenship's input on injecting slurry and building the impoundment. Sebok said Thompson would have to go back to the judge for permission to ask about the latter.

"Well, I am going to make my record," Thompson said.

"Fine," said Sebok.

"And I am going to ask my questions. Then we will go back to the court with a record. Okay," said Thompson.

Blankenship watched the lawyers bicker and smiled briefly.

Thompson asked a series of questions about slurry injection—had Blankenship ever been involved in deciding where to inject the slurry or when to stop injecting it? Every time, Sebok told Blankenship not to answer.

"Do you have any relevant questions to ask this witness?" Sebok asked. "If you don't, we are not going to stay here all day."

"I'm going to make my record. We are not going to stay here all day," Thompson said.

"Well, you better start making it," Sebok said.

"I am making my record to go to court, Al," Thompson said.

"Do you have any relevant questions with regard to the construction of the water line?"

"Yes, I do."

"Well, then I would suggest you ask those questions."

"Well, you can suggest all you want," Thompson said. "I'm going to ask three more questions."

"This is a narrow deposition, Kevin. You know that. This is just playing a game," said Sebok. "Ask the question."

"Mr. Blankenship, regardless of what your lawyer is telling you, is there any reason you don't want to answer these questions?" Thompson asked.

"I'm going to instruct the witness not to answer the question," Sebok said, initiating another round of quarreling.

"Stop testifying," Thompson said to Sebok. "Let him answer." Both

182

men were close to shouting, and without the judge in the room, it was unclear how the situation would get resolved.

"I will give you one more," Sebok said. "Are you going to ask a relevant question or not?"

Thompson paused to gather his thoughts. In a moment of clarity, he realized that his fury wasn't helping him. Sebok was shrill and unyielding. One time, Thompson had inadvertently been copied on an email from a Jackson Kelly associate referring to someone getting "Seboked." His own colleagues had turned his name into a verb. Jackson Kelly's other partners had probably known Sebok would irritate Thompson to the point of distraction, he thought. Facing Blankenship, who remained unruffled, he tried a new tack, asking calmly, "At some point did the water that you relied upon in the house that you lived in when you were the president of Rawl Sales begin to go bad?"

"No," Blankenship said.

"Water was always good?" Thompson asked.

"It was always bad," Blankenship said.

"It was always bad?" Thompson said, surprised.

"It depends on how you define 'good' and 'bad,'" Blankenship replied. "It was typical Appalachian water."

"How do you define 'good' and 'bad' in terms of water?" Thompson asked.

"I am not sure how to answer your question," Blankenship said. "You said 'good' or 'bad.' It depends on what you are using it for, I guess."

Blankenship said that he had occasionally used the water from the well at his house in Sprigg. He had bathed in it, and it was good enough to drink most of the time, once the iron had been filtered out with the treatment system at the house. Thompson asked if the well water had changed at all during the time he used it, and Blankenship said he didn't recall any change.

"Can you describe the characteristics of the water?" Thompson asked. "What did the water look like?"

"I don't know. It looked like water," Blankenship said.

"Was it clear water?"

"Most of the time," Blankenship said. "Sometimes it wouldn't be."

"When it wasn't clear, what did it look like?"

"It looked red."

"Did it ever turn any other colors?"

"Not that I recall."

"What did the water taste like?"

"I don't know. It tasted like water," Blankenship said. "It doesn't taste like perfect water, but it tasted like water."

"Did it have an iron taste to it?"

"Sometimes," Blankenship said.

Thompson handed Blankenship a blank sheet of paper and asked him to draw his house in Sprigg and the location of the well and septic system, and Blankenship took out his own pen. "Your lawyers have asked all of our clients to draw maps," Thompson said. "Let the record reflect Mr. Blankenship is drawing a map."

Thompson showed Blankenship three maps with the location of the Sprigg house relative to Matewan and the surrounding area. Sebok objected, but the blowup had faded. "Objection noted," Thompson said. He was beginning to enjoy himself, in the old way he used to feel during extemporaneous speech competitions in high school. He admired Blankenship's calculating intelligence. When Thompson noted that Matewan was in the right-hand corner of one map, Blankenship corrected him: "Well, it's in the right-hand quartile."

"Quartile," said Thompson, who loved precise words. "Right."

Thompson wanted to expose Blankenship's role in pumping slurry under the communities and then getting a water line for himself from Matewan. He wanted to put the CEO through everything Thompson's clients had endured in their own depositions. At the same time, in spite of his desire to hate Blankenship, Thompson felt an affinity for the CEO. While he had no affection for the man, their fates had become entwined. Both men had graduated from Marshall University and moved away from West Virginia. Now that they had returned, their lives and worldviews couldn't have been in greater opposition. Yet something had led them to be in this room together, in much the same way that Blankenship had said that his return to Mingo County to work for Rawl Sales had been predestined. It felt like it had always been just a matter of time before the outlaw coal baron and the crusading environmental lawyer met face-to-face.

Thompson could feel in the pit of his stomach how the people living in the hollows off Route 49 had suffered at the hands of this man. His clients were fighting a coal company, just as their parents and grandparents living in the same coal camps had. But maybe Larry Brown's vision was telling; it would be different this time. Blankenship was cool, but adrenaline was pumping through Thompson. After hundreds of depositions, this one mattered the most. It was a dry run for the trial, one week away, and he relished the moment. There was no one he wanted to put on the witness stand more than Blankenship.

Blankenship, who had a sharp recall for anything related to Massey's operations, said he had only vague memories of the water line's extension to his own home in Sprigg. Thompson asked for the date of the construction. "It wasn't there in '83, because I moved in after that, and when I first moved in it wasn't city water," Blankenship said. "But whether it was 1990 or 1996 or when it was, I don't know, because with the travel and the schedule I have, it's not something I focused on."

Thompson tried a different tack. "Did anyone in the house suffer from persistent diarrhea between 1983 and 1993?" he asked. Sebok told Blankenship not to answer.

Thompson ignored the other lawyer. "Have you discussed with your attorney any diarrhea you may have had?" he asked.

"One," Sebok said, "that is clearly attorney-client privileged. I am going to instruct the witness not to answer. This is just harassing, Mr. Thompson, and you know it."

"It is not harassing," Thompson said.

"Are you going to ask relevant questions or not? It's the construction of the water line," said Sebok. "If you want to ask if there is any type of illnesses they had that they tied to the well water, I will let you ask that one. That's the relevant one."

"Al, you are not letting me ask any questions," Thompson said.

"Well, today—"

"I'm going to ask any question I want, and you can advise your client whether or not he is going to answer," Thompson said. "And unless you have got a privilege, I don't think you can instruct him not to answer."

"Yes I can," said Sebok.

Thompson resumed his questioning. "Did anyone have persistent diarrhea linked to the water who has ever lived in your house?"

"Not that I am aware of," Blankenship said.

"Has anyone complained of persistent diarrhea?"

"I'm going to object and instruct him not to answer the question," Sebok said.

"Are you refusing to answer the question?" Thompson said, the edge returning to his voice.

"He is refusing. I have instructed him not to answer the question," said Sebok.

"He has to testify," Thompson said.

"No he doesn't have to testify. The court made an order," Sebok said. "You are harassing the witness."

"I can't think of a better witness to harass," Thompson said, before he thought better of it. "But while I have got him here, let me ask this—"

"Well, no. We are going to walk out of here with your comments," Sebok said angrily.

Thompson knew he had crossed a line. Blankenship looked uncomfortable on Thompson's behalf for a moment, while his lawyer defended him.

"Diarrhea questions is just harassment," Sebok said. "Now move on."

"It is not harassment," Thompson said, trying to regain his footing. "We have made claims for diarrhea. He has said that he had well water and then he had city water. Al, I let you speak. Okay. . . . So now let me explain to you what I'm doing. I'm going to go through the symptoms that we have linked to the water."

In separate questions, Thompson asked Blankenship if anyone in the Sprigg house, from 1983 until the arrival of city water, had complained about a list of health problems that they attributed to the water. Skin rashes. Boils. Cysts. Kidney stones. Cancer. Learning disabilities. Liver and kidney disease. "Not that I'm aware of," Blankenship said each time. Sebok objected whenever Thompson forgot to link the health condition to the water in his question. Then Sebok threatened again to walk out.

"Mr. Blankenship, Mr. Sebok asked every single one of my clients questions, probing questions, about their health. Are you going to allow me to do the same?"

"No, he is not going to allow you to do the same, because your plaintiffs are making claims for damages," Sebok said. "So I have every right, under the Rule of Civil Procedure, to ask those."

"If you leave I will ask for sanctions, Al," Thompson warned.

The threat of being punished by Judge Thornsbury through a fine or an adverse ruling didn't sway Sebok. "Well, you can do whatever you want, sir," he said. "But I'm going to tell you, this is harassment."

"This is not harassment," Thompson said.

"Yes it is," said Sebok.

"Al, harassment is—" Thompson started to say, when Van Bunch, who had been sitting silently the entire time, interrupted. "Kevin, just go on," Bunch said wearily.

"Okay," Thompson said. "Thank you, Van."

Thompson asked Blankenship why he had decided to put the water line in at all.

"Because city water was thought to be preferable," said Blankenship: water was more thoroughly treated at municipal water plants than by home filter systems.

"Did you feel that city water is safer?" Thompson asked.

"Didn't think about safety, but I guess it is," Blankenship said. But he said he had never been hurt by iron water and had drank it a lot over his life. He hadn't known of any environmental threats to his well water before switching to the Matewan system.

Blankenship said that by his recollection, he was aware that city water might become available at some point and told Massey people that he wanted to switch if that happened. He said he only recalled that he had spoken to someone in engineering nearby. Since his assistants paid his bills, Blankenship said, he didn't know if he personally paid for the water or if Rawl Sales did.

When Thompson handed Blankenship invoices from the Matewan Utility Board to Rawl Sales for the Sprigg house, Sebok objected, noting that he didn't think they would help Blankenship's recollection.

"Well, thank you, Al," Thompson said sarcastically.

Had Blankenship ever had any tropical fish at the house, and had they ever died prematurely?

"They always die," Blankenship said.

Thompson circled back once more. Why did Blankenship want to get connected to the Matewan water system if he had no problems with the well water?

"The only thing I recall is that at times we would have trouble with the well, either because of the pump or because of the old line or because of the tank, and that, generally speaking, whoever was there, whether it was the yard guy or one of the people from Rawl, the engineers that were trying to figure out what was wrong with it, they were made aware that, you know, it would be good to be on city water if the opportunity arose."

Blankenship said that the well sometimes went dry in the summer and that its pump burned out on occasion. He said he didn't know if it was a shallow hand-dug well or a deeper drilled well. It had been there since he had moved in.

"Is it possible, do you know, to take a sample of that well?" Thompson asked.

"I don't know, but I would think that the casing and, you know, it's still there, but—"

"It's not plugged to your knowledge?"

"To my knowledge," Blankenship said.

"It could be, but you don't know?"

"That's true."

"So that's literally something below your pay grade?" Thompson said.

Sebok objected. Blankenship answered anyway, looking at Thompson without raising his voice. "I'm as Appalachian as anyone in here," Blankenship said.

More than any other answer, the statement was a window onto how Blankenship saw himself. In spite of his wealth and power, he belonged to this place as much as the pastor and the retired miners and others in the room. His words also carried a challenge. He wouldn't back down any more than they would.

Blankenship said Thompson was making the decision to put the water line in more complicated than it had been. "I mean, the well breaks down. A bunch of guys are standing around. I say, if we get a chance to hook the city water in here, we ought to do it," Blankenship said.

Thompson asked if it would have occurred to Blankenship to have the water line extended up to his neighbors.

"It probably would have occurred to me, but I wouldn't have taken the time at that time to do it," Blankenship said. "I have done similar things but didn't do that."

"Why didn't you do that one?"

"Probably had a lot of problems on my mind," Blankenship said.

Thompson asked if Blankenship would do it today.

"I don't know," Blankenship said. "It depends on what it costs. It depends on lots of other factors."

The truth was, Blankenship could have gotten the water line run from either Matewan or Williamson to the four communities years ago. He might have even considered it, he had just said. Yes, it would have cost a few million dollars. But he could have either paid the construction costs himself or helped speed the process along at the state level. Naturally it would have been a mistake for him now to say that he wished he had taken action. Massey was arguing that its slurry injection hadn't contaminated the aquifer and that the water hadn't harmed anyone's health. But it was clear that of all the people in the county, Blankenship had possessed the money and political connections to have resolved the issue years ago. It would have cost roughly what he had spent to help elect a justice to the state Supreme Court in 2004.

When Blankenship confirmed that there weren't any well tests done on his house—or any well water complaints in Rawl Sales' files that played a role in his decision to get public water—Thompson told him, "You are free to go until we get you back again."

Blankenship had successfully avoided every question about his knowledge of, and involvement in, the slurry injection. As the room emptied out, Larry Brown came over to Thompson and said, "He dodged you pretty good." But Thompson knew Blankenship's obvious involvement in decision-making at the company would play differently in front of a jury, as would the uncomfortable fact that Blankenship had approved construction of a city water line to his own home when it took his neighbors twenty years to get the county and the state to build them one. During that time, Thompson would argue, they had a toxic soup—sometimes discolored and foul-smelling and other times as tasteless and odorless as arsenic—coming from their taps.

Bunch thought it was good that Blankenship called the water at his house typical Appalachian water. How could these people who are living in it tell the difference between typical Appalachian water and the poison that's coming out of their spigots? Don Blankenship couldn't.

CHAPTER 21

Days before the February trial date, with all of Jackson Kelly's motions to dismiss still pending, Thornsbury bumped all the plaintiffs to the May date. Once more, Thompson and his team had to fan out to the communities and deliver the news that the trial had been postponed yet again, with the threat of dismissal hanging out there like a black cloud on the horizon. Some people doubted there would ever be a trial.

In March, Thompson deposed a father and son who had worked at Rawl Sales and were intimately familiar with the slurry injection and said it had really started because the old filter press system couldn't keep up with higher volumes of coal. "It worked, worked good, until they started running all that tonnage," said Scotty Cisco. He said one injection hole had lasted fifteen minutes before the black sludge shot up and ran all over. He said slurry lines had blown apart several times, and he guessed there had been between thirty and fifty injection holes. His son, who went by Robbie, was running the injection pumps in 1984 on the night of the Lick Creek spill. Robbie thought the equipment was pumping too much, but he was told by his boss that everything was fine. "Come to find out, the line had blown in two and I pretty well blacked the river up," he said, with a mix of wonder and regret. The company had fixed the line and continued to inject slurry, Robbie Cisco said. It was all powerfully damning testimony from two men who had participated in the slurry injection.

Judge Thornsbury ordered a mediation to see if Jackson Kelly and Thompson's team could reach a global settlement, and in early April they met with a mediator. After three days of intense negotiations in Charleston, Thompson and his partners emerged believing they had a deal, assuming all the plaintiffs approved, to settle the entire case for $40 million.

Thompson's partners were thrilled to be close to reaching an end of the war, but he was conflicted. He had lately been playing around with a settlement calculator he had designed, plugging in different dollar amounts, and $40 million was near the low end. What he and Wussow and Ellsworth and the others from the Treehouse really wanted was a trial in front of a Mingo County jury, where Thompson would give the opening statement he had been practicing for years.

Even so, Thompson and his partners took his staff to a Chili's restaurant, where they ordered margaritas to celebrate. Thompson called Stuart Smith and put him on speakerphone. Smith, in his raspy voice, started singing the verses of "We're in the Money."

On April 27, a Monday, all the lawyers were back before Judge Thornsbury, and the courtroom was filled. Thompson felt excitement but also regret as he eyed the empty jury box. He wouldn't put Blankenship on the witness stand or get to repeat the evidence he had recited at the January hearing, when he felt he'd beaten back Jackson Kelly's dismissal motions. Still, he approached the bench, along with Stickler and the other lawyers, for a sidebar conversation with the judge.

"Your Honor, we have a deal," Thompson later recalled saying as the lawyers huddled before the judge.

Without missing a beat, Stickler said, "No, Your Honor. We don't."

Thompson felt a jolt. The judge asked if Massey's insurers had been unwilling to come up with the settlement money, and Stickler said that was the case. Judge Thornsbury asked if Thompson had gotten every client to sign a settlement demand, a document containing an amount each plaintiff would accept to settle their individual claim. Thompson hadn't done that—he believed the two sides had reached a global settlement for the entire case, and that the money could then be distributed by hiring a third party to come up with a formula for doing so.

"You're having a community meeting tonight?" the judge asked.

"Tonight," Thompson said.

"Get demands on an individual basis tonight," the judge said.

"I can't do that, Your Honor. There's no way," Thompson said. He made another plea to resolve the case through a global settlement.

"I was going to take my entire day Thursday in dealing with them," the judge said.

"Really?" Thompson said.

Five minutes earlier, he believed he had settled the entire case. Now he had to get individual approvals from the more than five hundred adult plaintiffs in the case in less than three days, and he had to find a way to get them all to the courthouse. Judge Thornsbury said anyone who didn't settle individually on that day would remain in the case. He wasn't canceling the May trial date: "It's number uno."

Thompson thought again about Massey's hundreds of millions of dollars in insurance coverage, and he pressed again for a global settlement. "There's a lot of coverage if they want to do the right thing," he told the judge.

But the judge and Massey's lawyers seemed to be moving at a different speed, eager to push ahead with an individual settlement plan. The remaining cases would "become manageable at that point," the judge said. Thompson was to have all of his clients at the courthouse Thursday morning at eight thirty.

When the lawyers returned to their counsel tables, the judge announced the news to the courtroom. He reminded everyone that there were motions for dismissal pending. "It may well foster settlement that those motions are there and in the breast of the court prior to ruling," he said. In other words, some people might want to grab what money they could now.

Thompson suggested that his out-of-state clients could give him the authority to settle their claims by phone.

"No. They've got a case here in Mingo County and you've got plenty of time to call them and tell them to make travel arrangements," the judge said. "They're going to have to travel sooner or later, and it's better they travel Thursday, because we might be able to settle some of these claims."

Back at room 409, Thompson and Bunch held an emergency meeting. Everyone sat around the long table next to Thompson's desk.

"What the fuck just happened?" Thompson asked. He began listing things they had to do immediately, starting with calling every family that lived out of state. They had to know that if they didn't show up Thursday they could be dismissed from the case. Thompson assigned himself the task of drafting a settlement authority document. He would have to get every adult client to sign one in the next three days. Meanwhile children under eighteen would need attorneys appointed to represent them. Thompson had no idea how the judge planned to handle that. Within the next sixty-nine hours, Thompson would have to sit down with every adult client to determine how much they would accept from Massey. He decided to gather as many of them as possible at the meeting that evening.

Why had the global settlement fallen apart? Thompson believed that either a major insurer had balked at paying or Blankenship had decided against it. The CEO had no doubt made his own calculations. Weeding out individual claims in a single day made sense if it led to a smaller settlement later. Thompson assumed Massey and its lawyers believed many of his clients could be bought off cheaply.

That night, about 120 anxious people filled Bo Scott's church in Rawl Bottom, a narrow space with red pews and purple carpeting. Some people stood along the walls. For more than two hours, Thompson tried to ease people's fears. He explained that they had reached a tentative settlement but it had fallen through. People were upset that after years of delays they were now being told to show up to possibly settle their claims on three days' notice. Thompson had to shout to quiet the crowd at one point. He had his own misgivings. After years of letting the case play out, the judge was now bent on settling as many claims as he could in a single day. In the past, he'd allowed people to join the lawsuit and to stay in even after they missed several dates for depositions or medical exams. Now he was saying that if people didn't show up to court on Thursday they would be out. Where had the urgency come from? A growing number of people didn't trust the judge, they certainly didn't trust Massey, and now they didn't trust Thompson.

Thompson and Bunch wanted a medical monitoring fund, a remedy available under state law that would provide medical screening for years to come, but it was hard to convince the room. Thompson said that medical testing would be important to the entire community, but the crowd was divided into two camps. Some older people were against creating a separate fund because it would cut into their individual settlement. Many parents with young children were for the testing.

Brenda McCoy, who lived in Merrimac and worked as a paralegal, was more familiar than most of her neighbors with the legal process. She had a teenage daughter who was excelling in high school but had suffered from a series of mysterious illnesses. McCoy, who had had cervical cancer and thyroid problems, understood why some people wanted the biggest settlement check they could get. She had known poverty herself. She had grown up in a house built out of ax-hewn boards, with no running water or electricity, and had been beaten once as a girl for cooking with too much flour. But she was now all for the medical monitoring.

"They thought Kevin was raking in millions of dollars in interest that was accumulating on this money. And him explaining, no, I'm not making money off this," she recalled later. "They were pretty tart at times, very openly saying, you're just selling us out."

Thompson spent the next two days meeting with clients in a room off the lobby of the Mountaineer. He talked about their claims and how much they could reasonably seek in compensation from Massey, one after another, past the point of exhaustion each day in the warm room. He tried to reassure people about the strength of the case, while explaining the legal details of the choice they faced—settle their claim now or put their fate in a jury's hands. Without his settlement calculator, the task would have been impossible in three days. Even so, everyone from the Treehouse was busy day and night, booking flights for families traveling from as far away as Seattle, corralling people in the lobby, and driving out to Rawl and the other three communities to find others who couldn't be reached by phone.

Since the courtroom could hold only about a hundred people, Thompson got the county's director of emergency services to make the Williamson Field House available. A bus company would shuttle people in vans from the old gymnasium to the courthouse, about a mile away. On Thursday morning, by 8:30 a.m., lawyers for some sixty insurance companies had gathered in the courthouse's grand jury room. People from Rawl, Lick Creek, Merrimac, and Sprigg began to arrive at the courthouse and the field house.

The judge had ordered people whose last names began with A and B to come to the courthouse. Melissa Ellsworth tried to arrange them in alphabetical order in the courtroom. Steve Wussow was there helping Thompson with his documents. Wussow's job would be to usher people to another room, where Thompson, Bunch, Massey's lawyers, and the judge would be waiting. Mathis and Getzen, meanwhile, were stationed at the field house, to check people in and then ferry them to the courthouse.

By 9 a.m., the temperature was already rising in the crowded courtroom. Thompson and Bunch were starting to sweat in their suits as they waited for Judge Thornsbury to arrive. No one working in room 409 had slept much in three days.

The judge came in wearing his robes. Rather than take his seat, he stood in the middle of the courtroom to address everyone. He said he didn't expect to settle everyone's claim that day. But people needed to think now, if they hadn't already, about what they were willing to accept. They would have three or four minutes to decide once they were in a room with him, so there wouldn't be time to hesitate. He added, "I will tell you, by way of history, folks that have sat in the chair you're sitting in right now—that have went to settlement conference—very few have fared better at trial than they could have at settlement conferences. Many in the last group of cases turned down offers and then received either zero verdicts or substantially less than what they were offered at settlement conferences. Some received more by way of a jury verdict. Again, it depends on your case and the settlement, but it's time to give this case and your case serious thought."

Seated among the crowd were the families of Larry and Brenda Brown, Ernie and Carmelita Brown, Donetta Blankenship, and James Berlin Anderson. They listened as Judge Thornsbury said he was going to be as fair to them as possible. "But I really want you to know that this is going to be sort of fast and furious," he said. "The bailiff will be running you in and out and I'll know very quickly whether the case is going to settle or not going to settle."

An Associated Press reporter, Vicki Smith, was in the courtroom, taking down the judge's comments. She noted his "assembly line efficiency" and his plan "to shuttle hundreds of plaintiffs through his courtroom." Yet it promised to be a long, hot day. "Away from the courthouse, about 500 plaintiffs were packed in a community gymnasium with no air conditioning in temperatures that hovered around 80 degrees," Smith wrote.

In fact, the assembly line came to a halt almost as soon as it started. Amy Bailey, Larry and Brenda Brown's daughter, was the first plaintiff to enter the small room, and when she heard Massey's offer she asked the judge whether the money included medical monitoring. Her question threw the day into chaos.

Judge Thornsbury called a recess and met privately with lawyers for Massey and its insurers to discuss funding a medical monitoring program. When he emerged, Thompson and Bunch met with him in a hallway outside his chambers. They said a program that would provide years of medical screening in the communities would cost $5 million to fund. The judge asked them to waive a fee, and he said that Massey and its insurers would do the deal only if they waived any fee for generating the fund. Thompson and Bunch expected to receive a fee of roughly $1.7 million for their work on that part of the case, and they wanted the fee to be paid by Massey or its insurers separately to keep the $5 million fund intact. When the judge asked them again to forego payment for their work, they refused once more. The judge then told them, according to their separate recollections, "Don't worry, boys. At the end of this, there's going to be a pile of money for everybody."

Thompson believed the judge had suddenly shown an interest in funding future medical testing only because it might entice more people to settle their claims. "He never believed in the medical monitoring. He thought it was bullshit," Thompson recalled later.

Yet in the moment, Thompson took it as a good sign that Thornsbury was willing to consider the issue. The judge went by himself to the grand jury room, where lawyers for Massey and its insurers were waiting. For the next five hours, the judge hashed out a medical monitoring settlement between all the parties. He approved a $5 million settlement to create a trust that would pay for plaintiffs' medical exams for years to come. The judge told Thompson that if he didn't get 100 percent of his clients to agree to the settlement of this issue, he would consider a request to certify a class, which would allow people to opt out of the program. Thompson addressed all of his clients in the courtroom and asked for approval of the trust. Every hand went up in favor.

At the field house, however, he didn't even get a chance to poll the crowd. People had been waiting for hours in the warm gymnasium; they were sweaty and agitated, it was well past lunchtime, and they wanted to know why the process was taking so long. Standing in the middle of a group on the hardwood floor, Thompson took a microphone and again tried to explain the importance of the medical monitoring fund. Someone asked what would happen if they got sick years later. A murmuring in the room grew louder. A few people began saying loudly that Thompson had sold them out.

One man grabbed the microphone from Thompson's hand and said, "So if I get cancer, Massey wins!"

People drew closer around Thompson, and bodies were suddenly up against one another, with arguments breaking out. Mathis was unable to do anything to calm the crowd. Bo Scott waded into the scrum and raised his arms up. "Peace!" he called several times. People started shoving, and a few threw punches. Carmelita's brothers Ira and Roscoe and another man pulled Thompson out of the melee. As soon as he was outside, where two deputies had been posted, Thompson called Ellsworth.

"Talk to the judge," he said. "Tell him to send more deputies right away."

"Excuse me, Judge," Thompson heard her say. "Kevin said he needs deputies."

"What?" Judge Thornsbury replied. "He already has deputies."

"He wants more," Ellsworth said.

She tried to hand her phone to Judge Thornsbury, but he wouldn't take it. Seconds later, Thompson heard sirens in downtown Williamson. He said into the phone, "You got to certify a class, Your Honor."

Ellsworth relayed the message, and through the phone Thompson could hear the judge announce, "I hereby certify a class!"

The class for medical monitoring allowed people who didn't want to participate in the program to opt out, while allowing their claims that the water had harmed them to still be handled as individual complaints. Thompson went back into the field house and said, "The judge certified a class action for medical monitoring!" A cheer went up in the room. Two deputies led Thompson out of the auditorium again. Before Thompson left, he looked around the gym for the elderly and sick and anyone else struggling in the heat and brought them to the courthouse.

Back in court, Thompson thought Stickler and Sebok looked like the most defeated people he had ever seen. He considered the $5 million medical monitoring fund a major victory.

"Your Honor," Sebok said, "just, again, this would also include attorney fees, costs, expert witness fees?"

"All claims of any type of nature, yes," the judge said. "Do you understand that?"

"Yes. We understand," Thompson said.

But he didn't. He thought that Sebok was saying that under the terms of the settlement, attorney fees for the medical monitoring trust would be allowed and paid separately by Massey; Sebok, however, was saying, and the judge was confirming, that attorney fees from this medical monitoring settlement would be taken out of the $5 million fund. The exchange was ambiguous, much like the dispute over the scope of Blankenship's deposition, and it would soon help put the entire case at risk.

For now the judge was ready to get his assembly line moving again. The next family agreed to settle two claims for a total of $15,000. A string of people after that declined. Massey was offering some people $5,000 to settle their claims, with some offers as high as $25,000. When Larry and Brenda Brown entered the room, the judge didn't bother to say what Massey had offered. Larry later recalled he hadn't been willing to settle his personal claim for less than $155,000. The judge said he'd pass that information along to the company's lawyers and let Larry know if they came any closer to his number. Ernie and Carmelita Brown turned down Massey's offer, as did Frank Coleman, Don Dillon, Maude Rice, and Bo Scott. Tom Jervis, whose wife, Opal, had died since the lawsuit was filed, said no, as did the parents of Chastity Dawn Prince, who had died of kidney cancer when she was four.

"They wanted to give us $9,000 for Chastity," Virginia Prince told a reporter later. Then, referring to either Thompson or Bunch, who were in the cramped room all day, she said, "One of our attorneys was sitting at the end of the table and he shook his head no."

Judge Thornsbury swept in and out of the courtroom, his robes flowing behind him. Even with the rapid-fire offers, the process was painfully slow. Ellsworth and the judge's staff stopped trying to line people up in alphabetical order. They had people sign a sheet and pointed them as quickly as they could toward the settlement room. In the first group of clients, there were more than two dozen Blankenships present, none apparently closely related to Massey's CEO.

Soaked in sweat, Thompson peeled off his suit jacket in the settlement room. Bunch motioned to him to put it back on. Earlier, Bunch had asked to take off his jacket, and the judge had said no—he had to wear his robes, after all. "Hell no, I'm not putting my jacket on," Thompson said to Bunch. The judge looked at Thompson, but Thompson just glared back.

In the courtroom, Ellsworth was conducting triage, trying to decide who was sicker and less able to handle the situation. She told one client with a broken back who was wearing a protective turtle shell that he could go to a doctor's appointment. Many others didn't want to leave the courtroom—even to use the bathroom—for fear that the judge would dismiss their claims. People had been wilting in the stifling courtroom all afternoon. The approach of evening meant cooler temperatures, but nerves were so frayed that it hardly mattered. There were restless children, and parents and grandparents trying to calm them. A few people were attached to oxygen tanks, and Ellsworth wondered when those would begin to run out.

Then, finally, a man leaned over and fell to the courtroom floor. His wife announced that he was diabetic. Passed out between the rows of benches, he began to turn blue. Ellsworth went over to him gripped with panic. His wife loosened his shirt, as a crowd closed in around him. Several people began praying aloud. A woman began to talk to Jesus, raising her hands and speaking in tongues. A few others laid their hands on the man. Someone shouted to get him some water and a candy bar. Ellsworth relaxed a little when she saw that at least half the people in the courtroom seemed to know how to revive him. Several people dialed 911, and an ambulance came to take the man away.

Thompson missed the commotion, but after the dinner hour passed, he lost his cool. "This is bullshit. You don't have to be here anymore," Thompson told some people individually. In the settlement room, he found himself speaking for some clients and saying they wouldn't take the company's offer. Bunch had spent most of the day and night in the room. He had watched Thompson hugging people since the morning and told him, "You are going to get so sick."

Just before midnight the judge saw the last of the people who had remained.

The next morning, Thompson woke up to his phone ringing, and it didn't stop all day. Reporters in West Virginia were calling for comment. Jackson Kelly called him to complain about Vicki Smith's AP story, which included confidential settlement offers. The article quoted Brenda Brown: "I'm through with it. We helped organize this and keep this going, but it's torment. That's exactly what it is." Brenda had claimed earlier in the day that she was ready to settle, but she'd declined Massey's offer. James Berlin Anderson told Smith he'd rejected a $30,000 offer and would've settled for $210,000. "We're just a bunch of dumb hillbillies. That's what they think," he said. He wanted to go to trial "to take something from them, because they've taken something from me." Ernie Brown and B.I., Bo Scott, Don Dillon, and others were similarly offended by Massey's lowball offers. They didn't intend to quit the case anytime soon.

Thompson lay on his back on the floor of his room for hours, picking up the phone when it rang. Having barely slept since Monday, he drifted in and out and his voice sounded detached. When Smith called to pursue her follow-up story, he declined to say how many people had settled their individual claims or for how much. But he told her the settlements had likely shaved weeks or months off the upcoming trial. A total of 185 people had, in fact, accepted Massey's offers, and they were now out of the case. And yet, if Smith had asked, Thompson would have told her he didn't feel any closer to the end.

CHAPTER 22

A week later, the bitter feelings were still fresh. It was finally May, and the trial was a few days away. In Thompson's view, the recent ordeal—sweltering heat, endless waiting, and chaos—had re-traumatized many people. And now he had to go back to court for a hearing to deal with Jackson Kelly's complaints about the process.

Stickler and Sebok told the judge that plaintiffs who hadn't attended the settlement conference should be dismissed from the case. In fact, they were still arguing that the entire case be dismissed. Thompson stood up to defend his clients. One of them, he reminded the judge, had suffered a diabetic seizure right there in the courtroom; another had gotten violently ill while she was taking care of her grandchild and had to leave; a third had stayed until she had gone to her father's funeral in the evening.

Likewise, Thompson rejected Sebok's assertion that he had failed to show there was any real problem with the water in the community. "Ernie Brown, stand up," Thompson said, looking to the back of the courtroom. "Ernie Brown's well is one of the most tested wells in the world," Thompson continued. "The French government has tested his well. The American government has tested his well. The West Virginia government has tested his well. Their experts have tested his well. We have tested his well, Your Honor, and every one of those well tests is different. The point is this is a groundwater system with this slurry percolating through it. We have videotapes of water turning from clear to milky to orange to black while it's running out of the same spigot and every one of those moments would have yielded a different result had we taken a snapshot in time."

Thompson reminded the judge that the Browns' well was at the base of the Lick Creek Syncline, "a sluice where this entire ground-water system comes out." He argued that it was entirely appropriate to use averages across the community because the water quality was constantly shifting.

The water contamination had happened over the course of more than twenty years, well before Thompson found out about it in February 2004. "This red, black, stinking water with all of the heavy metals associated with coal slurry is bad for you," Thompson told the judge. "This isn't about some hypothetical risk, Your Honor."

Before the hearing concluded, he had one more question. "Your Honor," Thompson asked, "are we going to trial Tuesday?"

"We're going to trial Tuesday," Judge Thornsbury said.

But they didn't. On Friday, May 8, the rain started, and it didn't stop. By Saturday morning, roads were covered by mud-brown floodwaters. Creeks had become rivers. Mobile homes had been lifted up, swept into the creeks, and battered. More than three hundred homes and other structures were destroyed in Mingo County; more than three thousand had major damage. Governor Joe Manchin declared an emergency across six southern counties, including Mingo, which experienced the worst of the flooding. Water filled one coal mine in the county up to the roof in places, trapping seven miners for twenty-four hours before they were rescued. The roads into communities were underwater for days. Thompson and others had blamed surface mining for the increasing severity of floods like this one. The mountains had been stripped of trees and plants whose roots hold water, and the rains had nowhere to go but into the narrow hollows where people lived. It was the nineteenth significant flooding event in Mingo County in eleven years.

In Rawl, the creek came up to the houses on the left side of Dick Williamson Branch Road. The floodwaters tore off part of the garage and porch of Donetta Blankenship's house in the middle of the night. She and her husband, Orville, heard the water lapping at the house and got their son and daughter into the front of the house before the structure came apart.

Nick Getzen visited the family to let them know the trial had been postponed, and Filippo Piscopo and Lorena Luciano, who had traveled to Williamson to cover the trial for their documentary, instead captured the shattered buildings and devastated hopes of Thompson's clients.

"So we got more bad news. The trial got pushed back to October," Getzen said to Donetta. He explained that nothing was going to happen with the case for the next three or four weeks because of the floods, and now the trial was another five months away.

Donetta was picking through debris with Orville. "It's not ever going to be over with, is it?" she said.

In room 409, Thompson and everyone else regrouped around his desk. Still reeling from the sudden postponement, they went over what needed to be done in the coming months. As they discussed how the medical monitoring settlement would work, Thompson and Bunch disagreed on a critical point: whether people could bring a new lawsuit against Massey later if they developed an illness like cancer that could potentially be tied to the slurry.

"Nobody said anything about future medicals being pulled off the table," Thompson said.

Bunch was certain the settlement meant people couldn't sue later. "If they're future claims, they're extinguished. I guarantee you, that's the law," said Bunch. "I wish it wasn't that way. I'm just telling you the way it works."

As it turned out, Bunch was right. If their clients got sick in the future, the medical monitoring program would hopefully catch the illnesses early. But no one would be able to file a new lawsuit.

In June, Thompson met with everyone who had accepted Massey's settlement offers. More than a hundred people had come in from the rain and crowded into the Brass Tree Restaurant on West Second Avenue. Before they could receive their checks, he and Jackson Kelly needed to cosign their release forms. Thompson worked to get through all the paperwork—the judge had set a deadline for 4:30 p.m.—and raced three blocks to the courthouse through the rain with an associate from Jackson Kelly. They were dripping wet as they passed through the metal detector.

The clerk received and date-stamped the documents. The judge couldn't sign them that day—he wasn't in the courthouse—but at least the paperwork had been delivered on time. Then Thompson watched as the clerk called a Jackson Kelly attorney, Erin Stankewicz. When the clerk hung up, she took out a bottle of Wite-Out and began to paint over the date stamps.

"You can't do that," Thompson later recalled saying.

The clerk claimed she could: they were Erin Stankewicz's documents. Still soaking wet, Thompson watched in disbelief as the clerk erased, one by one, the dates on all the documents she had previously stamped to show when they had been received. He worried that if the judge thought he had missed the deadline, it could cause another delay in distributing the settlement checks. His clients were already frustrated because it was well beyond the thirty days when they were supposed to be paid. What disturbed Thompson more was the clerk's apparent deference to Jackson Kelly. Was the judge's staff deferring to the law firm on other matters?

That same month, the medical monitoring trust reared its head again at another hearing that Thompson couldn't attend—he was home in New Orleans, laid up with bronchitis. He'd been sick on and off ever since Bunch had predicted he'd get ill from overworking and then hugging hundreds of his clients at the settlement conference. When Judge Thornsbury brought the courtroom to order, Bunch was sitting at the plaintiffs' table by himself.

This was supposed to be a routine hearing about the representation of minors whose claims had been settled. But Bunch noticed Jackson Kelly's attorneys passing around a document—something about the medical monitoring trust. When he asked for a copy, a Jackson Kelly lawyer refused to give him one, but he stepped over to the defense counsel table and took one for himself anyway. It was more than fifty pages long.

At the judge's direction, the bailiffs removed several local newspaper reporters from the courtroom. In fact, they removed almost everyone—it was a sealed hearing. Bunch turned around and saw the cleared benches.

In the mostly empty courtroom, Stickler began describing how Jackson Kelly had drafted the medical monitoring plan, incorporating some changes suggested by both the insurance companies and Thompson and Bunch.

As Bunch skimmed through the document, trying to get his bearings, Stickler said the judge needed to appoint three parties to set up the trust. "One is the grantor," Stickler said. "We have made the recommendation that the court be the grantor of the trust."

"That's the way it's going to be, so ordered," the judge said, dropping his gavel.

"Okay," Stickler said. "Secondly, we have proposed that Christopher Beckett, who is a local—"

Judge Thornsbury brought his gavel down again. "Already discussed it with him, so ordered," the judge said.

"And the trustee would be the Community Trust Bank," said Stickler.

"So ordered," the judge said, rapping his gavel a third time.

Bunch was uncomfortable with the rapid-fire appointments. The judge had just made himself the grantor of the trust; he'd sealed the hearing without warning. And who on earth was Christopher Beckett?

Outside the courthouse, Bunch found a local reporter who was upset about being forced out of the hearing. She had already learned several details about the trust document, and she gave Bunch a quick tutorial on Mingo County politics. Beckett, who had just been named fund administrator, was a doctor in town as well as Judge Thornsbury's campaign manager. The judge and Beckett were partners in a real estate investment company called Williamson Renaissance Development, she explained. They owned several buildings on East Second Avenue, including one with a wine shop and apartments where visiting lawyers frequently stayed.

When Thompson caught up on the hearing, a queasy feeling began to grow in his gut. He feared the judge and Jackson Kelly had discussed the trust appointments in private before the hearing. From Bunch's recounting, the rulings sounded scripted. When Thompson got the transcript from the judge's clerk, he saw that when Stickler proposed Beckett as administrator, the judge hadn't even let him finish his sentence. "Already discussed it with him, so ordered," the judge had said.

Thompson and Bunch had thirty days to sign off on the medical monitoring plan. In that time, Thompson set out to learn as much as he could about the judge and his friends and business partners.

CHAPTER 23

As the sole circuit court judge, Thornsbury was the most powerful elected official in Mingo County. That is, with the possible exception of H. Truman Chafin, who was serving his seventh-straight term as state senator, one of the longest runs in West Virginia history. They had become the heads of two warring factions of Democrats in Williamson. Thompson figured the best place to start digging into Thornsbury's local connections was with his chief political enemies, Truman and his wife, Letitia, who had a joint law practice in the city. It had been several years since the Chafins had appeared before Judge Thornsbury, and that was partly his doing. In March 2004, the judge had written a letter to the state Supreme Court citing judicial harassment by the couple and voluntarily recusing himself "in all present and future matters" involving them.

"What do you know about the judge?" Thompson asked Letitia, who went by Tish. The couple's law offices in the post office building, two blocks from the Mountaineer, contained relics from the 1920s: a dusty old courtroom, a jail, and an oversize safe. (Blankenship's girlfriend had her own office there and shared a secretary with the couple.) The atmosphere—and the air of political intrigue—were like something out of an Appalachian noir.

"Buddy," Tish said, "you're going to have to narrow that subject, because there's a lot of ways that conversation can go."

The judge's business partners, Christopher Beckett and Jarrod Fletcher, owned much of the block that Starters was on, including the wine shop, Tish explained. Tish thought owning the shop was a conflict of interest for the judge because he sentenced people on alcohol-related offenses. Earlier that year, the judge had appointed Fletcher foreman of the county's grand jury, which she also thought was ethically questionable.

Tish didn't know whether Don Blankenship had ever been friendly with Thornsbury, but she doubted it. In her view, Blankenship would never participate in any schemes at the courthouse. Thompson asked if his staff at the Mountaineer was in any danger. Tish Chafin couldn't say for sure, but if he was concerned, he could trust Lonnie Hannah, the Mingo County sheriff.

Until recently, Thompson had thought Judge Thornsbury had been reasonable and even sympathetic. For years the judge had allowed Thompson to keep adding people to the case, over Jackson Kelly's objections. He had been reluctant to dismiss them whenever Jackson Kelly argued they should be dismissed. Early on, the judge had even indicated that he believed the evidence tended to implicate Rawl Sales for contaminating the drinking water in the four communities. All along, he had said he had wanted a fair trial and to keep the train from coming off the tracks. But Thompson was troubled by the judge's apparent change of attitude, especially his having set a settlement conference on three days' notice. Then there was his statement that by the time the case was over there would be a "pile of money" for everyone. Thompson knew that Bunch thought the judge was a crook and had finally shown his hand.

Thompson had always respected the judge's grasp of the facts, his written decisions, and the way he ran his courtroom. The judge had a sharp mind, but it was also clear he was no natural politician. Some of his longtime friends described him as the kid who couldn't get a date to the prom in high school. Thornsbury had come into power after federal prosecutors had indicted Johnie Owens, Larry Hamrick, and others in the 1980s. By sweeping out nearly all the officeholders in Mingo County, prosecutors cleared a path for Thornsbury, then a Williamson lawyer, and about fifty other political novices to vie for local office in 1988. Thornsbury ran for a seat in the state House of Delegates as a reform candidate. "It's up to the people this time," Thornsbury said then. "They can choose the old way, or they can take the best opportunity they've had to vote good, honest candidates into office."

Thornsbury lost that election, however, and he lost a subsequent bid to become mayor of Williamson. Eager to get into politics, he found his opening in 1996, when Elliott "Spike" Maynard, who had been a judge since 1981, won a twelve-year term on the West Virginia

Supreme Court of Appeals in Charleston. Truman Chafin and Spike Maynard, Blankenship's longtime friend, engineered Thornsbury's ascent from lawyer to circuit court judge.

As Chafin told the story, Thornsbury came to his office one day, pulled a handkerchief out of his back pocket, lifted his glasses, and dabbed at his eyes, saying he wanted to become a judge. "He told me he got beat and really wanted to be in politics and he couldn't win anything. If I would consider him, he would do a great job, be a really good judge. Dedicate his life to it. The usual sob story," Chafin said. "So I went back to Spike and told him he seems like a pretty good guy. University of Kentucky graduate. He's got the credentials and he's good as a lawyer, and we really don't have anyone that wants to do it."

As part of the deal, Thornsbury agreed to retain Maynard's secretary, who was Ben Hatfield's wife. Governor Gaston Caperton appointed Thornsbury to fill the post. In the view of some county leaders, Thornsbury never learned to handle the power of the office with the grace or goodwill of someone like Spike Maynard, whom Chafin and others had liked. "The worst thing you can do to any individual ever is have a lot of people praise him," said Chafin. "This is a guy that couldn't get elected dogcatcher and now everybody is going, 'Oh, Your Honor. Nice to see you.' You start praising a man. That can be a dangerous thing for a person that doesn't absorb it well." It didn't take long before Chafin regretted his involvement.

Once he got in office, Thornsbury consolidated his power, and the Chafins said he showed bias against them in his courtroom. Nearly every day at lunch, Thornsbury sat at the head of a reserved table in the back of Starters, with a basket of Club crackers in the middle. He was joined by a shifting group of lawyers, county commissioners, and political appointees. People didn't have to know what the judge and his friends discussed. Anyone could plainly see who ran the county.

"They weren't hiding anything. They were letting people know where they stood," Carmelita Brown said. "They were buddies. Lord, how do you think they got where they were?"

Voters liked Thornsbury well enough to keep him in office when he came up for election in 1998. In 2000, he ran unopposed. Ernie Brown and B.I. had helped him campaign in the hollows along Route 49. Thornsbury had been to their homes. Carmelita had gone to high school with his wife, Dreama. "As a man, as a friend, I liked Mike," Carmelita said.

On the bench, the judge was known for his efficiency. In September 2004, he conducted 117 civil and criminal hearings in a single day, a Mingo County record. He was known for meting out harsh sentences on occasion. He sent a man to prison for up to ten years for threatening a judge from another county. "Keep thy tongue from evil and lips from speaking guile," Thornsbury told the man at sentencing, quoting Psalm 34. Yet Thompson, who sometimes watched the judge handle criminal cases, thought that for the most part he was lenient with people who had committed minor crimes and tough when the community needed to be protected.

The judge set another record in 2004 for overseeing the longest jury trial in the history of the county. Remarkably, Thompson discovered, it was another well water lawsuit. A community in Delbarton, nine miles north of Rawl, alleged that Massey's underground mining had caused seventy-six wells to go dry. The state DEP had required Massey to provide replacement water; Massey appealed, and Thornsbury ordered the company to provide the water. The trial lasted five weeks.

The jury deliberated for forty hours before finding Massey liable for $1.6 million in damages. By that time, the company had hooked the residents up to a municipal water line and made lump sum payments to residents for the loss of their water. Thompson believed it could be a template for the Rawl case, even if Rawl was far more complicated. In Delbarton, the wells went dry soon after Massey opened a new mine. Still, the people had won some justice from a Mingo County jury with Judge Thornsbury on the bench. That case had given Thompson hope. He hadn't seen any reason, until now, to doubt the judge's integrity inside his courtroom.

CHAPTER 24

After he spoke to the Chafins, Thompson sent Getzen to the courthouse to dig through the judge's records. Thornsbury's 2009 financial disclosure with the state ethics commission confirmed that his business interests included stock in Williamson Renaissance Development, the company that refurbished and rented properties in downtown Williamson. Getzen pulled at least fifteen deeds for downtown properties the judge co-owned. Thompson was stunned to learn that his business with Beckett, the local doctor, had a $1.6 million deed of trust at Community Trust Bank. Beckett also had an agreement with Massey to treat its employees for a $5 co-pay.

To Thompson, it seemed unlikely at best that Jackson Kelly had suggested that Beckett and Community Trust Bank have some role in the medical monitoring trust without first consulting the judge. This set off alarm bells—the same doctor who would be entrusted with looking after his clients' long-term well-being also had a business arrangement not only with the judge but with Massey.

Thompson tried to keep his inquiry quiet, but people in Williamson soon knew what he was up to. Over the next few weeks, he started getting tips about the judge late at night. His answering service sent them to him as text messages. Most tipsters remained anonymous and unreliable. One night, however, B.I. Sammons called Thompson directly. A state police officer he named was going to plant cocaine "on your young people's cars tonight," B.I. said. Thompson wasn't sure how reliable the tip was, but as the news rippled through his staff, Ellsworth and Wussow packed up some hard drives and stayed for a few days at her parents' house in Shepherdstown. Thompson, Getzen, and Mathis remained in Williamson.

Then Thompson got a call from Jack Spence, a retired police chief from Delbarton, north of Matewan. Spence said he had seen Thornsbury and Blankenship having lunch together at Starters in mid-April. Thompson thought of the date and realized it was shortly before the marathon settlement conference, when the judge had suddenly seemed eager to settle as many claims as possible. Spence signed an affidavit under penalty of perjury saying that he had seen the Massey CEO and the judge socializing at the restaurant.

Thompson knew that his clients—who were already suspicious about Massey influencing the court—would no longer have any confidence in the judge once they heard about his lunch with Blankenship. In the end, Thompson hoped that Thornsbury's failure to disclose his ties to the medical monitoring trust would be enough for the state Supreme Court to remove him from the case. If the court disagreed, Thompson risked the judge's wrath for having tried to remove him. He and his colleagues made the tough choice to file a recusal motion. Stuart Smith, who called in from New Orleans, warned: "If you're going to shoot at the king, you better not miss."

Thompson discussed the matter with Larry Brown, B.I., Don Dillon, Bo Scott, and others. He talked it over with Ernie and Carmelita. Even though she had liked Thornsbury, Carmelita believed he couldn't be trusted with the case. She told Thompson he was doing the right thing. "We need to get it out of Mingo County," Carmelita said, and Ernie agreed.

"Sometimes I wish I had fallen off the back of that four-wheeler when Ernie was taking me up the mountain," Thompson said.

A few days before the filing, Thompson walked into Starters by himself. The restaurant was in a building at the heart of Judge Thornsbury's real estate holdings, he now knew. Above the storefronts were suites where visiting attorneys stayed and paid money to a company co-owned by the judge. Thompson sat down at the bar and ordered a beer, and he felt the power of the allegations he was making against the judge. He began to feel uncomfortable among the familiar faces. He didn't know how the judge would respond or how the judge's allies, or even the staff at the restaurant, would treat him going forward. The ground was already shifting, as though from the undertow of a tidal wave about to break over the courthouse.

Thompson filed his disqualification motion to the state Supreme Court on the afternoon of Friday, July 17, and he also marched a copy over to the courthouse. It had been thirty days since the medical monitoring hearing. Thompson and Getzen brought the filing to the judge's clerk on the second floor and watched her stamp it "Received."

"Salvo fired," Getzen announced when he and Thompson got back to room 409. "World War Three had to start somewhere at some time. Mingo County seemed like a decent place today."

As Wussow and Ellsworth packed to leave, Thompson leaned back at his desk, lost in thought. He had taken off his jacket and loosened his tie. Behind him, a recent edition of the *Williamson Daily News* was tacked to the wall. The front-page headline read: "Rawl Residents Question Strange Sludge." In a photograph, Larry Brown held up a jar of black water.

"Fuck, I'm far from home," Thompson said.

Thompson's motion said the judge's impartiality had come into question: he hadn't disclosed that Beckett was his business partner, that Beckett had served as his campaign manager, or that Beckett was a contractor with Massey. The judge was alleged to have steered potentially large fees to his business partner in violation of judicial ethics canons and had demonstrably communicated with Jackson Kelly prior to the hearing. Furthermore, Thornsbury had consistently tried to protect Blankenship from being deposed; Thompson even claimed that the court had provided a transcript of the massive settlement conference to Jackson Kelly but refused to give it to Thompson's staff. And, of course, the judge had been seen having lunch with Blankenship at Starters.

In a phrase later used in articles that ran statewide, Thompson called the judge's actions "cronyism at its worst." He said Beckett's appointment had "sinister overtones." "Hundreds of residents and former residents of Mingo County are facing off against the largest coal producer in the state. They are concerned about their health. . . . It has been essential for the Court to scrupulously avoid showing bias, avoid acquiring an economic interest, avoid all appearance of impropriety and hold a balance between the litigants. Yet the judge has utterly failed to do so in ways both small and large," Thompson concluded.

Even in good times, Williamson could make a person feel claustrophobic. With the courthouse a few hundred feet from the Mountaineer, and Starters across East Second Avenue, the city was now uncomfortably small. Thompson had walked up to the line of accusing the judge, and by extension his allies, of corruption. He might run into one of them anytime he stepped out of the hotel. It was the first time since the 1980s that anyone had shined a light so publicly on allegations of malfeasance in the courthouse. A random act of violence in the city had always felt possible at night. Now Thompson felt exposed in the daytime.

After Thompson filed the recusal motion in the courthouse, he met with Sheriff Lonnie Hannah, whose office was on the second floor, like the judge's. Hannah, who was allied with the Chafins and no friend of Thornsbury's, took Thompson's concerns seriously. He didn't have probable cause or the manpower to post a deputy at the Mountaineer. But the hotel wasn't the safest place in the world for Thompson or his staff to be at the moment. Ominously, Hannah said he couldn't protect them from the state police. "You never know what people will do. You don't know," he said. "People are mad. Everybody's tense and upset."

Getzen and Mathis both planned to stay in town at their rented house. Wussow and Ellsworth had already decided to leave. Before they left, Thompson mapped out a plan. He said he wanted Wussow and Ellsworth to call all the clients once they got to her parents' house.

"You got to explain to them that Van and I have lost faith in the judge," Thompson said, as they sat around his desk in room 409. He said they needed to reassure people. They didn't know for sure if the judge was corrupt. But there was an appearance of impropriety. "It's absolutely necessary, because the clients are going to be upset. Some of them might be mad at us, because the judge is popular. Some of them might be scared. We've got to take care of that."

"I think you'd be crazy to stay," Wussow said.

What the clients needed, Ellsworth said, was for Thompson to be safe and coherent and alive. She urged him to get away from Williamson, though she knew it wouldn't be easy. "You don't even have a car that works," she said.

They all laughed at the absurdity of Thompson's position. His current car, his mother's old Crown Vic, which he'd nicknamed the Vada Vada in her honor, was at a mechanic's on West Second Avenue. It was fixed, but Thompson couldn't pay the bill.

Ellsworth asked Thompson if he felt naive, given his past admiration for the judge.

"He's the best judge I've ever practiced in front of until this came up," Thompson said. Then he added, "I don't feel naive. I feel like these conflicts were hidden from us."

A train passed through the city, but none of them heard the whistle anymore.

"This means we're not going to have this place," Thompson said. A sadness hit him as he realized they'd have to find a way to move the entire operation to Charleston. It wouldn't only mean losing the office. It felt like the end of an era for them in Mingo County.

Thompson decided to pack up and leave too, but he couldn't shake the feeling that he was abandoning Ernie and Carmelita, Larry and B.I., and hundreds of other people still relying on him. When he pulled out of Williamson with the young couple, the afternoon sun was still pouring into the city. They didn't stop for food or gas until they had crossed the Mingo County line.

CHAPTER 25

Two days later, Judge Thornsbury sent his response to the justices in Charleston, arguing against his removal from the case. He said that he had presided over hundreds of cases involving Massey in the past thirteen years and that he had no relationship with the company that would require his recusal. He denied that he had spoken to Jackson Kelly about Beckett's appointment, and he expressed "extreme confidence" in the doctor: he had known him for many years and he had an excellent reputation in the community, had the facilities to handle the medical testing, and was the only area physician with electronic charting capabilities. The judge said he himself would have derived no economic benefit from Beckett's appointment. In any case, Beckett had turned down the opportunity, so the issue was moot.

Thornsbury expressed surprise at the claim that he had lunched with Don Blankenship. "If there was any type of actual close personal relationship between this Court and Mr. Blankenship, there would be ample evidence of the same, not a flimsy, false affidavit from a questionable individual," he wrote. He attached affidavits from an owner of Starters and two waitresses, one of whom served Blankenship that day, stating that he had dined separately from Blankenship. He attached another affidavit from Eugene Crum, the chief magistrate, who sat with the judge that day two tables away from Blankenship.

If Thompson was unhappy about the limits on the Blankenship deposition, he could appeal the judge's ruling. In short, Judge Thornsbury denied having any bias in the case, and he didn't plan to step aside. "The easiest course might be to voluntarily recuse given the present environment and to avoid the judicial responsibilities attendant with a very contentious matter, but it is not the right course, nor is it fair to any of the parties in this case," he wrote.

In his own response filed the same day, Stickler said Thompson's motion was a "thinly veiled" attempt to recover his fee for the medical monitoring settlement. Stickler denied that Jackson Kelly had had any improper communications with the judge regarding Beckett's appointment. Massey wanted a local physician to administer the plan, and Beckett was the obvious choice. Stickler also disputed Thompson's version of the clerk whiting out filings. He said Thompson had ripped up a document and behaved inappropriately and abusively toward the staff, without providing any more specifics. Stickler quoted Thompson saying in open court in January that he wanted Thornsbury to remain on the case. Thompson had said: "I'll do whatever I have to do not to lose you, the courtroom, and the jury, okay?"

"For all the foregoing reasons, defendants respectfully request that the hyperbole and drama of plaintiffs' motion be ignored and the plaintiffs' motion to disqualify be denied," Stickler concluded.

It was true that Thompson had said he wanted the judge to remain on the case earlier that year. But to his mind, no one had yet explained why the judge had spoken to Beckett and the bank before Jackson Kelly had even proposed them. He still felt that something had changed that spring, something that had turned the judge against him.

Ten days after "the exodus" from Williamson, as Thompson called it, he was in New Orleans. Just making it home had been a strange trip. After driving to Charleston, he had stayed at a hotel with Wussow and Ellsworth, who had a functioning credit card. The next morning, Thompson decided to go to his old friend John Alderman's house in a neighborhood overlooking the city. Alderman had said years earlier that if Thompson ever got in trouble there was an old car in his backyard that he could use. Ellsworth drove him there, and sure enough an old green Cadillac was parked in the grass. Thompson found the key, and the car started. As soon as he drove into Charleston to buy gas he was pulled over by a policeman who spotted the expired tags. Thompson had no valid registration, no insurance, and a Louisiana driver's license. Ellsworth pulled up in her own car and talked the policeman out of giving Thompson a ticket. The cop, who initially thought Thompson had stolen the car, let him go.

"You were going back to Mingo, weren't you?" Ellsworth said to Thompson, after she realized what he had been up to. Furious, she forced him to take the Cadillac back and drive with her to Shepherds-town. Wussow decided to go home to North Carolina. Getzen stayed back in Williamson, trying to find another way to recuse the judge.

When Thompson met Ellsworth's parents, he wondered what they must think of their daughter's employer, a lawyer who was broke and had been forced to flee his office in a hotel. Kathleen wasn't thrilled about the situation either. Her husband was stuck in Shepherdstown, in the eastern panhandle of West Virginia, staying with a young woman and her parents. Stuart Smith called to bail Thompson out once again and offered to buy him a plane ticket to wherever he needed to go.

Thompson flew to Huntington, West Virginia, where his brother-in-law picked him up, and he spent a few days with Kathleen and Kelsey in Gallipolis. For the third time in five years, he had no money and no immediate prospect of getting any.

Thompson made it home to New Orleans on Stuart Smith's dime, and he got one more tip. His client Raymond Fitch called and said that Thornsbury had once represented Rawl Sales in the 1980s in a case about blasting damage to Fitch's house. Fitch said he thought Thompson should know, since he was looking into Thornsbury's past. Getzen found the case file in the Mingo County Courthouse. In 1985, Fitch had alleged that Rawl Sales allowed "an unlicensed operator to set off massive blasts . . . which impacted me and my property." The lawyer representing Rawl Sales at the time was Michael Thornsbury.

The 1985 case was directly relevant because Thompson had argued that blasting had worsened the slurry contamination. In addition, Don Blankenship became president of Rawl Sales in May 1984, so Thornsbury had previously had a professional relationship with Massey's current CEO. Thompson started drafting a new motion, arguing that Thornsbury's involvement in the 1985 case should disqualify him.

Before he could file the motion, the acting chief justice of the state Supreme Court, Robin Davis, issued her ruling on Thompson's first recusal motion. She denied it: Thornsbury would remain on the case. She did, however, order Thornsbury to hold an evidentiary hearing into his appointment of Community Trust Bank.

Hours later, Thompson still hadn't filed his supplemental motion. But Thornsbury faxed a letter to the state Supreme Court citing his involvement in the 1985 Fitch lawsuit and saying it had "absolutely no relevance" to the water case but that he wanted to make the disclosure "out of an abundance of caution." Evidently someone had told the judge that Getzen had copied the case file. Any lingering doubts Thompson had that the judge kept a close watch on everything inside the courthouse disappeared.

It was a busy day for filings. Thompson sent his supplemental motion to the justices in Charleston. Thornsbury, meanwhile, issued an order in Williamson, saying he had "no intention of appointing Community Trust Bank" and directing Thompson and Jackson Kelly to be prepared to present alternative trust administrators in his courtroom at the hearing on August 4.

Thompson came back to Williamson ahead of the hearing. He avoided Starters now and barely left the hotel for the next several days. When he did go out, he had a tight feeling in his stomach. He received what he considered a "credible threat" from a trusted client in another case, who told him "they" were going to beat him with a tire iron until he couldn't talk right.

On August 4, with all the lawyers in the case present, Judge Thornsbury defined the scope of the evidentiary hearing he had been ordered to hold: to examine the appointment of Community Trust Bank and the setting of fees for the medical monitoring trust. Despite the tension in the courtroom, the hearing had an element of farce from the beginning. The judge, after all, was holding a hearing examining his own behavior. At one point, he asked Stickler how the bank was chosen: "Are you aware, as an officer of this court, whether or not this court, i.e., me, was aware of any of those negotiations?"

"No," Stickler said. "The court was not involved in any of that."

Stickler said he had filled in the blanks on the trust document himself but had never considered the fees that would be paid to the bank or to the trust administrator. A bank official testified that he had no idea how the bank was named on the document, and Beckett wasn't available to testify. The judge admitted he had made quick rulings but said he hadn't talked to Jackson Kelly ahead of time. Everyone seemed to suggest there had been no discussions behind the scenes. But Thompson remained unconvinced.

What Thompson didn't know at the time was that Beckett was

in business with Thornsbury because the judge and Jarrod Fletcher had bought out Beckett's three original partners. In fact, Beckett was unhappy with the judge as a partner because he wouldn't provide tax information Beckett needed to refinance the debt he held on his real estate holdings. Beckett recalled later that he had tried to steer clear of the feud between Thornsbury and the Chafins, calling politics in Mingo County "a contact sport." He later became friends with Eric Mathis, and supported his sustainability projects by putting solar panels on the roof of the health clinic in Williamson. "I got kind of raked over the coals by Kevin Thompson," Beckett said. "The only benefit I got from the judge was hanging on to a lot of debt."

At the hearing, Bunch told Judge Thornsbury they could have avoided many of the issues if the judge had disclosed his relationships with Beckett and the bank. "We ferreted out that information. The issue is nondisclosure. The issue is not whether we could upset the applecart," Bunch said. "The issue is whether the applecart should have existed in the first place."

On August 19, 2009, Justice Davis, the acting chief of the state Supreme Court, issued an order recusing Judge Thornsbury from the case.

The order hit Thompson's inbox before noon, and soon news outlets around the state carried the story. She cited the 1985 case: "Given the temporal and geographic relationship between the prior matter and the allegation and defenses in the current litigation, Canon 3E(1) provides that a judge shall be disqualified in a proceeding in which the judge's impartiality might reasonably be questioned, and Canon 2, which requires that the judiciary shall seek to avoid even an appearance of impropriety, are both applicable," Justice Davis wrote. She assigned the case to Judge Thomas C. Evans, from Jackson County.

There was a brief celebration in the Treehouse. It was as though the air in the office had been swept clean. Wussow skipped down East Second Avenue when he learned the news. It was the happiest Thompson had ever seen him. But the elation was short-lived. Thompson knew it was time to pull up stakes and leave Williamson. With the case now in limbo, and no telling how long it would take a new judge to get up to speed on five years' worth of arguments and evidence, let alone set a trial date, there was no reason for him to stay in Mingo County.

PART V

THE ADMIRAL'S DEN

SEPTEMBER 2009–SEPTEMBER 2011

CHAPTER 26

In September 2009, Blankenship helped organize a pro-coal Labor Day rally on a former mountaintop removal mine in Holden, thirty minutes north of Williamson. The "Friends of America" event drew an estimated seventy-five thousand people. Ted Nugent emceed from a full-size concert stage erected on the rocky ground. Between sets by Hank Williams Jr., Taylor Made, and Halfway to Hazard, Blankenship, Sean Hannity of Fox News, and others railed against President Barack Obama's coal policies. "I want to thank everybody for inviting me here today," Blankenship told the crowd. "It only cost me about a million dollars or so."

He had dressed for the occasion in an American flag shirt and a matching Stars and Stripes cap. He told the crowd that America's CEOs, many of whom he knew from the US Chamber of Commerce and the National Mining Association, harbored warped views on climate change, illegal immigration, government spending, and energy policy. "These guys think they're geniuses, and they brag about making liquid energy from corn," Blankenship said. "They don't know that in these hills we've been doing that for over a hundred years, and we call it moonshine." The line, his best of the day, drew laughter and enthusiastic flag-waving.

Yet Blankenship was an awkward public speaker. It was tough, it seemed, to rouse his voice to the volume or enthusiasm of a politician giving a stump speech. Blankenship was never in his life going to deliver a barn burner like Cecil Roberts, president of the mine workers' union, regularly did. But to the crowd, he was still the face of coal, an industry leader who created coal-mining jobs and told it like it was. Blankenship coined the term "reg-cession" and argued that the Obama administration's overzealous regulation was endangering the American middle class. China was stealing US manufacturing jobs, and the promise of green jobs was a fairy tale. He told the people gathered on the former mine that climate change was "pure make-believe," and he said environmentalists were job killers: "Next in line trying to give your jobs away are the easy-to-recognize environmental nuts. They're easy to recognize because they're the ones chained to your equipment or hanging in trees." Blankenship said regulators sought power over coal miners, instead of protecting them. "As someone who has overseen the mining of more coal than anyone else in the history of Central Appalachia, I know that the safety and health of coal miners is my most important job," he said. "The very idea that they care more about coal-miner safety than we do is as silly as global warming."

The crowd cheered. As it turned out, it was the last time he would be so welcomed by so many families of miners.

Meanwhile, Thompson had retreated to New Orleans. He went with Kathleen to the House of Blues in the French Quarter, where Stuart Smith had hired the B-52s for his fiftieth birthday party. Smith strutted onstage with the band during "Rock Lobster," and for a few hours, it felt like old times. "Stuart was fucked-up," Thompson said. "It was great."

But while the Rawl lawsuit was on hold, Thompson and Dave Barney spent most of their time trying to bring in money from small personal-injury cases. Most of their clients had extraordinary luck. One miner backed a rock truck over a berm and tumbled down a hillside. He was thrown from the cab, and witnesses thought he had been killed. But the empty bed of the truck landed on him, protecting him from being crushed, and he escaped with a few scratches. A father and son were literally blown up in a house after methane from a natural gas fracking site collected under their home. They too had only minor injuries, even though their house was destroyed. A third client totaled a car, and managed to only chip a tooth. Thompson pretended to rue this good fortune, and the small damages he and Barney collected. "If you know us, by God, you will miraculously survive every accident," Thompson joked.

Once again, he was scraping bottom financially. On February 5, 2010, a friend emailed to ask if he wanted to join another water contamination case in West Virginia. "I'm sort of dead now, dude. I'm not sure if I'll be around at all anymore," Thompson wrote back. "These cases have just strung me out way too far beyond my means. I've literally been living on leftovers from Nick, Steve, and Melissa."

Three days later, Thompson learned that Don Dillon's wife, Mary, had died, and the entire weight of the case came back to him. He and Ellsworth drove to Rawl for the funeral.

Mary Dillon was seventy-five when she died. The immediate cause of death was sudden cardiac arrhythmia, but she had suffered from chronic kidney problems and had been diagnosed with a liver disorder in 2004. She had suffered for years with skin rashes and gallstones; her gallbladder had been removed. In the final weeks of her life, her organs had finally failed as her body wasted away. She had been too weak to climb the stairs at their house in Rawl in the weeks before she died, and she was so light that Don Dillon, who was himself seventy-three, would carry her up and down the stairs and help her get dressed.

Don always believed he was the healthier of the two because he had spent thirty years away from home working in the mines, even showering at the mine's bathhouse. Mary had been exposed to the house's water whenever she made a pot of coffee, drank a glass of water, or took a shower. One sample from the couple's well had found high levels of iron, manganese, and aluminum.

The funeral was held at the Baptist church on the Kentucky side of the Tug Fork across from Merrimac. Before he was born again, Dillon used to drop his wife there on Sunday mornings and then go play cards up the road at a house not far from a McCoy family cemetery where an infant born to a McCoy and a Hatfield in 1881 was said to be buried.

Several other clients had passed away since the case started, but for some reason, Mary Dillon's funeral haunted Thompson the most, and he dreamed about it again and again. Every time, he felt the same overwhelming sadness. As soon as he walked through the doors of the church, everyone turned toward him. The memory filled him with dread, but there was another intangible feeling in the dream, which might have been the reason for its return. Something his unconscious mind wanted him to know. Thompson, who normally wanted to be in the spotlight, recoiled at having everyone's attention focused on him in the simple church with the light streaming in. He didn't want to be a distraction from the funeral for Mary Dillon. Or maybe it was something he wasn't willing to admit in his waking life: that their eyes were asking more of him than he could deliver.

Then, on April 5, 2010, Massey's Upper Big Branch Mine exploded. Initial news reports of the accident flashed across televisions in West

Virginia that afternoon. Just over two hundred miners worked at UBB, and people across the southern half of the state were soon trying to account for miners they knew. Ambulances parked on the shoulder of Route 3, south of Whitesville, their red lights sweeping the hills. By nightfall, dozens of news vans lined the road in front of Marsh Fork Elementary School, the same school where Thompson was fighting for families who complained that their children were at risk from Massey's nearby coal silo.

The accident occurred just after 3 p.m. on the Monday after Easter, as miners on one shift were leaving the mine and others were entering. At the portal, a rectangular entryway, miners felt a breeze coming from the bowels of the mountain. It gathered strength until the men had difficulty standing. With the force of a hurricane, the wind blew dust, buckets, and debris out of the mine. Once it died down, the president of Performance Coal Company, the Massey subsidiary that operated the mine, and three other managers and an emergency medical technician took a low-slung vehicle called a mantrip into the darkness, in violation of multiple mine-safety protocols. They had meters to measure explosive gas levels but no mine-rescue equipment. They first saw the headlamp of a man, the light shining through the dust suspended in the air. He said there had been an explosion and that he had tried to put emergency oxygen masks on a crew of men. All the men had pulses except for one when he had been forced to leave them to save himself. The Massey officials walked up to a mantrip with seven miners who were unresponsive. An eighth man was laboring for air. The officials brought them out of the mine, while the president and another manager walked farther in. Rescue crews trained to enter mines that might collapse or explode arrived on the scene and began their meticulous search for survivors.

Massey initially reported seven dead and nineteen missing at 8:10 p.m. By 1:40 a.m. on Tuesday, it said twenty-five miners were dead and four were missing. Later that day, a black helicopter landed on the school's ball field. Blankenship stepped out and was swarmed by reporters as he made his way to a mine building that had become a gathering place for the families of the miners, including those who weren't yet accounted for. Inside, angry relatives yelled at Blankenship. While loved ones waited for news from the mine-rescue teams, Governor Joe

Manchin led news briefings at the elementary school beside officials with the Mine Safety and Health Administration.

The coal-dust explosion, which had swept through more than two miles of underground tunnels, was among the most destructive in the history of coal mining in the United States. On the fourth full day of searching, as midnight approached, rescuers found the last miner under debris. Manchin stood at a podium and announced that there were no survivors. The death toll stood at twenty-nine, making it the worst US coal-mining disaster in forty years, since thirty-eight miners were killed in an underground explosion in Hyden, Kentucky, in 1970. It took another four days to bring out all the bodies, some of which had to be carried a mile and a half underground. The days and nights of waiting were over, and the news trucks left Route 3 for somewhere else. The funerals were just beginning, as was a reckoning that would take years to unfold.

As Ken Ward Jr. at the *Charleston Gazette* noted, regulators had ordered all or parts of the Upper Big Branch Mine to shut more than sixty times in 2009 and 2010, and had repeatedly found that highly combustible coal dust in the mine had been allowed to accumulate. Reporters also asked MSHA why it had allowed a mine with such serious problems to keep operating. Massey defended the company's safety record, and Blankenship argued that just before the accident, MSHA forced the company to use a ventilation plan that cut in half the volume of fresh air pumped through the mine. A week after the accident, when federal and state investigations had barely begun, President Barack Obama called the accident "a failure, first and foremost, of management." The statement absolved MSHA of responsibility, even though the agency had an inspector at the mine every day of the year, including the day of the accident. The president of the United States had implicated Blankenship himself.

Two days after the accident, Massey's board had convened by phone and agreed it was unlikely that any of the miners had survived. On the call, Blankenship and the board decided to offer $3 million to each family to head off a wave of litigation and wrongful death claims that hadn't even been brought yet.

Soon Blankenship was under sustained and increasingly personal attack. In May, the UMWA held a rally of several hundred miners and retirees outside Massey's annual stockholders' meeting in Richmond, Virginia. The union's president, Cecil Roberts, with his neatly trimmed gray goatee, shouted through a bullhorn, and, straining his high-pitched voice to the limit, called Blankenship "an Appalachian Pharaoh!" and said he should be in prison. A few days later, members of the US House of Representatives held a hearing in Beckley, West Virginia, and miners and family members testified. One miner who got knocked down by the wind that blew through the mine, Stanley "Goose" Stewart, said the section that exploded had been "a ticking time bomb"; it wasn't getting enough fresh air. He blamed Blankenship for defeating the union at the mine, which had led to a culture of fear. Miners knew they'd be "marked men" and fired if they complained about safety problems. Stewart said he wouldn't work underground again. "Been through a lot in thirty-four years, and always stood tall and went back," he said. "I can't go back this time."

That same month, at a US Senate hearing in Washington, Blankenship and Roberts, who had been enemies since the 1985 strike at Rawl Sales, sat three feet from each other. Blankenship expressed sympathy for the miners' families with the same flat affect that he had used when Thompson deposed him a year earlier. He called for an independent investigation, instead of allowing MSHA to investigate a situation it had overseen. As Thompson had done, Senator Robert Byrd asked Blankenship to speak more loudly and clearly into the microphone. With Massey's general counsel, Shane Harvey, and a criminal defense lawyer sitting a few rows behind him, Blankenship said, "Let me state for the record, Massey does not place profits over safety. We never have and we never will. Period."

Blankenship looked tired but was firm in defending himself and Massey. The company's safety record, measured in accidents that required time away from work, was better than the industry average in seventeen of the past nineteen years, he said. He didn't mention that the company had long been accused of encouraging workers to report to work after getting injured, which kept down the accident rate. Just a few days before the explosion, MSHA officials had signed off on a quarterly inspection of the mine and found no outstanding safety conditions, Blankenship said. Others would go on to question MSHA's role in policing the Upper Big Branch, including its apparent failure to fully address earlier releases of natural gas into it. Blankenship would continue to argue that the explosion was fueled by a sudden release of gas from the floor of the mine, and say that MSHA forced the company to use a ventilation plan that cut airflow by half, making it more likely to explode.

At ninety-two years old, Senator Byrd was in failing health. Participating in the hearing seemed to require all of his remaining strength. Hunched toward his microphone, he was determined to hold Blankenship to account. Twice he asked Blankenship if he was listening. He said he was concerned about Massey's safety record, spelling it for emphasis, R-E-C-O-R-D. Then he spoke a language Blankenship could understand. Between 1995 and 2006, Senator Byrd said, Massey mines had a total of 1,998 injuries and 24 deaths. Massey mines were cited for 31,000 violations. Over that decade, on average, a Massey miner was injured every other day and there were 10 safety violations every day. "This is a clear record. A blatant—B-L-A-T-A-N-T—blatant disregard for the welfare and the safety of Massey miners. Shame." The final word hung in the high-ceilinged subcommittee chamber.

"Mr. Blankenship, why, why, why so many fatalities at Massey mines?" Senator Byrd asked. "I helped to write the laws, in 1969, 1977, and 2006, to improve safety in our coal mines. The responsibility to comply with those laws is yours, Mr. Blankenship."

The Senate hearing focused on safety at Massey and the culture Blankenship had created there. Left unsaid were the outside forces weighing on the company and the coal industry, especially in West Virginia, where cost-effective coal was disappearing after more than a century of mining. The Upper Big Branch Mine had been one of Massey's most profitable. In 2009, miners there had churned out 1.2 million tons of high-quality steelmaking coal for the US and export markets. The mine had a longwall machine, the industry's most productive piece of equipment, cutting through the coal seam in thousand-foot-wide swaths. The machine operated during two 10-hour shifts per day, seven days a week, producing $2 million worth of coal every day. Every hour it had to be shut down for maintenance at Upper Big Branch cost Massey about $100,000.

On the day of the accident, the machine had been down from about

11 a.m. to 1:30 p.m. MSHA investigators would discover that the long-wall machine had been operating with seven water spray nozzles missing and that it had been cutting through sandstone, which generates sparks. A crew of miners had shut the machine at 3 p.m. when a pocket of methane gas had ignited. The gas burned for some two minutes in a cloud of flame, and apparently when the miners realized the ignition couldn't be controlled they started to run. According to MSHA's findings, a second pocket of gas exploded before touching off loose coal dust the company had allowed to accumulate, creating a massive, cascading explosion that swept through the mine.

At the hearing, Senator Byrd noted that in addition to civil investigations by state and federal regulators, there was a criminal investigation into the accident. "Perhaps these will provide some solace to the families who are looking for accountability," he said. The senator died a little over a month later, on June 28. But his words would prove to be prophetic.

Thompson was in Morgantown in a mediation for another, much smaller water contamination case when he learned about Upper Big Branch. The depth of the tragedy was apparent to him immediately. He had been studying the ravages of coal for years. Since 1900, more than one hundred thousand miners had been killed in the United States, many in the mines of West Virginia. Nearly seventy thousand miners had died since 1970 from coal workers' pneumoconiosis, their lungs blackened and scarred from breathing coal dust. Almost all of the families that Thompson represented in and around Rawl had a close tie to coal. Some had worked in the mines or hauled coal. Or they had a father, brother, or other close relative who had done so.

Days later, when Thompson was back in Williamson, he could feel how the shock of the disaster had reached the community. Those who already disliked Blankenship were outraged by another example of his ruthlessness, while others didn't believe he was to blame and maintained that the company as a whole wasn't like that. There was enough anger and heartbreak among Blankenship's neighbors living along Route 49 that someone delivered a box of rattlesnakes to his house in Sprigg and left it in the sun so the snakes would be angry when he opened the package. At least, that was the story that passed through the community. Blankenship was rumored to be getting death threats just as he had during the 1985 strike and that out of concern for his safety, he was moving between the Sprigg house and the Massey property on the Kentucky side of the river.

The accident saturated the news in West Virginia for weeks. In Thompson's view, the entire state was in "a Blankenship frenzy." He thought the Rawl case would be a historic rebuke, not just to Blankenship but to the entire coal industry in the state. "Every time someone flips on their lights, they need to know that that electricity is paid for in someone's blood, communities like Rawl, or the twenty-nine Upper Big Branch miners," Thompson said later, reflecting on the connection between his case and the mine disaster.

Room 409 was just as Thompson had left it the prior year. The aerial photograph of Rawl with tabs marking his clients' homes was still tacked to the wall behind his desk, and on the other walls were the *Dark Side of the Moon* poster, Stickler as Chef Boyardee, and a poster for the Rough-N-Rowdy Brawl, a bare-fisted boxing match held at the field house. Hundreds of client files and binders filled the second room. The wooden sign that said "REVIVAL NOW IN PROGRESS" still hung above a doorway. But Thompson's world had been in flux since the beginning of 2010. Wussow had recently moved to New Orleans to go to law school; he and Ellsworth had broken up. She had moved into an apartment in Charleston. Getzen was still living in a house with Mathis and helping him run a sustainability nonprofit he had founded in Williamson called the JOBS Project. All four kept working for Thompson in varying capacities.

In May, Thompson was agonizing over whether to file a motion to disqualify the new judge assigned to the case. He liked Judge Evans, but the judge had disclosed that when his daughter Talia Markham had won the Miss West Virginia pageant, Massey had helped sponsor the competition and contributed to a children's charity she was involved with. It was just one more event that Massey sponsored, but now it didn't look good. "It's like a whole bunch of good shit that they've tainted," Thompson said. "There should be nothing wrong with any of it. But it is an appearance of impropriety." He informed the judge in a letter that several of his clients weren't comfortable with him presiding over the case. The judge then recused himself.

Although he knew it was for the best, Thompson was sorry to see Judge Evans go. In addition to spending hundreds of hours reading the Rawl case file, the judge had started applying a new term—"sentinel symptoms"—to the rashes, diarrhea, and kidney stones that many people had. The judge's rationale was that these milder symptoms could precede more serious ones like kidney failure and cancer, according to Thompson. He kicked himself for not thinking of the idea, which gave new weight to the lesser health issues, and he started using the term himself.

The state Supreme Court then handed the Rawl case to five judges from the state's Mass Litigation Panel, and Thompson waited for a first hearing to be announced. The court typically appointed panels of judges to handle sprawling asbestos, tobacco, and flood cases. This was the best hope yet that the Rawl case would finally make it to trial.

By summer, Thompson, still running low on money, got another lifeline from Bruce Stanley, the Pittsburgh attorney who had represented Hugh Caperton, the coal operator who said Massey drove him out of business when it canceled a contract, and the widows of the two miners killed in the 2006 Aracoma mine accident. Stanley persuaded his partners at Reed Smith LLP to invest more than two hundred thousand dollars in the Rawl case. Adding another law firm diluted Thompson's control and his financial stake. But he felt he had no choice. As soon as Stanley came on board, Thompson sent a check for twenty-five thousand dollars to a bank to keep his house in New Orleans out of foreclosure.

Thompson was happy to have help from Stanley, one of the few lawyers who had beaten Massey in court more than once. Normally polite and almost deferential, Stanley would become red-faced talking about Blankenship. Stanley had grown up in Mingo County in Breeden, a thirty-mile drive north of Williamson, and like Blankenship, he had known the poverty of coal camps and his share of tough characters. His fight with Blankenship and Massey was personal in a way that it wasn't for Thompson.

Now Thompson wanted to depose Blankenship a second time, with Stanley there. He knew Stanley was possibly one of the few people Blankenship feared or, at least, respected as a combatant. Stanley had gotten Blankenship on the witness stand in November 2008 during the Aracoma trial. After the CEO's weak performance, Massey's board had settled the case before a jury could return a verdict, and the company paid each of the widows an undisclosed sum in the seven figures. During the earlier Caperton trial, lightning struck the courthouse while Stanley was asking Blankenship about the bonuses he had gotten while he urged managers to cut costs and keep the coal flowing. A power surge hit the court reporter's computer, and twenty-five minutes of Stanley's cross-examination of Blankenship were permanently lost from the record. At the time, Blankenship turned to the jury and quipped, "Must have been all those numbers he was asking about."

"Bruce controls the weather," Thompson joked when he told the story. But it was also a story about Blankenship's arrogance and how to show a jury that the company's board had lavished pay and benefits on their CEO, even as he risked miners' lives.

The Mass Litigation Panel brought a new focus to the case. After a year's hiatus, there was a sense among Thompson and his partners that they were all in the fourth quarter, and the clock was running down. Thompson wanted the ball so he could make the big play to end the game.

On August 20, 2010, a full year after Judge Thornsbury was removed from the case, Thompson was sitting at a counsel table in the Ohio County circuit court in Wheeling, West Virginia, in the northern panhandle between Ohio and Pennsylvania. Wheeling's own 1960s-era courthouse was just as drab as Williamson's. It had old water fountains in the hallways and scuffed beige walls. It was the new home of the case, where James P. Mazzone, the county's district court judge, would lead the panel of judges. Sitting next to Thompson were Bunch, Barney, and Stanley.

At the other counsel table, Stickler and Sebok sat near the attorneys for Massey who were still suing its insurers for coverage. The insurance company lawyers had shown up en masse again: more than fifty filled most of the courtroom. Some insurers were continuing to challenge their need to provide coverage under clauses in Massey policies that said pollution wasn't covered. The insurers didn't even know yet the full extent of Massey's insurance coverage; they were, as one lawyer put it, "a loose confederation of tribes."

Mazzone sat on a dais in the middle of the other black-robed judges who had traveled from around the state. Thompson picked out their most noticeable characteristics and, by the end of the day, had a shorthand to describe each of them. Mazzone had heavy-lidded eyes, and Thompson joked that he could never tell if the judge was falling asleep. To Mazzone's left, Judge John A. Hutchison had a mustache and a handsome, weathered face; Thompson called him "Hutch" in a way that made him seem like he'd stepped out of a western. Judge Jay M. Hoke, on the other side of Mazzone, had a squinting smile and a brush-like mustache that hung over his mouth. Thompson referred to him as "David Crosby." These three judges were preparing to oversee the trial.

The two judges sitting at either end of the dais would try to mediate a settlement. Judge Alan D. Moats said he and Judge Derek C. Swope were going to try to avoid a complicated trial if they could. Moats had close-cropped white hair and the bearing of a country doctor, gentle but unflinching. Judge Swope, with big-lensed glasses, called himself "just an old plaintiff's lawyer" who had mediated car-wreck cases. He offered unvarnished observations and asked pointedly why a settlement hadn't already been reached. Moats was the good cop to Swope's bad cop. Thompson packaged them together as "Moats and Swope," as if they were partners in their own law firm.

In truth, Thompson respected all the judges. It was a relief to have five judicial minds engaged in a case they clearly thought was important to the state of West Virginia. The panel's first act was to announce that they were going to rule against 180 motions Jackson Kelly had filed to dismiss people from the case who hadn't shown up to the massive settlement conference day in April 2009. There were still hundreds of motions pending. But it was time for the people of Rawl, Lick Creek, Merrimac, and Sprigg to have their day in court.

Thompson said there were 545 people headed to trial, and 748 covered by the medical monitoring settlement, which was still in dispute. Of the 545, there were 26 people with serious medical conditions: brain cancers and kidney transplants and liver failures. Another 519 had sentinel symptoms, which Thompson now described to the judges: "Strange rashes; consistent, explosive, continuous diarrhea for years on end; and then kidney stones." (Stickler said his staff thought there were 556 people going to trial, and Thompson conceded that Jackson Kelly was probably right.)

Thompson wanted the judges to know that his team, unlike Jackson Kelly's, had been working on the case all year, keeping up with clients, though some were hard to find. "Many of them don't have phones. They're spread throughout eastern Kentucky and southern West Virginia and we hunt them down. One by one they move, they do a lot of couch surfing, and we find them." Thompson wanted to convey the difficult conditions some of his clients had been living in while the case dragged on for years.

Offering his own summary, Stickler reached for his favorite metaphor: "This is like a train that left the station and at every crossing people were added in, cases were added in, theories were added in."

The panel of judges set a trial date for August 1, 2011, nearly a full year away. It was still an ambitious timeline. The judges had twenty-six boxes, each containing thousands of documents. "I know it's taken some turns along the way, but that's why we commit to you, we are going to do what it takes to resolve these things sooner rather than later," Judge Moats said.

Meanwhile, Moats and Swope set a mediation date for November 15. All insurance carriers needed to send someone with the authority to write a check, Stickler needed to have authority to write a check, and Thompson needed to have all of his clients there. The location hadn't been decided yet.

Judge Moats said it wasn't a matter of trying. "There is no doing your best," he said. "You either do, or you don't." Stickler said it sounded like a line from *Star Wars*.

"Yoda," Judge Moats said. "You're a Yoda fan."

"Yeah, I'm a Yoda fan," Stickler said. "I know that. It's thrown at me a lot, I can tell you that, by my coworkers."

"Well, I'm glad you didn't call me Darth Vader," Moats said.

"I did not," Stickler said. "The black robe is— We're getting there, Judge."

"We can't choke them like that," Judge Moats said, referring to Darth Vader's ability to choke people using only the power of the dark side.

"That's right," Stickler said. "We don't have that power."

CHAPTER 27

On November 14, the day before the mediation, Thompson was sitting at his desk in the Treehouse. Bluegrass played from a radio. It was a little after 6 p.m. and the office was crowded with people. Bunch had recently driven in from Chattanooga. Getzen was on the phone at his desk, and Ellsworth was typing at her laptop. Two young activists Thompson had asked for help, Bobby Mitchell and Katie Lautar, floated in and out of the office. Stuart Smith had also sent an associate from his firm named Sean Cassidy to help Thompson and keep an eye on his investment. While Cassidy leaned back in a chair casually observing the Treehouse in action, he and Thompson commiserated about working for Smith.

Once again, the prospect of settling the Rawl case stirred mixed emotions in Thompson. But he also relished being a field general on the eve of a major deployment. "We're invading the capital," he said.

Over the past week, Thompson had spent entire days meeting with people again to go over their claims, just as he had before the marathon settlement day in 2009. By 9 a.m., he had to have all of his clients at the civic center in Charleston. This time, the judges had given him weeks to make travel arrangements and get settlement authority documents signed by everyone.

Thompson dialed people who had so far refused to give him a final figure they'd be willing to settle their case for. Neither he nor Bunch wanted a settlement to be held up by unreasonably high demands. He wasn't getting through to anyone. "Hm. I wonder why the refusals are the most likely not to answer the phone," he said. He reached B.I. and it was a short conversation. When Thompson put the phone down he smiled, but it was more of a wince. To a reporter, B.I. said he thought the entire case would be worth $1 billion at trial, partly because there were so many people involved.

As people moved through the narrow office, Thompson said he thought someone had tried to break into room 409 recently. There were scratches around the keyhole, and all of their keys felt different in the lock. Surveying the papers piled throughout the office, he said, "They probably came in, said, 'Oh my God,' and left."

Ellsworth handed Thompson a stack of papers she had just printed that listed the major claims for the 556 clients still in the case.

"Whoa! You did it!" he said.

Ellsworth rattled off a checklist of things they still needed to do that night. "I'm bringing the consent binder. Blank forms. Box of supplies. A sign-in sheet. What they need to ask people. Info cards. Name tags," she said.

"Summary graphics binder," Thompson said, adding to the list. "Star plaintiffs. Ernie Brown. Power of attorney. Consent and residency binders. Want to bring the printer? It's too important. If something happened to it, we'd be fucked."

Bunch came back into the room, and Thompson said, "We're going over the final checklist right now. We got lanyards. I think we've got everything. Damn, we're usually not at this place until three or four in the morning. We better add some stuff. We better redo something. We're way ahead of schedule."

Over dinner at El Azul, a Mexican restaurant across the border in Kentucky, Thompson plotted the next day's assault on Charleston. He insisted that the buses loaded with clients should pull up to the civic center so that news cameras stationed there could see the people stepping off while holding jars of black and rust-colored water from their wells, which he also wanted the two judges to see. When Thompson said the buses might have to drive the wrong way down the street, if necessary, to get the right look, everyone laughed. "We can't have people coming around the bus. It's a fucked-up shot," he said, to more laughter.

After dinner, everyone went back to the Mountaineer, sat on a few chairs and the bed in Thompson's room, and passed around beers.

"It's just awful," Thompson said. "In August, we began to see that the people were beginning to get sicker faster . . . their digestive organs are just failing in lockstep. There's the gallbladder, the pancreas, the liver, the kidney. Just *bam-bam-bam*. There's one young guy, the doctor told him he didn't expect him to live ten years. There's another guy about the same age, his body failed and he ended up in Pikeville for ten days. If you look at the report, you'll see. What that report doesn't include are these general stomach problems. There's dozens, if not hundreds, of those."

Getzen turned off the lights except for a single lamp, so Katie Lautar could read a poem describing what it was like to interview people in Rawl about their health. For five minutes, everyone listened to Lautar fill the darkness with her impressions about the people in the hollows a few miles away. "Today's calls yielded barren women, babies with cancers, and their sons, their sons have arsenic in their blood," she read. "On this day, they are counted in the cost of how coal keeps the lights on."

When she had finished, Thompson broke the silence. "I thought that was awesome," he said.

"Damn right," said Bunch.

Thompson said he hoped Judge Moats and Judge Swope would see that real people had suffered, rather than think of them as claims to resolve. It was seven months since Upper Big Branch, when lives had been lost in an instant. Thompson's clients, meanwhile, had been suffering for years, and he believed some would later develop illnesses caused by the water. Massey had offered a $3 million settlement to each of the Upper Big Branch miners' families, but Thompson expected the company to continue to fight the Rawl case.

For a moment, though, he allowed himself to consider what would happen if they negotiated a big settlement the next day. He recalled that when 185 people had settled their claims in 2009, the bars in Williamson filled up the night that people finally got their checks. In a few cases, the celebrations had gotten out of hand with partying. "Good God. If we do hit it out of the park, there'll be another fucking drama," Thompson said.

He told the story of one troubled young man who had decided to settle. In the small room off the courtroom, Judge Thornsbury had suggested that Thompson's client leave town and start over once he got his check. It was a genuinely helpful suggestion, in Thompson's view, and the guy's excitement was palpable. "There was a lot of drama in that room," Thompson said. Over the next few weeks, the young man went to the library and used Google Earth to chart a course to his grandmother's in Virginia. He had to stay off the main roads, because he had lost his driver's license for drunk driving. But he knew someone who had a dirt bike he planned to buy, and he had found gas stations along the way. As the weeks went by, he asked Thompson regularly about when his check would arrive. It was June, but he was worried he wouldn't be able to make the trip once the weather turned cold.

"He had talked to his grandmother. He aspired to a job. He was going to get a job as a grocery bagger. He was telling me this. He said, you know, 'I can bag groceries. I can live at Grammy's. I won't get involved in things.' He was all for it. And he had it all planned out, man. He was going to do it right."

Thompson continued, "By God, he got the money. Fucking had a bunch of parties. Pilled up. And then in one last blaze of glory, he went to Hurley's Drugs. Decided he'd get into business. He bought himself a big prescription a pill doctor gave him and walks outside and sells it. He had a deal. . . . Does not look to his right and did not see a deputy in a cruiser. With lights on it and everything. Not an unmarked car. A deputy who saw the whole transaction. He got out of jail about a month ago."

Here was another life slipping away. Thompson had argued for years that the metals in the water contributed to some clients' problems, like attention deficit disorder and difficulty holding a job. But he also saw the damage done by the pain pills that seemed to be raining down on Williamson. That spring, federal investigators had raided the Mountain Medical Care Center, a notorious pill mill blocks from the Mountaineer. Prosecutors said hundreds of people went to the clinic daily and paid $150 to $450 for pain medication like oxycodone. It had taken in $4.6 million in cash in 2009, an astounding sum in an old coal town on life support. Thompson had seen a line of people waiting for the clinic to open in the morning. Many cars had out-of-state plates. But he knew the pills also ended up in local homes.

The next morning, the sky was still black when everyone left the hotel. Out of the darkness, a Norfolk Southern train pulled around the curve at the end of West Second Avenue, the thunder of its engines echoing off the buildings as its wheels screeched, steel against steel.

At the field house, four white charter buses were waiting. Thompson expected several hundred people. But as the sky lightened and the fog began to break into patches clinging to the hills, only a handful arrived. Bunch and a few others joked nervously. What if no one showed? After days of meetings and phone calls, lining up transportation, and distributing letters to every household, Thompson climbed aboard a half-full bus and told the driver to head for Charleston. "I guess the one question everyone forgot to ask was, Do you need a ride?" Bunch said.

When the bus pulled into the civic center, Thompson was relieved to see hundreds of clients already there. Many had decided to drive up on their own, so they could leave when they wanted. News cameras were also on the scene. The Upper Big Branch disaster had made any Massey-related story major news in the state. Thompson never got his shot of people stepping off the buses. But people had brought water from their wells, as he had asked. Dozens of plastic bottles and mason jars lined the sidewalk, because the court's staff wouldn't permit them inside. The water was rust-colored and gray—just as it had been on Thompson's first visit to Rawl.

A seven-hundred-seat auditorium was more than half-full with residents from Rawl, Lick Creek, Merrimac, and Sprigg. Some were milling around in the hallways, along with lawyers in suits. Babies were crying as people found their way to seats. Families sat together, many dressed casually in jeans. There were middle-age mothers in slacks and neat blouses and scruffy young men wearing camouflage sweatshirts and hats. B.I. and his family sat along one wall; Larry and Brenda Brown, Ernie and Carmelita, Donetta, Don Dillon, Bo Scott, and others who had become like an extended family were scattered throughout the first few rows. Sitting among them were dozens of others who had been less involved in the case but who were also counting on Thompson.

On the stage, Moats and Swope in their black robes sat at a table draped in red fabric. Judge Swope looked out at everyone through the big lenses of his glasses and introduced himself with the easy delivery of a trial lawyer. "I understand we have folks come not just from Mingo County but from out of state. We appreciate you coming in here today," he said. "This is not an attempt to put a hardship on anyone.

But frankly it's the best hope that we have for everyone, for all parties involved, to resolve these matters, all matters, once and for all. That's our hope and our prayer for the session we're going to have here today and as many days as it takes to get this resolved in a way that's satisfactory to everybody."

Judge Moats opened a discussion about the lawsuit in a reassuring tone. "You can watch the grass grow faster than you can experience a lawsuit move forward in many instances," he said. "So when we talk about resolving this as quickly and efficiently as possible, that doesn't mean it can be accomplished overnight. . . . I pledge to you that our Mass Litigation Panel will do everything in our power to resolve this case."

Judge Swope started taking attendance, with people calling out that they were present. Then he was interrupted and announced that there was a special guest. He introduced Chief Justice Robin Davis, who had disqualified Judge Thornsbury a year earlier. She strode to the center of the stage in a blue dress, and the crowd dutifully applauded. A petite woman, she addressed the crowd in a high, formal voice that was jarring after Moats's and Swope's homey cadences. "Our court has worked extremely hard and spent a lot of money and time to hopefully get all of this resolved for the people of the great state of West Virginia," she said. "So on behalf of the court, I thank you, and good luck."

Once the speech was over and attendance was taken, Thompson's clients started gathering around him near the stage. The mediation hadn't begun and he was already sweaty, his tie loose around his collar. Several people asked if Massey was going to agree to a settlement.

"I wouldn't trust Don Blankenship any further than I can throw a bull," Thompson said, before heading into the mediation.

After two and a half hours, Thompson returned to the stage and took the microphone. People were getting restless. When B.I., with a white cap perched on his head, asked from his seat if people had to stay, Thompson said everyone was free to leave. Thompson thought for a moment and then said that if people chose to stay it would help their cause, but they could also go if they needed to. "I love seeing that white hat," he told B.I.

"I can't really tell you anything other than we're staking out positions," Thompson said to everyone. "That's what we have now. Things are progressing."

There was some commotion in the crowd. A woman with a child on her lap was not amused. She said to herself, "He's full of hisself. He's full of malarkey. Malarkey."

Many in the auditorium were fed up. And they had good reason to be, it turned out: the next day, the second of the planned three-day mediation, negotiations ended without a deal. Disagreements over the medical monitoring trust helped keep the two sides apart, and the dozens of insurance companies couldn't agree on how much each was willing to pay. The "loose confederation of tribes" had fallen into dissension. Until the insurers resolved their positions, there was little chance of reaching a settlement.

By the end, Thompson was deflated. But a part of him was glad the process had broken down. He wanted to beat Stickler at trial next August.

There was one more impediment to a deal. The attention of officials at Massey, up to and including Don Blankenship, was still far more focused on the ongoing fallout from the Upper Big Branch explosion.

From his earliest days at Rawl Sales in the 1980s, Blankenship had taken an antagonistic position toward the mine workers' union, the UMWA, and the federal mine-safety agency, MSHA. In the fall of 2010, his old foes threatened to be his undoing at the company.

Though Upper Big Branch was a nonunion mine, the union planted itself at the center of the federal investigation by serving as a "miners' representative" for some workers there. That role, written into federal law, gave the union a seat at the table whenever miners were interviewed about conditions inside the mine.

Pressure had mounted quickly on Blankenship. Massey suffered a loss of $88.7 million for the second quarter, mostly because of the accident. The mine had been one of the company's most profitable, and it was now unlikely to reopen. Within two weeks of the accident, the widow of an Upper Big Branch miner sued the company for wrongful death, and a New York–based trust that owned Massey stock filed a shareholder lawsuit, alleging that Blankenship and other board members were exposing the company to "a substantial threat of monetary liability." In its second-quarter results, the company said it took a $128.9 million one-time charge against earnings related to benefits it expected to pay to families, to the expense for lost equipment, and to the cost of the investigation and litigation. The company also soon faced challenges from other shareholders, including another lawsuit brought by the powerful California State Teachers' Retirement System, which sued Blankenship and the board for financial damage inflicted on the company because of the accident. The lawsuit alleged that Massey had failed to make a series of companywide safety improvements mandated by an agreement reached after the 2006 Aracoma fire.

Shareholders had lost millions of dollars. Massey's stock price had fallen 11 percent the day after the explosion. Through much of July and August, the stock was down more than 40 percent from its pre-accident level. In August, Massey added two board members to focus on the shareholder litigation, diluting Blankenship's power on the board. Yet a company spokesman said Blankenship wasn't considering retiring; he was focused on running the company. After the Aracoma fire, Massey had paid $4.2 million in civil and criminal penalties, on top of the settlement it paid to the two widows Bruce Stanley had represented. In the coming months, it was likely to face far larger civil fines and potential criminal charges.

Three months after the accident, in July, Massey announced that a massive inundation of natural gas had fueled the explosion. Upper Big Branch was known to be a gassy mine, and it had suffered outbursts of methane in 2003 and 2004, according to MSHA's own records. Under Blankenship's theory, the natural gas inundation was either something the company couldn't foresee, or it was something MSHA itself had failed to prevent by not accounting for the earlier outbursts in the ventilation plan it had forced the company to use.

In October, Massey posted a twelve-page letter on its website insisting that MSHA had cut the airflow in the mine by half according to its computer simulations, just days before the mine blew up. "MSHA has not done a very good job of conducting its own investigation. It's as if they really don't want to find out what happened," Blankenship said. "It's MSHA-gate, which basically means cover-up."

As he attempted to shore up his position, it became imperiled from another direction. Blankenship had known for months that another coal company wanted to acquire the weakened Massey. In the days after Upper Big Branch exploded, Alpha Natural Resources' chairman, Mike Quillen, and its CEO, Kevin Crutchfield, called Blankenship several times to offer their support and sympathies. When they tried to buy the company a short while later, Blankenship and Massey's board weren't interested. But Crutchfield hadn't given up. Massey was attractive because it had 1.3 billion tons of reserves of steelmaking coal, more than any US mining company.

The Massey board's lead outside director, Bobby Inman, was growing weary of the fighting that seemed part of Blankenship's DNA. Blankenship didn't help his cause with his antagonistic statements about MSHA. By the time merger talks with Alpha rekindled in August, three other companies had approached Massey about a potential deal, including Wilbur Ross's International Coal Group. Alpha's CEO, Crutchfield, began dealing directly with Inman, who advised him not to worry about Blankenship's unwillingness. "That's my problem," Inman wrote in an email to Crutchfield, "it will be dealt with." Soon Blankenship was complaining that someone inside Massey was feeding Alpha financial information, circumventing his authority.

In October, Massey had settled wrongful death claims with at least eight Upper Big Branch families, paying each $3 million; that same month, it settled lawsuits with nine miners who had survived the 2006 Aracoma fire. Then Massey shut all of its underground mines for two shifts to reinforce to miners that they needed to follow federal laws. It was partly in response to a surprise inspection at a Massey mine the prior month in which inspectors had found serious safety violations, prompting the company to fire three workers and suspend nine others. More than five thousand miners would watch a video in which Blankenship said that safety was more important than production at the company.

But it was too little too late. A day after the safety stand-down was announced, the *Wall Street Journal* reported that Massey was exploring a sale of the company. Everyone in the coal industry knew a sale would likely mean Blankenship's departure from Massey. On November 6, seven months after the accident, the *Journal* broke the news that Massey was considering a buyout from Alpha Natural Resources. Massey's stock price shot up 11 percent that day, recovering several hundred million dollars in value within a few hours. Blankenship continued to fight, offering new evidence at a mining conference in New York in mid-November that the explosion was caused by an inundation of natural gas. He told shareholders privately that the company could be sold for a higher price after it resolved its problems stemming from the accident. He had initially been interested in a deal with billionaire Wilbur Ross. But when he learned that Ben Hatfield would lead the combined company, and not him, "he instantly dropped any interest," Bobby Inman said later. Inman realized Massey's board had to take control of the process. It committed to paying Blankenship a rich severance package. If he agreed to leave the company before the end of the year, he would reap a big tax savings.

Blankenship's public image had hit a nadir. On November 29, *Rolling Stone* posted a profile of him by Jeff Goodell under the headline "The Dark Lord of Coal Country," and the Mephistophelian nickname stuck, just as it had for Devil Anse, another Mingo County villain.

On December 3, Massey issued a press release: Don Blankenship would retire at the end of the month. "After almost three decades at Massey it is time for me to move on," Blankenship said in the company's release. He negotiated a $12 million cash payment, in addition to other performance awards and benefits. The company gave him the option of buying the house in Sprigg, and it turned over the title to a 1965 blue Chevrolet truck. It was the truck Blankenship had driven from Colorado to Georgia through an ice storm years ago to spare himself the cost of shipping some wicker furniture.

Hours before Blankenship's retirement was announced, Thompson had been in the US Attorney's office in Charleston talking to a young prosecutor named Steve Ruby who was investigating the Upper Big Branch accident. Ruby, who had an earnest boyish face and a surprisingly deep voice that lent him a certain authority, was eager to know what Thompson could tell him about Massey and Blankenship. Like Thompson, Ruby had competed in statewide extemporaneous speech competitions in his youth before going on to become a lawyer. Both men's families had roots in Lincoln County. Ruby's went back to before the Civil War, and Thompson's parents had both been born there. Thompson handed Ruby binders of information about Massey's slurry operations, which Thompson considered to be criminal, and the two talked about Thompson's time in Mingo County and the stories he had heard over the years.

That same afternoon, Nick Getzen and his girlfriend were surprised to see Blankenship inside the Walmart off Route 119 in Logan, north of Williamson. They thought it was odd that he left without buying anything, and they followed him across the big parking lot to a Bob Evans restaurant. Getzen waited outside. Inside, Blankenship chatted with Getzen's girlfriend and asked her how her day had been. He told her his hadn't been so great. The conversation made its way back to Thompson that evening. Once again, the initial rush of victory shifted. Thompson had been giddy when he learned that Blankenship had been ousted. Then he felt a twinge: he would miss having Blankenship as an adversary. Somehow the CEO's retirement threatened to diminish the war Thompson had waged all these years against Massey.

The day after the announcement of Blankenship's exit, Thompson sat in the Charleston airport, waiting for a flight home that was delayed by heavy snow, and he jotted down a few notes to Kelsey. "It's quite a time; but of course time is the issue, isn't it?" he wrote. "I've spent so much time; time away from you; time doing w/o; time invested in a war that at times seemed to have no possible end . . . I can't wait to get home. You'll hug me; so will mom. Blue will kiss my face right off."

CHAPTER 28

At the beginning of 2011, Thompson moved his operations to a brick house in Charleston, a few blocks from the gold-leaf dome of the state capitol. His new office on the first floor had the close, dark feel of a ship's cabin, and he called it the Admiral's Den. There was room enough for his desk, a table with a green-shaded lamp, a threadbare Persian rug, and a dark-red faux-leather couch. Leaving the Mountaineer represented the end of an era, the most hard-fought, painful, and thrilling years of his career so far. Thompson would still say how awful it had been, but he obviously didn't regret a single moment. And the Rawl suit was still very much alive. He transplanted the case files to the house, and packed as many as he could into the room. Dark-wood shelves from the floor to the ceiling held folders stuffed with depositions and other documents. He was surrounded by the case on three sides. On the folders were the names of dozens of key players in the case, from Blankenship and other Massey executives to medical, toxicology, and engineering experts and dozens of clients. Wall sconces with electric candles added to the ship-like ambience. When Thompson worked late into the night, the Mardi Gras beads he had hung from a chandelier almost seemed to sway.

The house on Kanawha Boulevard was in a quiet neighborhood of law firms and business associations wanting easy access to the capitol. Once the private residence of a former head of the West Virginia Coal Association, the office was partly hidden by a tall holly tree; across the boulevard was the placid Kanawha River, where towboats pushed coal barges past the city. Thompson didn't hang out a shingle. The house was a refuge, and he didn't want to advertise his location.

On the day they moved in, Melissa Ellsworth bought gauzy blue-and-red curtains at a Walmart and hung them on the windows in the Admiral's Den. Dave Barney put his desk and two others in an open room on the first floor that was painted the blue of a swimming pool. The floor creaked, and in a corner plaster dust was gathering beneath a ceiling slowly crumbling from water damage. Upstairs, a spacious room with a fireplace held a long conference table; a tiny adjoining room had a wet bar dating from the 1960s or 1970s. Thompson slept in a corner room barely big enough for a twin mattress that had been donated to him by the Southern Appalachian Labor School. A lamp with a dented shade sat on the floor, and plastic crates held his clothes. He taped his *Dark Side of the Moon* poster on the only wall big enough for it.

Ellsworth put a note on the front door of the house stating that firearms weren't allowed on the premises. She taped another note above the light switch in Thompson's office: an image of Blankenship with cherry-red lips surrounded by floating red hearts and a light bulb, with a message asking people to conserve energy. "LIGHTS ON = HAPPY DON (BLANKENSHIP). PLEASE TURN OFF ALL LIGHTS WHEN LEAVING A ROOM. PLEASE TURN OFF ALL LIGHTS AND ELECTRONICS WHEN LEAVING FOR THE DAY. SCREW THAT GUY, SERIOUSLY. THANKS!"

There was a freedom to being out of the pressure cooker of Williamson. But Thompson was also suddenly much farther away from clients like Ernie and Carmelita Brown, and he didn't see or talk to them as often.

Even without Blankenship around, Massey and Jackson Kelly weren't backing down on any lawsuits. In March 2011, Thompson faced Stickler in front of a jury in the case involving the Marsh Fork Elementary School—and lost.

To Thompson, the case was a matter of common sense. In 2003, Massey had built a coal silo fifty times larger than its previous one and put it 235 feet from the elementary school so that the company could load coal trains one minute faster. He and Simonton had found coal dust inside the school, and when the wind blew toward the school, air monitors detected higher concentrations of dust in the air. Because there had been so much uproar in the community, the state was, in fact, in the process of building a new school miles away. Thompson wasn't suing for damages. He wanted the jury to make Massey pay for a medical monitoring program. He told the jury of six women that the case was all about risk and that they had a chance to do something no other jury in the state had done by forcing Massey to pay for medical testing that could detect if any children developed asthma or pneumoconiosis.

At trial, Stickler argued that there were no health risks, and he noted that the EPA and state regulators had signed off on the silo and that it never had any air quality violations. He called it the most inspected coal facility in the world. In his opening, Stickler held up an enlarged photograph of a train being loaded with coal, and there was no visible dust. "Where's this coal dust? It's not there," Stickler said. "Make them prove it's there." He said Thompson couldn't point to a single person who had an illness caused by attending the school or working there.

Stickler tried to dismantle the testimony of Thompson's experts. His relaxed manner seemed to suggest that Thompson's outrage was misplaced. Massey's own experts, including professors from Harvard who earned a thousand dollars an hour to testify, said the increases in dust measurements could have been caused by humidity, which could swell the dust particles like dried beans soaked in water. The air monitors Thompson had used were sensitive and prone to bumps in readings, they said. One monitor at the school's playground had registered higher readings, but Massey's experts said those could have been caused by a calibration problem.

Thompson believed trials were most often won during opening arguments, but this time the closing was pivotal. "You have the power to give the children of Marsh Fork Elementary a fighting chance against the disease risk caused by Massey's negligence," he told the women in the jury box. At one point his voice rose to a near shout as he rapped his hand against the podium facing the jurors. Then he settled down and concluded, "This case is about risk and truth. It's about them putting the children at risk so they can save money. It's about them exposing the children to coal dust, and then it's about a pack of mistruths, untruths, and hidden evidence. That's what this case is about: risk and truth."

After Thompson finished, Stickler maintained his bemused, avuncular demeanor. He stood up and said, "I'm exhausted," as if commiserating with the women on the jury. After arguing that Thompson hadn't made his case, Stickler calmly tapped the thick résumés of Massey's experts. He said the company had sought out experts that were the best in the world in their fields and that they were worth the fees they charged.

Then he held up a single sheet of paper each for Thompson's environmental and medical experts and read off a few citations to academic papers that had nothing to do with coal dust. He said Simonton was part of a team Thompson had that was fighting Massey across the state, as if Thompson and Simonton were engaged in a nefarious plot. He called the case political, as he tried to tap a feeling that the coal industry was under siege from politicians and activists.

When it was time for Thompson's rebuttal, the judge said he had fifteen minutes, instead of seven, because Stickler had gone over his allotted time. Thompson abandoned his plan to do nothing more than walk the jurors through the verdict form. Instead he attacked Massey's experts and defended his own, saying Simonton wasn't a crazy activist out to stop industry but a fair man. Then he argued once again that Massey had lied on its original permit. He tried to rebut Stickler's claim that the case was political, by clumsily comparing Massey to Russia during the Cold War. He recovered and went on to say, "Nobody but Massey has had the audacity to build something like this next to a school." Finally he concluded: "People don't expect their children to get black lung because children aren't supposed to go to school 235 feet from a ten-thousand-ton silo," he said. "Where on earth can six women stand up to power and put truth to lies?"

Later, he believed it was overkill. Thompson compared himself to a quarterback who has a lead with twenty seconds left on the clock. Rather than take a knee, he goes for a touchdown, gets picked off, and loses. The jury returned a verdict the next day in Massey's favor, and Shane Harvey, Massey's general counsel, didn't hide his pleasure. The trial was widely covered across the state, and he told reporters Thompson had relied on "junk science, hype, and fear," and that Massey had "a lot of hard evidence and reputable scientists." Harvey added: "This was an important victory. The out-of-state attorneys who brought this case are behind numerous other attacks on coal, such as the claims of well water contamination in Mingo County. These attorneys try to sway West Virginians with hype and publicity, but the jury focused on the facts. We live in these communities and support our local schools and take great care to operate responsibly."

Thompson made a point to shake Dan Stickler's hand in front of the news cameras after the verdict. He knew he had been outgunned.

But he also thought he had learned a valuable lesson. Thompson had thought the case against Massey was obvious—and therefore would also be obvious to a jury. Now he saw that Stickler's experts had presented their science at such a level of complexity that the jurors believed what they were saying even if they didn't understand it fully. Now he planned to hire several new experts for the Rawl case.

"Plaintiffs' attorneys say we can't get down in the weeds with them [jurors]," Thompson said when he was back in the Admiral's Den, obsessively reflecting on his missteps with Ellsworth and others. "Dude, you got to get down in the weeds with them. We're going to get way down in the subsurface. Little ants crawling around in the weeds."

After the loss, Stickler loomed larger as an adversary. Over the past seven years, Thompson had spent countless hours in rooms with Stickler, but now he'd started noticing uncanny similarities between the two of them—trivial coincidences, but hard to ignore when taken together. Like Thompson's family, Stickler was from Lincoln County. Both had their first teeth cleaning by a dentist there named Lester Wilkerson, who happened to be a cousin of Thompson's. Stickler's primary legal assistant was named Melissa, as was Thompson's. One day Thompson said he liked to drink bottled Starbucks Frappuccinos—except they were so small he tended to gulp them down. A few days later, he heard Stickler say he loved Starbucks Frappuccinos, the bottled ones, even though he tended to gulp them. Thompson said both men drank bourbon. At the restaurant inside Tamarack, a cultural center outside Beckley, Thompson liked to order grilled trout, collard greens, and fried green tomatoes. One day after he ate there, Thompson listened to Stickler tell a court clerk that whenever he went to Tamarack he always ordered the grilled trout, collard greens, and fried green tomatoes. Thompson practiced CrossFit; Stickler told Thompson that his son owned a CrossFit franchise in Charleston. They each said their favorite exercise was the burpee. That explained why the balding, sharp-eyed older man with the salt-and-pepper mustache was so fit. Thompson still had a mostly intact head of auburn hair and about fifteen years on Stickler, but he wasn't sure if he could take the other lawyer in a fight. He had once suggested it to Stickler, who looked back at him without replying.

Even the two lawyers' concerns about the coincidences became a coincidence. Stickler's assistant Melissa said that Stickler himself was disturbed by the similarities. "They say the same things," Thompson recalled her saying. "One will say something completely out of the presence of the other and twenty minutes later the other will say the exact same thing."

When the Mass Litigation Panel issued an order with a schedule culminating in an August 1 trial date, another confrontation between the two lawyers seemed inevitable. "I think the ultimate battle is set up between Luke and Darth, you know," Thompson said. He joked that Stickler had cut off his hand at Marsh Fork. The Empire had struck back. But Thompson would return stronger now. "The stage is set. Nothing is going to stop it now."

After the mediation at the civic center had failed, the three trial judges divided the health claims of all 565 people still in the case into seven categories based on illness—from a category for cancer and renal failure down to a category for the sentinel symptoms of chronic diarrhea and rashes. Thompson and Jackson Kelly would each submit one client for each of the seven categories. The judges would then pick one of the two names at random per category.

The judges had also decided to hold a trial in two phases. In the first phase, the jury would decide if Massey was liable for contaminating each of the seven plaintiffs' wells. A second phase would determine compensatory and punitive damages for each plaintiff. The process could then be repeated with groups of seven plaintiffs. Thompson wanted to cut the process short—win the first liability phase, and then hold it over Massey like a sledgehammer to force the company and its insurers into a big settlement.

In April, a circuit court clerk in Wheeling picked seven names out of a box. Thompson got only two of his choices: Donetta Blankenship, whose liver had nearly failed, and Rebecca Elaine Roberts, Carmelita Brown's sister, who had lived in Rawl and also suffered from sentinel symptoms like chronic diarrhea and rashes. Stickler got five: James Berlin Anderson, who had grown up in Rawl and was claiming for cognitive impairment; a woman who had lived in Sprigg and suffered several bouts of skin cancer; a woman who had lived in Lick Creek and had had kidney stones; a woman from Merrimac who had had boils and cysts; and a man named Ed Cline, who had lived in Merrimac and had also suffered from sentinel symptoms. Each client was also claiming for property damages, from water filtration systems to wrecked hot water heaters and coffeepots.

Some of Stickler's choices had less severe illnesses, and Thompson assumed the Jackson Kelly lawyer would argue that plaintiffs like Anderson, who had a good-paying job driving a coal truck, hadn't suffered any financial hardship. He also expected Massey's experts to try to muddy the science of water sampling, exposures, health consequences, and the flow of water underground, while Stickler argued that many people had been unhealthy all their lives and the water had nothing to do with it.

Thompson developed a strategy for each client's evidence and tactics for handling them on the witness stand. After a while, he started to think of Ed Cline as one of the most important trial plaintiffs, because he was the least exceptional: a delivery truck driver who'd hurt his back and started collecting disability insurance. Like other people in the case, Cline's symptoms had improved when he moved away from the area for a while, according to Thompson. He planned to make this a major point at trial: when his clients had moved or finally had access to clean water, their rashes cleared and stomach problems subsided. Their health improved.

Cline was among about two hundred people still in the case whose claims related to sentinel symptoms rather than major medical issues. This group figured largely in the cold calculus of the value of the case: they would factor heavily in the overall amount that Massey would have to pay. To Massey, the claims of the Ed Clines were worth about five thousand dollars each, Thompson believed. He thought the figure should be much higher. "What's it worth to be poisoned?" Thompson asked. "Is it worth five thousand dollars, or is it worth a hundred thousand?"

Thompson wanted Ernie Brown, Don Dillon, and Bo Scott, among others, to testify as fact witnesses to the devastation from the water and to the area's history. He still wanted to show the jury Don Dillon's photograph of his father with a rifle over his shoulder in 1920 when he was living in a tent colony along the Tug Fork. In his opening statement, Thompson planned to say that people had been able to drink the water in the four communities for a hundred years but had also been fighting coal companies just as long. "They all had guns because they were standing up to coal companies. Same war, different battle," he said.

Ernie and Bo could testify that they had worked in some of the mines where Rawl Sales later pumped slurry. They could describe the concrete blocks used to build underground seals that were supposed to hold the slurry in place. Thompson expected Jackson Kelly to object to his clients' providing testimony as fact witnesses, but he believed the judges would allow it. At the same time, the case had taken so many turns, it had become utterly unpredictable. The only constant was the heartbreak, which had been with Thompson now for years.

Late one night, he pulled a thin book from a shelf in the Admiral's Den. It was Sun Tzu's *The Art of War*, which offered pithy wisdom for leading an army, often against superior forces, like those that Massey and Jackson Kelly had brought to the Rawl lawsuit. Around the sixth century BC, the Chinese general had categorized nine varieties of ground on which battles are fought: dispersive ground, facile ground, contentious ground, open ground, ground of intersecting highways, serious ground, difficult ground, hemmed-in ground, and desperate ground.

"I think that's why we fought so hard," Thompson said. "We were always on desperate ground." It was well past midnight, and Thompson's voice was failing. But in the chalky light, he read aloud Sun Tzu's description of "desperate ground": "Ground on which we can only be saved from destruction by fighting without delay," he said. "On desperate ground, fight."

CHAPTER 29

On June 1, 2011, Alpha Natural Resources acquired Massey for $7.1 billion, and the ninety-one-year-old company ceased to be. Alpha's executives had won their prize, but in the process, they had taken on all of Massey's civil and criminal liabilities, including those related to the Upper Big Branch accident and the Rawl lawsuit. Even so, Thompson wanted to do everything he could to keep Blankenship, whose reputation was in tatters, at the center of the case.

Over Jackson Kelly's objections, Judge Mazzone ruled that Thompson and his partners could depose Blankenship a second time. They had to steer clear of questions about the health of Blankenship's family and everything else covered in the first deposition.

The day before the June 2 deposition in Charleston, Thompson told local TV reporters when to expect Blankenship to walk from Jackson Kelly's offices at the Laidley Tower to the Embassy Suites hotel. Thompson knew reporters wanted Blankenship's comment on the just-completed acquisition. It was another way to screw with him.

Sure enough, when Blankenship crossed the street to the hotel, reporters with cameras converged on him. Thompson had also directed Ellsworth's new boyfriend, an AmeriCorps VISTA member whom Thompson and others referred to as "shirtless Gary," to serve Blankenship with a subpoena to appear at the upcoming trial. While Blankenship declined to answer questions from reporters, Gary—who had put on a shirt for the occasion—stood up from a bench where he'd been sitting casually and handed Blankenship the subpoena. Blankenship kept his arms at his sides, and the papers fell to the ground. This was also captured by the local news cameras.

The deposition itself got underway in a conference room, and Ernie Brown and Don Dillon had driven up at Thompson's invitation to witness the interrogation. Blankenship appeared to be enjoying his semiretirement. He sported a lime-green golf shirt and a tan.

Blankenship's face registered a flash of surprise when it was clear that Bruce Stanley was going to be asking the questions. Once they went on the record, Thompson didn't say anything. It would be Stanley's show for the next three and a half hours.

As a trial lawyer, Stanley, like Thompson, sometimes wore his emotions on his sleeve. But he could also be deferential in a way that Thompson typically wasn't, and he maintained a soft-gloved approach during the entire deposition. His politeness even seemed to lull Sebok, who roused himself only a few times with weak objections. But step by step, Stanley created a record of what Blankenship knew about the slurry injection process at Rawl Sales when he had worked there, beginning in 1982, when Blankenship was first hired.

"So when you arrived was there an impoundment in place?" Stanley asked.

"No," Blankenship said.

"What was the primary means of dealing with the refuse fines?" Stanley asked, using another term for coal slurry.

"I guess they were pumping some of it underground, and they were trying in some cases to create combined refuse," Blankenship said, referring to the plant's attempt to dry the slurry into a cake that could be dumped into a fill. "But I don't think it worked very well."

"I think that that plant was designed for something called a vacuum filter system," Stanley said. "And . . . the vacuum filter system was having a difficult time keeping up."

"Well, it was having a difficult time keeping material dry and handling it," said Blankenship.

"So as a supplement to, or an alternative to, that there was underground injection going on? Which would you characterize it as, an alternative to or supplement to?"

Blankenship glanced down at the table in front of him and smiled slightly as he pondered the distinction between the words.

"I don't know, I think an 'alternative to' at points in time," he said.

"At points in time," Stanley said. "The vacuum filter system was essentially abandoned?"

"I think so," said Blankenship.

"And the refuse that was being pumped underground, are you aware of what mined-out seams . . . it was being pumped to?" Stanley asked.

"To my knowledge, it was mostly Pond Creek, but sometimes Alma," said Blankenship.

Thompson was seething as he followed the exchange. He wanted to rile Blankenship. Ernie and Don were in the room. Both men had watched their wives suffer from debilitating illnesses. Thompson wanted the CEO to know that the slurry injection had caused real harm and to admit that the company had made a mistake. At the very least, he wanted to ask questions that would make Blankenship confront this truth. But Stanley kept his emotions in check. His approach from the start was almost willfully fact-based.

Blankenship drank from a glass of water from time to time, and he rubbed the left side of his face as though he had a toothache. Even when Sebok objected and advised Blankenship not to answer, this time Blankenship went ahead and said what he thought. The interrogation remained cordial.

When Stanley ran through the minutiae of the Rawl Sales operation, Blankenship had immediate recall. He knew the names of seven mines that had fed the Sprouse Creek prep plant and whether each one sent their coal by rail or truck. And he appeared to have a clear memory of the issues surrounding the slurry injection, all issues that Sebok had shielded him from two years earlier. Blankenship said that when he had arrived at Rawl Sales, the fear was that there wouldn't be enough capacity underground to store all the slurry that the plant was producing. He remembered that there was a constant effort to improve the slurry lines and prevent them from freezing and breaking. He said the company had added monitors that would alarm if there was a break in the line somewhere. But when Stanley asked if Blankenship knew how much slurry had been injected by Rawl Sales, he said he didn't.

"Would a number as large as a billion gallons surprise you in any way?" Stanley asked.

"I'm trying to calculate in my head what that would mean in density and so forth," Blankenship said. "But no, it wouldn't surprise me."

Stanley asked if the total amount might be twice as high, or three or four times as high. Sebok objected, because it called for speculation.

Blankenship said he'd have to know how many tons of solid waste had been disposed of at the plant and then calculate it by how many solids were dissolved in a gallon of water. But he didn't rule it out. He remembered Erkan "Doc" Esmer's work on the impoundment design at Rawl Sales. But he didn't recall the disagreement Esmer had described over the fifty-five-thousand-dollar expenditure to expedite construction of the impoundment.

"I find it hard to believe," Blankenship said of the dispute. "But it's possible."

He also remembered the slurry spill in Lick Creek in 1984 and using straw bales in the creek during the cleanup. "A lot of enhancements came as a result of these incidents," Blankenship said. That's when he had monitors installed on the slurry lines.

"I appreciate that," Stanley said. "And the reason for that is because the goal is to minimize the amount of environmental destruction or damage that occurs as a result of the spills. Is that a fair statement?"

"Yes," said Blankenship.

"And that's because slurry is not good for the water. Is that a fair statement?" Stanley asked as Blankenship was lifting his glass to take a drink.

"I don't know whether it's good or bad, but it looks bad," Blankenship said. "And I assume that in high concentrations it's bad. I don't know about individual elements over the long term." He took a drink and then set his glass back down.

Thompson continued watching with growing frustration. During a break, he took Stanley aside and asked him what the hell he was doing. "You're supposed to hate this guy," Thompson said. "You're supposed to be the Blankenship killer. Pull a fucking knife on the guy." Bunch also urged Stanley to be more aggressive. But Stanley kept to his game plan, which was to engage Blankenship's intellect. He knew that it was Blankenship's habit to answer any question put to him and that the CEO would talk more if he thought he was engaged in a debate. He didn't need pages of hair-raising testimony from the CEO. He needed only one or two revelations that would play well before a jury.

After three and a half hours, Stanley asked Blankenship whether he had discussed the water contamination with his neighbors.

"You mean drive up to Lick Creek and stop at the houses and ask them?" Blankenship said, and laughed. "No, I haven't done that. I've talked to one or two of them when they run into me on the street but I don't even know which ones I talked to."

"Have you discussed with any of them their health problems or any of the concerns that they have as a result of their exposure to the slurry?" Stanley asked.

"I wouldn't see any purpose and wouldn't be qualified to discuss it with them, and it would be outside the realm of what counsel would want me to do in these circumstances," Blankenship said. "I'm sure nothing good could come out of it other than being accused of trying to tamper with them."

Stanley said he would let Blankenship go for the day. When the lawyers were preparing to leave, Stanley said to Thompson, with a good-naturedness that bordered on humility, "I know you're not happy with me. I think if you look at the record you're going to see that we got some good stuff."

Once Thompson cooled down, he agreed they had good material. Even though Blankenship doubted that he and Esmer had argued over spending fifty-five thousand dollars to build the impoundment, he had stated on the record that the company needed to inject slurry and feared running out of space underground. When Thompson had sued Rawl Sales in September 2004, the company had downplayed the amount of slurry it had injected, saying it had been a limited amount in two or three boreholes. After seven years of litigation, Blankenship himself had finally admitted that the slurry injection was vital to the company and to agree that a billion gallons or more of the waste could be in the hills around the communities.

That evening, Charleston's WCHS played video footage of Blankenship getting swarmed on his walk to the Embassy Suites. Blankenship refused to answer any questions. "Not going to say anything at all?" asked reporter Bob Aaron. "Not a thing," Blankenship said. Then a clip was played of Gary approaching Blankenship and the subpoena falling to the sidewalk in slow motion. "The big ambush came at the door of the hotel, where a process server bagged him with a subpoena for the August civil case over allegations Massey polluted underground water supplies," Aaron said in a voice-over. "Blankenship treated the paper like a hot potato." Thompson watched the clip over and over, savoring the absurdity. As far as Thompson was concerned, any day he had Blankenship answering questions under oath was a good one.

At the same time, Thompson had to deal with a low-level revolt. Like many clients, Ernie was frustrated that he and Carmelita weren't among the seven plaintiffs whose claims were going to be tried in August. Ernie's dissatisfaction had been building for months as he watched others join the case. Some, he said, weren't true Mingo County residents; they had only lived in FEMA trailers set up in Lick Creek for a short time after the 1977 flood.

Ernie had come to blame Thompson, who, in his mind, had wanted the case to grow because it would ultimately mean a bigger payout for the lawyers. But Ernie reasoned that the more people who joined with less exposure and fewer health problems, the weaker the case got. When Thompson lost the Marsh Fork trial, it was proof that Stickler was outmaneuvering him.

Now that the Rawl trial was approaching, Brown thought Thompson risked losing without his strongest clients at the forefront. Massey's lawyers would make it look like Thompson was trying to get money for people who didn't deserve it. "Massey is putting forth the hogs. They done their homework," said Ernie. "They don't want people like me and Carm . . . They're going to take these people in the court of law and make Kevin look like a stink bug."

Thompson never stopped digging for evidence to strengthen the case. In early June, the panel of judges gave him permission to depose two former Rawl Sales officials now in Kentucky.

One of them, a former chief engineer of Rawl Sales in the late 1990s, mentioned that he had seen slurry injection holes on a series of maps that he called "sepias," or Mylar maps, which were kept at the company's mine map vault in Sidney, Kentucky. Thompson had never heard any company official refer to these injection maps, and he told Stickler at the end of the deposition that he wanted to see them as soon as possible. Three days later, Jackson Kelly turned over four maps that showed injection holes into the Alma seam, with the dates and durations of the injections. Thompson was livid. He'd never seen maps with that information before. The maps were exactly the kind of evidence he had asked for in his initial discovery request in November 2004. With help from Stuart Smith's associate Sean Cassidy, he filed a motion to the panel asking for immediate access to Massey's mine map vault.

"This last-minute production has exploded the lid off Pandora's Box with myriad wide-reaching impacts," Thompson wrote. "In short, this production directly demonstrates that Defendants have withheld, and more than likely continue to withhold, information and documents that are material and responsive to Plaintiffs' *initial* set of discovery propounded seven years ago." He asked for sanctions, including an instruction to the jury, and to be allowed to re-depose Blankenship and other officials with the information he should have already had.

Thompson argued that the maps undercut the central theme of Massey's defense—that the slurry injection had been limited and far enough away from the communities. One of Massey's experts had said he believed that injection into the Alma seam had occurred only near the prep plant, but the maps showed injection holes far closer to the communities in that coal seam. Thompson said there must be similar maps for the Pond Creek and other seams. "Defendants have finally realized they can no longer hide these key documents which Plaintiffs have been chasing for the better part of a decade," he wrote.

Judge Mazzone granted Thompson "immediate, unfettered access" to the vault. He said the issue of whether Jackson Kelly had intentionally withheld documents could be determined at a later date. Thompson drove to Williamson early the next morning and met Bo Scott in front of the Mountaineer. The two drove from there in Bo's truck to Massey's operation in Sidney even before a Jackson Kelly associate could get there.

Thompson had been to the cinder-block-and-steel building in 2007 but had been granted access to only a single room. This time, he asked what was behind a locked door. A company engineer said there was a storage room with Coca-Cola products. Thompson demanded to see the room, and inside he found crates of soda. But there was also a staircase leading up to an attic space above the main room of the map vault. Thompson and Bo climbed up and found about thirty dusty banker's boxes marked "Rawl." For hours, they opened the boxes and pored over the papers. Two days later, Thompson had to return to Charleston to prepare for trial, but he kept a team of five people at the vault for the next three weeks, sorting documents.

They found surveyor notes that described Rawl Sales' slurry injection sites as late as 1992—five years after Massey had said the injection stopped. Maps with injection rates and volumes associated with boreholes contradicted the testimony of Massey's experts. Some maps put the slurry in places that experts hired by Massey apparently had no knowledge of.

Thompson believed Jackson Kelly had intentionally suppressed evidence, a serious allegation that he made to the Mass Litigation Panel. Jackson Kelly denied in a filing with the court that it knowingly withheld material, and the issue went unresolved as the August 1 trial date approached.

A few days before trial, Thompson and Bunch looked over dozens of the newly discovered maps in a hotel room in Wheeling. Thompson planned to present as many as he could to the judges at a pretrial hearing the next day. Bo had driven up to help read the maps, and Ellsworth took notes as Bo leaned over a table and unrolled them one by one.

The maps were the most detailed Thompson had seen of the area. One listed Merrimac Coal Company, which Scott said dated to the 1930s, if not earlier. The irony was clear to Thompson: earlier generations had labored to dig the coal from the hills, and those same mines were later filled with slurry that poisoned their descendants.

CHAPTER 30

At night in the Admiral's Den, Thompson gave his opening statement for Ellsworth and anyone else who wandered by at the time. He recited it as if he were addressing a jury and Ernie and Carmelita Brown, Larry and Brenda, B.I., Donetta, Don Dillon, Frank Coleman, James Berlin Anderson, and as many clients as could fit into Judge Mazzone's courtroom in Wheeling were watching him tell their story. He had revised the statement countless times over the years. Now it started this way:

> For 100 years, the water beneath Lick Creek, Rawl, Merrimac, and Sprigg sustained life for the families who have called those four hollows home. My clients, the seven families in this trial, and almost everyone else who has lived in Rawl, Lick Creek, Merrimac, and Sprigg began to file suit against Massey Energy and Rawl Sales and Processing because Massey knew they contaminated the water, did nothing about it, and have fought the people every step of the way.
>
> Make no doubt about it . . . Massey is a coal company. Make no doubt about it, Massey knew what was in their slurry—heavy metals that three decades later can still be found in the water pumped out of the ground beneath Rawl, Lick Creek, Merrimac, and Sprigg.
>
> And you will hear from the people that Rawl Sales and Processing always denied contaminating their water. You'll hear from the people that they used that water. They used it to quench their thirst, make their coffee, cook their food, take their showers, clean their clothes, mix their children's Kool-Aid, and bathe their babies.
>
> Think about it . . . water sustains life.
>
> Evidence of the end result of this injection will horrify you— medical evidence showing a population exposed for three decades

to unsafe levels of heavy metals suffering from diseases known to be caused by the very heavy metals injected by Massey.

You'll hear from the people themselves about diarrhea that came and never left. You'll hear about rashes and boils common to everyone. You'll hear about young and old alike suffering from kidney stones. You will learn the horrors about what lead and arsenic do to children's brains. You'll hear about cancer.

As the water got worse, the people got sicker. The people asked questions of the company and of the government. Massey greeted those questions with lies and denials.

And the government never had a chance to do the right thing because Massey never revealed the whole picture to anyone, not to the government and especially not to the people.

You'll see government report after government report, all based on Massey lies and none placing the blame where it belonged, on Massey's shoulders.

The first scientist whose data placed that blame on Massey lives right here in Wheeling, a Wheeling Jesuit professor of aquatic biology [Ben Stout]. His report, released around Christmas of 2004, linked Massey's slurry to the contaminated water because he did what no one had done before—tested the water looking for all of the same elements that are in slurry.

You will hear evidence in this case that it wasn't until April of 2007 the Mingo County PSD [Public Service District] finally ran a water line to Rawl with funding from the Abandoned Mine Lands fund and the Mingo County Commission. Before that the people had been receiving three gallons of emergency replacement water each week since the fall of 2006.

It is important evidence in this case that the community finally got safe, clean water. It's important evidence because it proves that the water was making people sick because after clean water came, fewer people were sick . . . Just as our scientists predicted.

Let me tell you . . . that evidence was not easy to come by. You're going to see maps and memos which refute Massey's excuses that we just got last week.

Now let me take a minute to explain who our expert witnesses are and what they are going to testify about to give you a road map of these scientific issues you will have to judge. Dr. Scott Simonton . . . Dr. Sam Kriger . . . Dr. Carl Werntz . . . Dr. Dawn Seeburger . . . Jack Spadaro . . .

And you're going to hear evidence from the people them-selves—evidence of suffering, evidence of loss and evidence of years of unrelenting anguish.

In the face of all of this evidence, what will Massey's excuse be?

Massey agrees the people are sick, but they say the water isn't contaminated in the first place. Thus, they can't be blamed for making the people sick.

Their next excuse—even if the water is contaminated, it's not Massey's fault. Massey contends their slurry can't seep out of old abandoned mines.

This case isn't about coal. It's about coal companies who ignore the promises made in the permits given to them by the State, by the people. Think about the word "permit." The people "permitted" Massey to get permits for Rawl Sales to process coal—provided that Massey's subsidiary kept the promises it made in the permit.

Massey knew what it had done.

You're going to hear that from Thelma Parsley. Her story and subpoenaed documents from the Matewan Utility Board drive home the point that Don Blankenship knew that he'd poisoned the water, that he didn't care about the people but did look out for himself. In the early 1990s, as the water in Sprigg was starting to go really bad, Ms. Parsley noticed a construction crew digging a water line from the direction of Matewan. Thelma watched as the line drew ever closer to her house. She watched as the line was run to Mr. Blankenship's house. When the water got too bad to drink, Don Blankenship made sure that his house got clean, safe water—his house right next door to Thelma Parsley's house.

And she never got a drop.

The question was, would he ever deliver the statement in front of a jury? Both sides were gearing up for trial. Dan Stickler had filed motions to try to keep a jury from hearing about Blankenship's water line, or the term "Forgotten Communities," because he argued both would be unfairly prejudicial. Moats and Swope ordered all the lawyers in the case, including those for the insurers, to show up for a two-day mediation starting on July 25 at the Embassy Suites in Charleston. The mediation, days before the scheduled trial, had a different feel from the failed one the prior fall. This time there was no attempt to put a good face on a troubled case. Thompson knew the insurance attorneys had been jockeying, trying to reduce their own exposure and foist costs onto one another. Kevin Crutchfield was now Alpha's chairman and CEO and would have the final say about whether to reach a settlement or keep defending a case that was more about Massey's past, just as he was trying to shed Blankenship's legacy. Those of Thompson's clients whose claims were scheduled for trial were invited to attend, along with their immediate family members, and some others like Don Dillon and Bo Scott were present. Most of the more than five hundred people still in the case were back home, anxiously awaiting news from Charleston.

The judges had finalized the medical monitoring trust details with Massey's insurers: they'd agreed to fund the trust with $2 million, adding as much as $3 million more over time. Now only the claims from the underlying case remained.

The first day of mediation started at 9 a.m. and lasted more than ten hours, Thompson recalled, with the judges calling lawyers for each side separately into a conference room during much of the day. Thompson was excluded from long stretches of negotiations when Jackson Kelly or the insurers' lawyers met with the judges, leaving him to pace the bland halls of the hotel when he wanted to be in the courtroom in Wheeling choosing a jury with Stickler. Thompson's team at the mine map vault in Sidney updated him throughout the day about documents they were finding, and he periodically slipped out of the plaintiffs' room to try to trade information with insurance attorneys. When Bunch found out about these forays, he banned Thompson from leaving their room without an escort, increasing Thompson's frustration at not being able to control the situation.

Thompson's team at Massey's mine map vault had found plans for the water line extension from the golf course to Blankenship's house in Sprigg. Then Thompson got a text that his team had found a document that showed that the well at Blankenship's house in Sprigg had been tested. When the well test was found, there was a muted celebration among an intern and a surveyor there for Thompson and associates from Stuart Smith's and Bruce Stanley's firms—the team didn't want to tip off a Jackson Kelly lawyer in the room about the discovery. Thompson hadn't seen the results but he hoped the very fact that the well had been tested—when Blankenship had said in his first deposition that he didn't know if it had been—would help his cause with the judges. "Blankenship had the water tested for his house in 1988," Thompson recalled later. "That was found in those boxes."

When Thompson met with the judges, he made a plea to require the insurers to kick in more money for a settlement that would cover the entire case. Judge Swope had been making *Star Trek* references, so Thompson identified himself as "First Science Officer Thompson." Judge Swope said he would enter the request in the captain's log.

On the evening of the second day, Thompson was sitting alone in the sports bar off the hotel's soaring atrium nursing a Maker's Mark and his frustration. His partners were eager to reach a settlement—and he, in his ambivalence, had started imagining ways to try to scuttle one. That afternoon, Thompson called Carmelita's sister, Rebecca Roberts, who was one of the seven trial plaintiffs, to update her. She was driving with Ernie and Carmelita in Tennessee on vacation, and they put Thompson on speakerphone. Thompson said he was ready to take the case to trial. Ernie spoke up and told Thompson he should accept a settlement if a fair offer was made.

Even in Thompson's office, the movement toward a settlement had been building for weeks, often in heated discussions between Thompson and Bunch and the other lawyers who had become involved in the case. Many saw a settlement as the only rational way to resolve the suit. Bunch had to consider that his partners had spent $2.2 million on the case, including just over a million in expert witness fees and $144,000 to obtain medical records. The decision would be put to the clients in the end. But Thompson and others discussed different scenarios. "If they offer us forty [million], I'll say fuck it," Thompson said on at least one occasion, to which Bunch replied sternly, "We are not walking away from forty [million]."

Thompson expected to run out of money again by mid-September, when they would be about six weeks into the trial. He figured Bunch would keep paying his hotel bill in Wheeling during the trial, and he would let the rent on his Charleston office go unpaid, if needed. If no one else came through with more money—if everyone abandoned him—he decided that he could try the case himself. Sitting alone at the hotel bar, he spun out his darkest fantasy. He could run his own graphics off his laptop; he had his black binders with five-inch spines containing more than four hundred trial exhibits—Rawl Sales' own reports showing hundreds of millions of gallons of slurry injected each year in the mid-1980s, lab results displaying lead and arsenic in his clients' wells, and medical records documenting the human toll: rashes, kidney failure, and cancer. The bourbon was working in his brain. He was a twenty-first-century Ahab, ready to fly his ship into the sun and disintegrate.

As soon as he saw Bunch, Barney, and Stanley walk into the bar, his fear lifted. He realized Ellsworth and the others would never leave him either.

Just before 6 p.m., Thompson got a text from an insurance attorney he had known for years. The lawyer said it looked like Thompson wasn't going to get his dream of a trial where he could put Blankenship on the stand. Thompson joined Bunch and the others at a table.

It was close to 8 p.m. when Judge Swope entered the bar and walked over to Thompson and his group and suggested that they stay there until they heard otherwise; it could be a while. While the judges met upstairs with the insurance lawyers and the plaintiffs who were present, Thompson and his crew had dinner and they kept on drinking. Across the room, Stickler, Sebok, Stankewicz, and the rest of their team sat at another table, nursing iced teas and sodas.

At close to 1 a.m., Judge Swope walked back into the bar and waved his arm to get Thompson's attention. With his raised hand, the judge made the Vulcan "live long and prosper" salute.

"They just got it," Thompson told his colleagues. "We're done."

"How do you know?" Bunch asked.

"I know," said Thompson. "I just got a sign."

As he left the bar, Thompson passed through a gauntlet of insurance company lawyers in a dizzying blur and high-fived as many as he could. All the lawyers were smiling and laughing. A cheer went up. For a moment it seemed like Thompson had sunk a three-pointer to win the game just before the buzzer sounded and then been carried off on his team's shoulders.

The final details had been worked out upstairs apart from Thompson and his partners. The settlement number was $35 million. In meetings with the judges, Thompson had been arguing for more than that to settle the entire case. But in the end, he had become one voice among many and he was unable to push the figure any higher. Even for some who had been present during the negotiations, the process was opaque enough that they couldn't say exactly how the final figure was arrived at. In the end, it was a number that Thompson and his partners couldn't say no to on behalf of their clients.

For the next three hours, Thompson drank coffee in the judges' room as he and the other lawyers read the tentative agreement. His initial rush faded. His clients had been expecting more, and it was going to be up to him to tell them that while they had reached a tentative settlement, no one was going to receive as much as they hoped. Dawn was approaching when all the lawyers finally finished signing the paperwork, and Judge Swope declared, "We have peace in our time!"

About sixty lawyers formed two lines to shake the judges' hands. Thompson didn't want to arrive at the front with Stickler, but he did anyway. They took turns shaking hands with Judge Moats and Judge Swope, and then, as if the scene had been choreographed, the two lawyers turned away without acknowledging each other and walked back down the lines of lawyers. At the end, Thompson came face-to-face with Stickler. He had reached out his hand to Stickler after Marsh Fork, when he knew he had been bested. In a moment of hesitation, Thompson had one impulse to shake Stickler's hand again and another to lunge at him. The two lawyers walked away from each other without speaking or shaking hands, and then they left the room by separate doors.

As Thompson was packing up at the Embassy Suites and considering his own financial position, his mood darkened even more. Given the settlement amount, once the other attorneys divided up the contingency fee and he paid off his debts, he would earn nothing at all from the case. He told Bunch and Barney and the others in the room that the settlement had ruined him financially and that he was quitting.

He said he'd no longer be able to pay his staff. He would be shutting down the Charleston office. It was a brief speech. "I said, 'This is what you did. There you go. Figure it out,'" Thompson recalled later. He left with Ellsworth and went back to the Admiral's Den, where his phone started ringing at 7 a.m. Many clients were anxious to know what had happened and how much they stood to receive.

In the light of day, the loss of the trial hit Thompson again. He came around to the reality that his team had won a significant settlement for his clients. But there would be no courtroom showdown with Stickler and no appearance on the witness stand by Blankenship, no cross-examining him on why he didn't want to build an impoundment to store slurry but later approved a water line to his house on Route 49. Thompson held to the belief that he would have prevailed in the first round of seven clients, proving the company's general liability, and then forced Alpha and its insurers into a far larger settlement.

Vicki Smith at the Associated Press reported that the people in the four communities had won $35 million, plus the $5 million in medical monitoring. She calculated that after attorneys' fees of 33 percent, individual plaintiffs would each get roughly $50,000 on average. Ultimately, Thompson would hire a retired judge to work out individual payments based on medical conditions and other factors. Meanwhile Thompson hatched a plan so he wouldn't come away completely empty-handed from the settlement. He started telling Bunch and the others that he would need a postwar debt-forgiveness plan, so he could earn a portion of the fee.

One piece of leverage Thompson had, and it was a big one, was that every client needed to agree to the settlement. Traveling to Mingo County and meeting with the clients as a group and individually, when many were sure to be unhappy about the settlement, was a job no one else wanted, and one only Thompson could do.

Bruce Stanley, who knew better than anyone what a Herculean task it was to sue a coal company in Mingo County, viewed the settlement as the best possible outcome. If approved, the settlement would put substantial money in the hands of residents in one of the nation's poorest counties and create a medical testing program that could shed light on the health effects of slurry injection to potentially inform future cases and regulations, while promising to finally bring an end to seven years of litigation. Stanley spoke from experience. After nearly a decade and a trip to the US Supreme Court, he was still trying to win back the $50 million that a jury had awarded to Hugh Caperton in 2002 but that had then been lost on appeals. To walk away with nothing in the Rawl case would have been devastating to the hundreds of people living along Route 49.

"If Kevin had had his druthers it would have gone to trial, but I believe that Kevin came to believe and understand that in the time, at the moment, the appropriate thing to do was to settle the litigation. Tough decisions had to be made on multiple levels to try to bring a rational conclusion to the situation," said Stanley. "That a significant recovery was achieved against a coal company for polluting the wells of its neighbors in southern West Virginia is no small feat."

The tentative settlement was reached early on a Wednesday morning. That Saturday, Thompson drove down to the field house in Williamson for a community meeting. On his way, he stopped at the regional jail in Logan County to discuss the tentative settlement with a client who was there on a drug-related charge. The client told Thompson, "They're going to try to kill you." Someone would be wearing a long coat and would move from the front of the room to the back before making his move, the client said. The threat sounded outlandish to Thompson but he didn't know exactly how upset some people might be about the settlement. So he went into the gymnasium where a riot had nearly broken out in 2009, in the odd position of worrying that one of his own clients might try to kill him.

As Thompson recounted, while he was addressing people's concerns about the settlement, he did, in fact, see a man in a long coat. Then he watched as the same two men who protected Thompson two years earlier by ushering him out of the field house now stepped next to the man in the coat as if to keep him from moving anywhere. Nothing happened. Back in Charleston that night, Thompson took everyone out for tacos, and they had a "We didn't die" party to celebrate.

Thompson went to Gallipolis for a few days for a family birthday party at his mother-in-law's house. Everyone congratulated him, and Kathleen herself was relieved that the saga had come to an end, even though she knew how precarious his financial position was. As soon as Thompson could, he headed back to the Admiral's Den. "I didn't want to be anywhere but here with my crew," he said. He tried to go on "strike" and got Ellsworth and Barney to stop answering calls and emails for a few days to show Bunch and the others that they would have to offer him a larger percentage of the contingency fee. But all three of them kept working anyway: there were simply too many settlement details to work through, including working with the retired judge to help determine how much each client should receive, which would soon become a source of complaints and bitterness—all directed back at Thompson.

"It was a few days of purgatory. Now it's something that gnaws at you forever," Thompson said of the settlement. "How many times do you have the chance to have absolute evil pinned so far back up against the wall? Where does that happen? I'll never have a chance like that again. As a lawyer, I feel like I was cheated. I think the people feel like they were cheated. You know, they were cheated out of their fight. Everybody wanted to tell their story."

The ceremonial courtroom in the Kanawha County Courthouse in downtown Charleston has dark wainscoting and high white walls. An arch of ivory-colored stone fixed to the front wall looks as though it was plucked from an ancient temple. On August 23, Thompson, Stanley, and Barney were in the courtroom in front of the Mass Litigation Panel judges fighting off a motion for sanctions filed by Stickler, alleging that Thompson had divulged the $35 million settlement figure to Vicki Smith at the Associated Press. Stanley was banging his fist on the counsel table when a rumbling passed through the building. Thompson wrote "earthquake!" on a Post-it and showed it to Barney, who nodded, thinking Thompson was referring to Stanley's performance. Within minutes, the building was evacuated. A magnitude 5.8 earthquake in Mineral, Virginia, was felt from Georgia to Maine by tens of millions of people. The judges dismissed Jackson Kelly's motion, and Thompson had another story about how Stanley could summon the forces of nature.

Just over a month later, on September 29, more than fifty people from the Route 49 communities filed into the room for a fairness hearing. They were joined by sixteen attorneys representing insurance companies and seventy-one attorneys representing minors. The three trial judges wanted to give people a chance to voice concerns about the settlement.

B.I. Sammons had gotten there early with his wife, Deborah, and their thirteen-year-old son and sat down next to Ernie and Carmelita Brown a few feet behind the attorneys at the counsel tables. Thompson already knew Ernie and B.I. were upset with the settlement amount. They thought the medical monitoring was mostly a waste of money that could've been distributed to people. Thompson had never turned anyone away who had lived in the area and been exposed to the water. Ernie and B.I. were among those who were incensed because, they said, dozens of people who had lived in the area for only a few months or years after the 1977 flood now stood to get a share of the settlement.

Thompson expected to get raked over the coals. Don Dillon and Frank Coleman were in the courtroom, as was Brenda Brown. A notable absence was Larry Brown, who had a medical appointment that morning. Thompson, already conflicted, was now stuck literally sitting between his partners and his clients. When the hearing began, Judge Mazzone called on Thompson to articulate the terms of the medical monitoring trust settlement—and he suddenly realized he was going to have to stand up and lay out the agreement that was now so unpopular with the people. He reached over to Stickler's table and grabbed a copy of the settlement. He launched into a perfunctory explanation, but his voice soon filled with emotion. He wanted to explain to the three judges that a critical-illness insurance policy needed to be added to the monitoring program.

"During the 2009 mediation, somebody had the microphone and said, 'So if I get cancer, Massey wins,'" Thompson told the judges. "At that point altercations broke out in the crowd. Families fighting each other, fistfights. We realized at that point . . . that the medical monitoring was not adequate for this population.

"My clients' concerns are valid. The medical monitoring only tells you if you're sick and it doesn't help you," Thompson said. He was pausing to keep himself from crying. "There's not enough to compensate for the injuries. But what I've— I've been— I've been to at least six funerals. Of the 587 people left, only 554 are alive today. . . . And Judge Moats pointed out, some of these people won't ever live to see any kind of compensation if this goes through trial and through appeal. He was right."

Thompson went on, "I'll tell you and I'll tell everybody, there's not enough money in this pot. It wasn't— It's not going to compensate these people for what they went through. But I'm very proud of the work that we've done to get the medical monitoring and the insurance. Thank you."

Thompson's speech, in which he came perilously close to admitting that the settlement was not fair or adequate, wasn't the one that Bunch or his other partners on the case wanted to hear. It wasn't what Stickler wanted to hear. At the same time, it wouldn't satisfy any of Thompson's clients who were upset with him either. But Thompson had let something genuine come through—and the judges, no doubt, could feel that.

"Well, Your Honor, I can't verify everything that he has said," Stickler said when he rose to address the court. "I can say this medical monitoring plan is the one we agreed upon. We're ready to put it into place."

Don Dillon was the first client to step to a podium in the middle of the room and speak out against the program, calling it "hogwash." When attorneys took an additional $1.3 million out of the $35 million settlement to account for their fee for the medical monitoring program, it would cut into his own settlement money. "It's hitting me $22,950 for something I don't need," Dillon said of the medical monitoring.

B.I. Sammons leaned in to the microphone and said, "Since we started this trying to get water and getting help from our attorneys, it took seven years and under the Constitution, you're supposed to have a speedy trial, a fair trial, on a timely basis, by your peers," he said. "There's a lot of us that wanted to have our day in court, but it was taken away from us. I didn't know that could be done. This is still America. People still rule this country and in our case— In our case, our rights were denied."

Ernie Brown said, "I've seen a lot of pain and suffering through our communities. And I'd like to thank our attorneys for what they did. They all worked, but somewhere along the line beyond this process, they lost focus on the real cause." He mentioned Carmelita going to the hospital for kidney stones; his children scratching themselves by rolling on the floor because the water had irritated their skin; and not being able to see when he got out of the shower because the water had stung his eyes. "Somewhere along the line we lost focus of what this was really and truly about." He finished by saying the settlement money should be divided equally between people who live in the community.

Bunch stood to try to turn the tide in the room, noting that 95 percent of the plaintiffs in the case had signed a letter accepting the settlement and noting that he and Thompson had never represented in writing or in any other way that they wouldn't get paid for their work. He reminded the judges that since the first complaint was filed in 2004, Thompson had won an injunction preventing Rawl Sales from injecting any more slurry and also helped get the state to fund the construction of the water line from Williamson to all four communities. "I know Mr. Thompson certainly has given his heart and soul to this case, at a manner and under the sacrifices that are far beyond what anybody buys into when they obtain a law-practicing certificate in this state or anywhere else. He's done so at great risk to himself financially. He's done so at great risk to himself, sometimes to his health. He has made himself available to all of these clients, not only as a lawyer, but as a personal counselor and friend. . . . To hear Mr. Brown suggest that a great injustice is being done is hurtful to me."

During the lunch break, Thompson never made it to the Jimmy John's where Bunch and everyone else had gone for sandwiches. Too many clients came up to talk to him. Don Dillon buttonholed him outside the courthouse to complain about the settlement terms, and then Frank Coleman walked up and playfully tried to put Thompson in a headlock. But Thompson twisted out of it and stole Coleman's wallet in the process, which Dillon thought was hilarious.

When the hearing started up again, a series of lawyers representing minors stated whether or not they approved of the settlement. The attorney for B.I.'s thirteen-year-old son said that while the family opposed the settlement, he thought it was fair.

B.I. stood up and said, "No. If this man thinks this is the best thing for my son, do it." After that, the mood in the room shifted, and more people agreed that the settlement was fair.

Stickler and Thompson sat at different counsel tables but were next to each other, like two generals whose usefulness was fading while the terms of the peace were being finalized. At one point, Stickler whispered, "September twenty-ninth. Buddy, we ought to be doing closing arguments right now."

Thompson replied, "Yeah, I know, I think about it all the time."

At 5:30 p.m., Don Dillon, who'd spent his career as an electrician underground in the mines around Rawl, had the final say. "I love everybody. I'm a born-again Christian. And my counsel here, I care for him," Dillon said of Thompson. Then he went on to question whether those who had fought the hardest and suffered the longest were receiving justice. It wasn't the testimony Thompson had envisioned when he planned to call Dillon as his first witness, holding up the photograph of Dillon's father as a young man in a soft-brimmed hat with a Winchester on his shoulder. Still, Thompson was right to think that his client would come across as humble and dignified. Dillon spoke at the end of a long day and a long seven years. He wore the same likable expression that his father had in 1920 when he'd been forced to live in a tent next to the Tug Fork. Thompson had wanted to show a jury that the people in these communities had been fighting coal companies for a hundred years. Instead Dillon delivered the closing argument for the people and cast his own verdict: they had failed to win justice yet again. "The people at Rawl is . . . ," Dillon said, and paused. "The residents is not getting justified."

That night in the Admiral's Den, Thompson leaned back in his chair and took long pulls from a beer. On a shelf behind him, mason jars of water from Rawl were lined up next to others full of clear moonshine that clients had given him as gifts. A few rowing medals with blue and red ribbons hung from the sconces. A shelf held his diplomas and family photographs, black-and-white stills of his father and mother. There were a few pictures of Thompson with Kathleen and Kelsey. In one photograph that predated the Rawl case, a much younger Thompson in a sport jacket and tie sits on a bench, looking carefree, as an eight-year-old Kelsey leans against him. Neither his wife nor his daughter had ever been to the Mountaineer or to his Charleston office.

Dave Barney sat on a wicker chair under the wall of Rawl files, and Melissa Ellsworth and several others filled the couch and two more chairs, sipping beers and rehashing the emotional day. Thompson's longtime executive assistant Pam Patai had driven up from New Orleans but had spent the day in the office. Bunch was already on the road back home to Tennessee.

Thompson, who was wrung out, said the day felt about twenty-two minutes long to him. He recalled snapshots—trying not to cry in the morning as he outlined the settlement to the judges, Don Dillon keeping him from eating lunch, and exchanges he'd had with Stickler.

"Don Dillon smacked us around. Ernie smacked us around. B.I. smacked us around," Thompson said. "The people I love and care about the most."

He asked if anyone remembered when B.I. had said the settlement was all right with him if the lawyer representing his son said so. "I thought that was a moving moment," Thompson said.

"I think it stemmed the tide," said Barney.

Thompson said he didn't have any problem with Ernie, B.I., or Don Dillon speaking against them or the settlement. "I didn't win the case. They had to live through it. They're the ones that suffered and got the cancer. I got to go off and have a great adventure against a fucking coal king."

"You did not lose," said Patai.

"We won," said Thompson, correcting himself.

Then he flashed back to the moment when he realized the case had been settled. "Do you remember when you walked out of the bar at the Embassy Suites when all the insurance lawyers were there?" he asked Barney.

"Oh yeah, that was embarrassing," Barney said.

"You found that embarrassing?" Thompson asked in disbelief. "That was one of the highlights of my life. That's on the final reel."

Thompson asked if anyone else remembered.

"There were sixty of those people following us around," he said of the insurance lawyers as he relived the moment. "So they were in the bar drinking. We were drinking. . . . I was as down as I could be. But I knew there was a lot of money involved, and I knew that everybody else thought I won the game. And I had. There were all these guys, these lawyers in the bar. Lined up. So I just went *shoosh, shoosh, shoosh, shoosh*! I high-fived them all, man. I high-fived, like, thirty-five lawyers on my way out of the bar. Hey, we're all smiling and laughing. It was a great moment in sports history."

EPILOGUE

The Mass Litigation Panel issued an order finalizing the Rawl settlement on December 7, 2011. A day earlier, Booth Goodwin, the US Attorney in Charleston, had reached an agreement with Alpha to resolve criminal and civil penalties it had inherited from Massey from the Upper Big Branch disaster—by paying $209 million in a landmark agreement, which included $80 million to improve safety at the company's underground mines and a total of $46.5 million in restitution to the families of the twenty-nine miners who were killed and two others who were injured. MSHA had fined Alpha a record $10.8 million for the accident, and issued a thousand-page report in which it said the company's culture was a root cause of the accident. Goodwin said a criminal probe of individuals was continuing.

In the Rawl case, the money from Alpha and its insurers was distributed to plaintiffs beginning in 2012. Thompson and his partners had wanted the settlement to fund a critical-illness insurance policy, but the plan was scrapped when people said they'd rather have the money added to their checks. Of Thompson's 556 clients still in the case, only one person didn't accept the settlement in the end. Thompson also finally got paid. Back in New Orleans, Kathleen and Kelsey spent an afternoon staring at Kathleen's laptop as the first amount was deposited into their checking account: $400,000. Most of that would be distributed to people Thompson needed to pay. But he called from Charleston and urged them to celebrate. The only thing they could think to do was go to Barnes & Noble, where they walked out with $300 worth of books. The next time he came home, Thompson bought his first iPhone and he spent $205 on two bikes, one for Charleston and the other for New Orleans. That May, he bought a five-year-old Jeep Liberty with 262,000 miles on it for $2,900 from a state surplus sale in Charleston. He didn't bother to fix the windshield after a rock flew up and cracked it from one side to the other.

In March 2012, Thompson attended a premiere with Kathleen of Filippo Piscopo and Lorena Luciano's film, which they called *Coal Rush*, and Kathleen met many of Thompson's staff in person for the first time. In August, a full year after the Rawl settlement, Thompson and the other attorneys on the case—Barney, Bunch, Stanley, and Cassidy—were runners-up for the Trial Lawyer of the Year Award given by Public Justice, a trial lawyers' group, for "holding Massey Energy and its then–chief executive officer accountable."

News from Williamson reached Thompson regularly, and most of the time it made him glad he didn't live there anymore. In September 2012, Dr. Diane Shafer was sentenced to six months in prison for running a pill mill in Williamson. She had been among the first to link the health problems in Rawl to the well water and had helped Thompson early on in the case. Shafer had pleaded guilty to leaving pre-written prescription pads in her office off Second Avenue, so that her staff could effectively sell them to people she hadn't examined. Prosecutors said that between 2003 and 2010, she'd written more than 118,000 prescriptions for controlled substances, more than several West Virginia hospitals during that time.

Over the next few months, a handful of people tied to pill mills in Mingo County, including four doctors, were prosecuted. The opioid epidemic had ravaged all of southern West Virginia, with Mingo County among the worst-affected counties not only in the state but in the entire country. For years coal left on trains from the rail yard outside Williamson, while prescription painkillers arrived by the truckload. From 2006 to 2016, two drug wholesalers shipped 20.8 million hydrocodone and oxycodone pills to the Tug Valley Pharmacy and Hurley Drug Company in Williamson, a city with a population of 2,900.

In April 2013, Eugene Crum, Lonnie Hannah's successor as Mingo County sheriff, was shot twice in the head at point-blank range while he sat in his police cruiser eating his lunch across the street from a pill mill that had been shut down. Crum had been an ally of Judge Thornsbury and a regular at his lunch table at Starters; hours before the shooting, he had asked the judge if he wanted to have lunch, but Thornsbury had said he had an appointment with an optometrist that day. Crum was killed a block and a half away from the Mountaineer.

The suspect in the shooting, Tennis Maynard, had fled the scene, and after crashing his car into a bridge about nine miles away in Delbarton, was shot multiple times by a sheriff's deputy. Maynard survived, but he has never stood trial, in part, it seems, because of questions about his mental stability. Rumors swirled in Williamson that someone had put Maynard up to Crum's murder. The suspicions only deepened after people discovered that the FBI had been investigating elected officials in the county for more than a year.

On August 14, 2013, Booth Goodwin, the US Attorney in Charleston, announced that Judge Thornsbury had been arrested on criminal charges. Federal prosecutors, led by Steve Ruby, charged the judge with conspiring to frame his secretary's husband for drug possession, grand larceny, and assault and battery. Prosecutors alleged that the judge had begun a relationship with his secretary in early 2008, around the time that Thompson and others had noticed that the judge had changed his wardrobe and diet.

According to the indictment, Thornsbury's secretary broke off their romance in June 2008. In response, the judge summoned a man to his chambers and instructed him to put a magnetic metal box that contained cocaine underneath the husband's pickup. Then Thornsbury arranged for a policeman to stop the truck, search it, and arrest the husband. One of the men backed out, and the plan was never carried out.

Thornsbury came up with a new plan in early 2009, prosecutors said, when he appointed one of his business partners in town to serve as foreman of the county's grand jury. Thornsbury crafted grand jury subpoenas to local companies so he could gather information about his secretary's husband. The judge secretly ordered a state trooper to file a criminal complaint against the husband for stealing scrap metal, even though his employer had allowed him to salvage the items. The judge had to abandon the second plot too, after his business ties to the grand jury foreman came to light—thanks to Thompson's motions to get him disqualified from the Rawl case.

Prosecutors pointed to yet a third plot: In 2012, after the husband got into an altercation outside a convenience store, Thornsbury instructed the Mingo County prosecutor to ensure that he got six months in prison. The prosecutor offered the husband a plea deal with those terms, but he refused. Charges were dropped only after security-camera footage showed that the husband had acted in self-defense when one man took a swing at him and another pulled a gun.

In September, Steve Ruby filed a second indictment, charging Thornsbury with conspiring with other county officials to cover up illegal drug use and other misconduct by the former sheriff, Crum.

In the months before Crum was shot, he owed three thousand dollars to a man named George White, a sign maker who had made yard signs for Crum when he was running for sheriff. Prosecutors said that rather than pay the debt, Crum had an informant buy three oxycodone pills from White. The county grand jury then issued an indictment against White, who was arrested on drug charges. White, however, approached the FBI with his attorney, telling agents that he'd provided Crum with narcotics in the past and that Crum had violated election laws.

In a convoluted scheme later outlined by Steve Ruby, Crum and two other county officials—the county prosecutor and a commissioner—met with White's brother and told him that if White fired his lawyer and got one of their choosing, Thornsbury would give him a lighter sentence. Thornsbury agreed, and White fired his attorney. But then the judge sentenced White to up to 15 years in prison anyway. White spent 240 days incarcerated before Thornsbury's indictment, and later said he feared for his life in Mingo County.

Thompson was home in New Orleans when the indictments against Thornsbury were handed down. Spike Maynard, Blankenship's old friend, called Thompson on his cell phone to ask where he was, Thompson recalled. Maynard had lost his seat on the state Supreme Court in 2012, and he was back on the bench in Logan County, where Thompson had just tried a case in front of him that involved the desecration of a Black graveyard by a natural gas company and a pipeline company. Thompson represented fourteen Black plaintiffs whose ancestors had been buried in the Crystal Block Cemetery in Sarah Ann, another historic coal camp. Not far away was the cemetery where Devil Anse, depicted in a life-size Italian marble statue, and other Hatfields were buried. Thompson had found Maynard to be fair and to show concern for the community, and he had won nine hundred thousand dollars on behalf of the families after a trial in which he alleged that a bulldozer driver uttered racial slurs to a resident who urged him not to disturb the cemetery. The victory earned Thompson another recognition from Public Justice as a finalist for Trial Lawyer of the Year. Now Maynard said he was concerned about Thompson's safety. "Thornsbury has been indicted. I wanted to make sure that you weren't in Mingo," Thompson recalled Maynard telling him.

While Thompson was talking to Maynard, Kathleen walked into his office. Taking the phone, she asked Maynard if Thompson had ever been in danger when he was living in Williamson. "Your husband was in grave danger," Maynard said.

The indictments justified Thompson's paranoia in the frenzied days when he was trying to get the judge recused from the case in 2009. After all, B.I. Sammons had warned him that a state trooper was going to plant drugs on someone's car—the same plot prosecutors accused the judge of cooking up.

Thornsbury pleaded guilty in federal court only to the conspiracy related to George White, the sign maker. The other charges were dropped as part of his plea deal. At his sentencing in June 2014, Thornsbury said, "I failed. I allowed the law to be clouded, the light of the law to be clouded by my loyalties, misguided loyalty, ambition, and pride." He had cooperated with prosecutors, providing evidence that would help send the county prosecutor and the county commissioner to prison. The night before he'd agreed to cooperate, a house Thornsbury owned in Kentucky had burned down; he took this as a warning against cooperating, but he did so anyway. A fire marshal determined that an arsonist set the fire, but no one was charged.

Ruby, the prosecutor, said Thornsbury's behavior was egregious. "This defendant sat on the bench, in a robe, flanked by the American flag, and adjudged George White guilty and sent him to prison for up to fifteen years," Ruby said. "Frankly, Your Honor, I've never heard of a case like this. If I weren't standing right here in the middle of it, I wouldn't believe it."

The judge sentenced Thornsbury to fifty months in prison.

Less than a month later, Thompson and Dave Barney found themselves in the bizarre position of deposing Thornsbury. The lawyers had agreed to represent both George White and a private investigator named Don Stevens, who had been beaten in his Mingo County home by masked men. Stevens alleged that he had been framed by county officials on wiretapping charges because they thought he was providing some kind of information to the FBI about Judge Thornsbury.

Thornsbury denied any knowledge of the situation involving Stevens. Under questioning by Barney, the former judge was less contrite than he had been at his sentencing. "I wasn't a dictator; I wasn't a Boss Hogg," Thornsbury said. Then, when the lawyers asked if he'd provided information to prosecutors about any other individuals, Thornsbury admitted that he had—about their own firm.

"Okay," Barney said. "What in particular about my firm?"

"Be obstruction of justice to go into the issue," Thornsbury said.

"Okay. Well, was anything—? There were certainly no indictments against my firm, were there?" Barney asked.

"Not yet," Thornsbury said.

Thompson had other things occupying most of his time while the corruption sweep was playing out in Mingo County. On January 9, 2014, a chemical spill outside Charleston contaminated the drinking water for the capital and about three hundred thousand people in nine counties. It would become one of the largest cases of drinking water contamination in US history.

That day, Thompson was in the Admiral's Den when his new assistant Tyler Collins, a tech-savvy recent West Virginia University graduate with a degree in political science, ran out of the office and vomited in the yard after drinking a mug of tea he'd made. Within minutes, the chemical spill hit the news, and Thompson could smell the heavy licorice odor wafting over Charleston. The contaminated water spread quickly through the region, and there were reports of others falling ill after drinking the water. Some people who bathed in it developed rashes and respiratory problems.

Thompson leaped into action, securing financing from Stuart Smith and hiring experts that same day. That week, he got another devastating piece of news. Kathleen was diagnosed with breast cancer, and she began a long road to treatment and recovery. As he tried to spend more time in New Orleans, Thompson outmaneuvered dozens of lawyers who filed small individual claims in state court. With help from Van Bunch, he filed a lawsuit in federal court and sought to represent everyone affected by the spill, including businesses. Along with Dave

Barney, Melissa Ellsworth was still on Thompson's team in Charleston. She would go on to marry her boyfriend Gary DeLuke and have two children with him, after getting a law degree from West Virginia University and becoming an attorney herself. Steve Wussow was already a lawyer based in New Orleans and kept working with Thompson. Nick Getzen had quit law school in Oregon, and he was playing in poker tournaments around the country.

The primary chemical that had leaked through a one-inch hole in a storage tank on the Elk River was used at prep plants to clean coal. The irony wasn't lost on Thompson or Ernie Brown, who had told state legislators that someday the problems at Rawl would visit them. After people bought up all the bottled water in Charleston, one man drove to South Williamson and bought 275 gallons, an entire pallet, according to a report in the *New Yorker*. It was from the same Big Lots where Ernie used to buy his own bottled water. Thompson sued Eastman Chemical, the manufacturer, claiming that it hadn't informed the storage company about the chemical's corrosiveness. He sued the water company, for failing to have an adequate emergency plan and a backup water supply in place as it had promised to do years earlier. The class action would cover more than 230,000 people.

Thompson had one good piece of news: the day after the chemical spill, Massey had agreed to voluntarily dismiss its defamation lawsuit against him, nearly eight years after it filed it. Thompson had spent twenty-eight thousand dollars in legal fees, but at least he no longer had the lawsuit hanging over his head.

In the end, three other Mingo County officials pleaded guilty to charges that included extortion, using public authority to violate a person's constitutional rights, and falsifying a voter registration application and were all sentenced to prison. As significant as these corruption cases were, in another sense they were merely a detour for Steve Ruby and Booth Goodwin, who were also investigating Massey and the deaths of the twenty-nine miners in the Upper Big Branch accident. They had already won guilty pleas and convictions against four Massey employees who had, among other charges, falsified a foreman's license and lied to investigators about it, covered up Massey's practice of warning underground miners whenever safety inspectors arrived (which would allow miners to clean up hazards and avoid citations and fines), and ordered a methane monitor to be disabled less than two months before the explosion. One employee admitted that the practice of warning miners about inspections had been going on for twelve years—and that it was discussed among employees at the company above him and below him. The judge asked for more specifics.

"The chief executive officer," the employee said, meaning Blankenship.

On November 13, 2014, the US Attorneys indicted Don Blankenship. It was extremely rare for a CEO of a major US corporation to face criminal charges following an industrial accident.

Blankenship was charged with a misdemeanor count of conspiring to violate federal mine-safety laws and felony counts that included allegedly lying to the Securities and Exchange Commission—and to his own investors—when he said that the company didn't condone any violation of federal mine-safety regulations. The misdemeanor count—for allegedly being part of a conspiracy to skirt safety laws by warning miners underground when inspectors were on the property and falsifying coal dust samples—carried a potential sentence of a year in prison. The felony counts carried a combined maximum sentence of thirty years. Blankenship pleaded not guilty and posted a $5 million cash bond.

Thompson was as shocked as everyone else when Blankenship was indicted. But most days, he was preoccupied with the chemical spill case, which now kept him in Charleston much of the time.

In August 2015, Alpha Natural Resources filed for bankruptcy. The company blamed sinking coal prices and debt from its $7.1 billion Massey acquisition. Alpha had posted four straight annual losses. Its stock was trading at $53.40 on the day it bought Massey; now it was trading at 24 cents. Other coal companies had already or would soon declare bankruptcy. Slowing steel demand in China helped tank prices for coal, and in retrospect, Wall Street analysts realized those record metallurgical coal prices in early 2011 that fueled acquisitions had been inflated from supply disruptions caused by massive flooding in Australia. Retiring when he did, Blankenship had gotten a golden parachute before anyone realized the plane was headed into a mountain.

On December 3, 2015, exactly five years after Blankenship announced his departure from Massey, a jury in Charleston convicted him of the misdemeanor of conspiring to violate mine-safety laws in the months prior to the accident and acquitted him of the two finance-related felonies, sparing him from a lengthy prison term. Prosecutors had secured damning phone conversations Blankenship secretly taped in his office. In one, Blankenship said he wanted to keep confidential a 2009 report about safety failings at the company: if the company were sued after a fatal accident, "it'd be a terrible document to be in discovery," Blankenship said in the recording, which was played for the jury.

Thompson was in the courtroom for the verdict so he could witness the once unthinkable moment in person. Like Bruce Stanley, he had long thought the CEO deserved jail time for a record of corporate malfeasance. Afterward, Thompson joined Ruby at a nearby bar where prosecutors were celebrating. Once again, the two men discussed corruption in Mingo County. Now the two lawyers had both survived cases involving Blankenship. Thompson noted that Thornsbury had been sentenced to fifty months in prison, while Blankenship was facing a maximum of twelve months. Thompson held his palms up, as if weighing the difference. "Thornsbury caused me more pain, so I guess that's fair," Thompson said. An FBI agent standing nearby objected. "Right, that's the measure of success for all convictions, how much pain was caused to Kevin Thompson." Ruby wasn't laughing. "That's a serious conviction," Ruby said of Blankenship's dizzying fall.

Ultimately, the judge in Blankenship's criminal case sentenced the former CEO to a year in federal prison, the maximum, and a $250,000 fine. "Instead of being able to tout you as one of West Virginia's success stories, however, we are here as a result of your part in a dangerous conspiracy," said the judge, who had herself grown up in the southern coalfields.

Blankenship spent most of his incarceration at Taft Correctional Institution, a low-security prison outside Bakersfield, California. He now owned a Spanish-style mansion with an infinity pool outside Las Vegas, and he was dating a Chinese-American businesswoman, Farrah Meiling Hobbs, who was waiting for him there. But soon after his release in May 2017, he returned to the hills along Route 49. Most former CEOs released from prison would have kept out of the public eye. But he returned to West Virginia to begin a campaign: he wanted to overturn his conviction. His prosecution, he believed, had been driven by the political ambitions of Booth Goodwin, who would go on to run unsuccessfully for governor. He felt that MSHA officials had destroyed evidence masking the accident's true cause, an inundation of natural gas, and that prosecutors had withheld exculpatory evidence. He wanted the federal government, now under the Trump administration, to reinvestigate the mine explosion. But he got little traction.

Blankenship was also planning an improbable US Senate run against Senator Joe Manchin, with whom he had always had a rocky relationship. Blankenship was still outraged that Manchin had said in April 2014 that Blankenship had "blood on his hands" from the deaths of the UBB miners. Blankenship's campaign also gave him an opportunity to drive home the point that his own free speech rights had been curtailed when the judge in his criminal case issued a gag order, and that, in fact, MSHA was to blame for the accident. Now, as he spoke stiffly from behind a podium, Blankenship joked that he had been born in the poorhouse, used an outhouse, dined at the White House, and lived in the big house.

Despite his conviction, he believed he knew the state's voters better than any pundit or elected official in Washington. In May 2016, Hillary Clinton chose Williamson as the place to apologize for a gaffe she had made on the campaign trail at a town hall event in Columbus, Ohio, two months earlier in which she said, "We're going to put a lot of coal miners and coal companies out of business." The coal industry and Republicans seized on the remark, even though Clinton had been saying that she didn't want to leave miners and their families behind as the nation moved toward renewable sources of energy. Clinton devoted an entire chapter in her book *What Happened* to the fallout, and she noted that Blankenship was in the crowd that day in Williamson.

"He should have been the least popular man in West Virginia even before he was convicted in the wake of the death of twenty-nine miners," Clinton wrote. "Instead, he was welcomed by the pro-Trump protesters in Williamson. One of them told a reporter that he'd vote for Blankenship for President if he ran."

In the days after his release from prison, Blankenship spent much of his time in West Virginia, visiting with his daughter's family there and tracking his investments, which now included a brand-new Golden Corral restaurant in Pikeville. He lived in his old home in Sprigg. According to a family member, the modest interior had barely been updated since the 1980s. Blankenship kept a TV in the first-floor den tuned to CNBC as he took calls from his broker. Perhaps he'd been studying the market in prison the way he had once memorized the stats on baseball cards. His investment calls had an oracular quality about them, as though he were reading from spreadsheets in his mind's eye. Leaning back in a recliner with his cell phone against his ear, Blankenship looked completely at home in Mingo County. At the same time, he was a total anomaly.

The house reflected this duality. It resembled the nicer homes of Thompson's clients. The den had a green leather couch and was connected to a modest kitchen with a pass-through. Yet there was also a room with expensive-looking exercise equipment and plush white robes. Broad windows looked out onto a backyard, and grass grew where a swimming pool had been filled in. The dining room had deep wall-to-wall carpet, a stylish dining set, and a portable popcorn maker in a corner. All these years later, Blankenship still owned a pair of German shepherds, and he would tell guests he wanted to impress that the dogs could easily tear them apart.

On many days, Blankenship drove a black Mercedes S65 V12, which he said cost $230,000, to Pikeville to check on the progress of the restaurant. Once again he monitored the preparations down to the finest detail, and he was frequently displeased with the performance of his managers. Leaving home, he drove past Merrimac, past Rawl, past the hidden spot where the road turns into Lick Creek. He drove through Williamson, crossed Second Avenue half a block from the Mountaineer, turned onto Route 119, and was soon past his old office in Belfry. He hadn't set foot inside since the day his retirement was announced in December 2010. Sidney, the site of Massey's mine map vault, passed next. On the four-lane, he pushed the car to ninety miles an hour, then one hundred, through the sweeping curves cut into the mountains, the walls of gray shale and orange sandstone bleeding past.

"Everyone in this part of the country knows me, by the way," he boasted on his way to the restaurant one day. "Even though some of them will shoot me and some of them will hug me."

Injustice was on Blankenship's mind these days. He said he had met people in prison who didn't seem to belong there. "There's 2.1 million

Americans in prison. The highest percentage of any nation in the world," he said. "It's a barbaric system because you have no chance. Most of the people plead guilty, just because they can't afford to defend themselves."

As he drove, he ruminated about his own prosecution. He believed the conspiracy charges against him had been cooked up because Steve Ruby hadn't been able to tie him to any corruption in Mingo County. "I knew he was offering plea bargains throughout southern West Virginia to tell him something about me," Blankenship said. He said he found the parallels between his own prosecution and Thornsbury's "odd and ironic." After a pause, he added: "They actually sent Thornsbury to prison for doing what they did in a sense. Thornsbury targeted an individual and framed him, they claimed. . . . They got Thornsbury with setting someone up, and then Booth Goodwin went and set me up."

He said that back in 1985 Thornsbury had represented some nonunion truck drivers for Rawl Sales when they would get arrested for trucks that were overloaded with coal. "That was the legal service he provided, getting them bailed out and defending them. But I didn't know him very well," Blankenship said. "They've made a big deal of me being in a restaurant with him in Williamson, but as you can see, in Williamson that's going to happen."

Blankenship defended himself and Massey. "It's a lie that I'm a bad guy. We had less violations than others. We did more to improve safety than others," he said, before he grew exasperated. "There's been so many lies told I can't ever straighten them out anyway."

He tried to argue that it wasn't accurate to say he was anti-union, even though he had broken the UMWA's strike at Rawl in 1985. "It was just that the union dominated who could be hired, what the wages were, all the things that the mine was trying to do," he said. "When we threw off that domination, they disintegrated, and they've hated me ever since." At the same time, he took credit for moving West Virginia from a blue state to a red one by defeating the union at Rawl. "What really converted West Virginia was the 1985 strike," he said. "Depowering the United Mine Workers is basically what caused West Virginia to move to the right."

Finally, when it came to the water lawsuit, Blankenship said slurry injection had been a common coal industry practice for decades. "Companies putting water underground has been the case forever and ever and ever," he said. "Water quality in this area has always been bad. It's naturally sulfuric, what they call red water. When I was growing up we had to boil the water and the red would come to the top and we'd skim it off with a cup. And you couldn't even wash your clothes. Otherwise your clothes would turn red. You couldn't drink it at all. So I don't know why the geology, or whatever it is, causes the water in this area to be bad, but it's just naturally bad."

He maintained that the Sprouse Creek processing plant had injected slurry closer to Sprigg than Lick Creek well before his house had been put on city water and that there was no connection between those discharges and the decision to get water from Matewan. To suggest otherwise was "a total lie."

He went on, "I knew Sprouse Creek pretty well, because that was the first operation I was over, and they were discharging water into the Pond Creek seam off the plant. But I was always told that it would not be impacting their wells because the wells weren't as deep as the coal seam and the coal seam was beneath the wells. I was told that the water would have to run uphill to get into their wells. So I don't know. We have so many frivolous lawsuits . . . as an industry you tend to get to the point where you're immune to it." He noted that the state of West Virginia had "to approve any pumping underground as not being damaging to the water underground. So you have to first assume that it would not be permitted if it was a risk to the water system." After a career of complaining that environmental regulators had been too zealous, now he was essentially saying that it was their fault if Rawl Sales had contaminated people's water.

When the Golden Corral came into view in a vast shopping plaza outside Pikeville, a look of irritation came on Blankenship's face. He had calculated that the restaurant, which had more than three hundred seats, should be able to generate about $4 million in revenue a year, with about a 20 percent margin. The breakdown in costs included 38 percent for food, 22 percent for labor, and 6 percent in Golden Corral corporate fees. The one measurement that a manager hadn't calculated properly was the height of the sign in the parking lot. Blankenship figured it was about twenty feet short compared to other fast-food chain signs off Route 119. "You can't see it from the highway. If you ask Siri about the restaurant, she'll tell you to come to this area, but you can't see it from the highway," Blankenship said. The oversight rankled. "I want them to see it when they cross the bridge." He figured it was going to cost about $6,000 to raise the sign twenty feet.

Everyone was deferential when Blankenship walked into the restaurant to look the operation over from top to bottom. It was a soft launch. A steady lunch crowd filed in.

"You Mr. Blankenship?" said an elderly man wearing jeans and a plaid shirt.

Smooth jazz was piped in through the ceiling, but the man's voice had an edge to it. There was a moment of uncertainty: Was this one of the people who wanted to hug Blankenship or shoot him?

"I am," Blankenship said back to the man. "How're you?"

The man gave his name. "I hauled coal for Massey for years," he said.

"Is that right?" Blankenship said.

"I lived up by Sidney for years," the man said.

"Is that right? You hauled for Sidney?"

"All of them," the man said.

Blankenship laughed and said, "I hope I didn't get your job when I put that belt line in."

"You did," the man said, breaking into a smile. "But they sent me right on somewhere else. They liked me."

"Oh, that's great," said Blankenship. He said he didn't want to hold up the line of people waiting to pay as they entered the restaurant. "But I'm always glad to meet people."

"I'm sorry what happened," the man said, referring to Blankenship's conviction and the year he had spent in federal custody. "I mean, that was a rip-off."

"It's terrible," Blankenship said.

The day before the restaurant's official launch, Blankenship visited again. Still unhappy with the pace of the preparations, he approached two Golden Corral corporate officials taking a dinner break.

"It sure looks better than it did two days ago," Blankenship said with a faint smile. "That was a total mess."

The officials said the employees were still on schedule. But that didn't reassure Blankenship. "Maybe I'll shoot everyone and let God sort 'em out," he said.

Blankenship smiled, while the corporate officials looked uncomfortable. It wasn't clear if they knew he was joking. Certainly they didn't know that he was echoing a sign union miners had posted on Route 49 during the 1985 strike at Rawl Sales: "KILL M ALL LET GOD SORT M OUT."

Driving between Pikeville and Williamson, Blankenship recounted the history of the area. Before there were any roads, "Devil Anse and those guys" used to make the trip between Logan and Pikeville along roughly the same path he was taking. Blankenship saw parallels between the 1985 strike at Rawl Sales, the 1920 Matewan Massacre, and the strike along Route 49 that lasted through 1920 and most of 1921, a piece of history he had spent three hundred thousand dollars to preserve by building a replica of Matewan's old train depot. After the 1985 strike, Rawl Sales had fired ninety unionized miners; it was the first time that had happened since 1921, Blankenship said. "It's such an amazing story of the shootout," Blankenship said. "The 1985 strike was almost as bad." He didn't know how to account for the violence of the county, except to suggest that some of the first miners in the region had been released from prisons to work there. "Maybe it's in their blood."

Soon he was back on Route 49, a road he had driven his entire life, in a place he knew as intimately as anyone.

"That's where I live," he said. "I can always go home."

In August 2017, James Berlin Anderson was talking about his disappointment over the settlement, still fresh in his mind six years later. "The truth's gonna stand when the world's burning," he said. Thompson had led him to believe that he stood to get as much as $1.6 million from the case, Anderson said. In the end, he walked away with less than $100,000. In the intervening years, he had been in a violent car accident that led to $82,000 in medical bills; a $17,000 insurance settlement hadn't come close to covering them. The house he lived in with his wife, Lisa, was in foreclosure. But there was more.

Anderson was sitting with Lisa and a family friend on the porch of their house, on the other side of Route 119 from Williamson, a few miles into Kentucky. He had on a grease-smudged baseball cap, a T-shirt, jeans, and a pair of untied white high-tops. His face looked drained. It was the color of the slate he'd hauled for years at the strip mine. A month after Blankenship had been released from federal custody, an oncologist had told Anderson, who was now forty-nine years old, that his renal cell carcinoma, first diagnosed in 2014, had returned. The doctor estimated that he had about four months to live.

As he sat on his porch and drew on a cigarette, Anderson said the cancer was through his lymph nodes in his chest, around his heart, and on the outside of his lungs. He had terrible headaches, which made him think the cancer had reached his brain. He had been given the option of another round of chemotherapy and radiation, but he said the treatments would just burn him up for three months and then he would die anyway. He'd rather enjoy his remaining days. "It's terminal this time," he said. "Unless God heals it. If God heals it, it's good. You know what I mean?"

Anderson had tried to reach Thompson several times over the past two years but hadn't gotten through. "He knew about the kidney, but he's not known anything else," Anderson said. "His wife got breast cancer, last I heard. So I figured he took some time off to be with her."

In fact, Thompson had started to draft a new lawsuit on Anderson's behalf in 2014. But the settlement had released the company from future claims related to the water. Since the 2011 settlement, the results of the medical monitoring program had been alarming: 83 percent of people who participated in the testing had health problems that required follow-up treatment, according to a report in January 2016. But only 20 percent of people were taking advantage of the testing. Many others feared receiving a diagnosis and not being able to afford medical treatment. The program was still well-funded and scheduled to continue through the middle of 2041. Thyroid disease was one of the most common problems found through testing.

James hadn't taken advantage of the program, but he didn't think it would have staved off the inevitable. He believed that his exposure to the water in Rawl in his youth had caused his cancer. "I can't help but think that that water thing started this junk," he said. "I can't prove it . . . But either way, that's sad, man, that they would take a chance on your life like that. Just to make money for them. Just to save money."

Anderson had lost sixty pounds and sometimes stayed in bed eighteen hours a day. He had qualified for disability benefits, but he wouldn't start receiving checks until December, when in all likelihood he'd no longer be alive. For some reason, on this day, his spirits were up. "I'm actually having a good day," he said. "It's too pretty to be sick today."

Sitting out on his porch in the mornings, he watched the five or six bucks across the road walk through a cut in the kudzu. And he recalled a day recently when he was free of pain for a few hours. He got in his truck for the first time in weeks and drove to an Arby's, where he got two roast beef sandwiches. Then he went home to sleep. When he woke, he was still free from pain and thought for a moment that Jesus had cured him. "You take so much for granted, man. So much, it's unreal," he said. "What you do. Breathing. Breathing."

He'd picked out his own casket, which he called "a Cadillac." "I'm telling you, if you come to my funeral, you'll see a nice box," he said. But he hoped to see his coworkers at the mine again. "I told Lisa, if I die tonight, all these people love me. I had some fantastic friends. I sure did. I can say that. Hopefully God will smile on that somewhere. I've heard it more than once. You preach your own funeral. When you leave here, people know you. They can tell about you. And they'll know if they mean it or not."

He had a glint in his eye. "I told my wife, I've lived almost fifty years. I know some buddies of mine didn't make it to thirty. As we was growing up they got killed early. And so I said, I'm fortunate, I got twenty years on 'em. So if the Lord lets me live another ten years, fantastic, and if he don't want me to make it through the night, that's fine too. I'm ready."

He remembered the poverty he'd grown up in. "We were poor, buddy," he said. "We were the type poor that we sit around the table in the evening, and we'd take a string bean and put a string through it and take turns swallowing it." He laughed at the absurd image. "That's poor, ain't it? That was funny. A buddy of mine taught me that years ago and I thought that was hilarious."

He had wanted to take a four-wheeler back into the hills behind Rawl, where he had drank beer and lit fires with his friends when they were teenagers. But he never ventured far from home again. His obituary would simply note that he died at home on December 1, 2017, from a lingering illness.

Fewer trucks loaded with coal barreled down Route 49, and fewer trains left the rail yard in Williamson. Most mines in the county had shut down. The green preparation plant at Rawl Sales had been idled again in 2011; the impoundment was drying out like an ash-gray lake after a long drought. The old Rawl Sales offices on Route 49 were fenced in and overgrown. In Matewan, the mine workers' local, born out of the massacre there in 1920 and decimated by the 1985 strike, no longer had a single member working as a coal miner. Some worked in a hospital in Pikeville. Once again, on the road between Williamson and Matewan, life had settled down after a bitter fight. The rhythms of the place were in the green uneven ridges, in the trees leaning over the Tug Fork, and in the kudzu taking back the land. For the first time in more than a century, it was possible to look at the mountains and imagine a time after coal.

In Rawl, some people had used their settlement money to replace the green metal roofs on the old company houses; they still looked brand-new. Pickup trucks edging up and down the narrow hollow were newer models. Bo Scott's Chevy Silverado had a black decal above its front grille, and he drove through the mountains keeping a busy schedule of preaching and organizing food drives for residents in the county: "Psalm 118:8." The verse—"It is better to trust in the Lord than to put confidence in man"—could have been a comment on the water lawsuit, the state's judicial system, environmental regulators, state and local politicians, or the coal companies and investors who had shaped the last century and a half of human activity along the Tug Fork.

Several families had moved to Tennessee, which Thompson said was a kind of Promised Land for some of his clients. Others, like Donetta Blankenship, B.I. Sammons, Maude Rice, and Frank Coleman, remained in the area. Donetta still sold clothes at makeshift markets by the side of the highway; her husband, Orville, worked on cars all day beside their house. In their front yard, there were a dozen red bird feeders that Donetta had set up. Hummingbirds darted between them.

In Lick Creek, B.I. spent most of his days laid up on his living room couch, the TV blaring a few feet away, as his son and daughter came and went and his wife, Deborah, brought him meals on a tray. In his seventies, he still had wispy white hair slicked back on the sides of his head, and he said he was in pain most of the time. "I've had a couple strokes, and there's things that I used to remember that I can't remember anymore," he said. He maintained that many people hadn't wanted to settle but felt forced into the decision. "We ended up not even getting a tenth of what we was supposed to have got," he said. "It's just one of those situations where a lot of money changed hands."

Maude Rice, whose parents had lived in the old tent colony near the mouth of the hollow where the top of an old white steeple now poked out from some trees, still lived in her brick house a few doors up from B.I. She said she too had been angry at first about the distribution of the settlement money but that her days really hadn't changed. She said she hadn't touched the money she had gotten. "I bet every one of them's got theirs spent, but not me," she said with a hint of mischief. "*Uhn-uhn*. It's in the bank. My son tells me, Mommy, why don't you spend some of it? But, you know what? You never know how times are going to get yet."

A new generation was coming up, and some saw opportunities far beyond Mingo County. Amber McCoy, who was eleven in 2004 when Thompson arrived in Rawl, had gotten a scholarship to the University of Pennsylvania. After she graduated magna cum laude, she hopscotched again to the University of Virginia, where she would receive a law degree in 2018. Her well water in Rawl had been orange and black and awful smelling. Whenever possible, she still only drank distilled water. She was seeking medical attention for several health issues, but she didn't like to discuss it much. Amber had never traced her lineage through her father's side back to the feud. She was looking to the future. A McCoy in the twenty-first century, she was armed with a law degree, and she said she wanted to help people like those she had grown up with. She had known both Don Blankenship and Kevin Thompson in a glancing way. Blankenship's daughter had been her babysitter, and Amber could recall seeing his guard dogs at the family's house in Sprigg. She also remembered peeking through the windows of Blankenship's corporate retreat across the river in Kentucky. She had met Thompson only a few times when she had gone with her mother, Brenda McCoy, to meet him in his office on the fourth floor of the Mountaineer. She had never seen Thompson in court, and she had played no role in the lawsuit, except for being one of the children it was intended to help. When she was a teenager angry that her community had been exploited for forever, Thompson had made a strong enough impression on her. She remembered seeing him go up to people at their houses to explain what was going on with the lawsuit. He was the reason she was becoming a lawyer.

"He never made people feel ignorant. He made people think there might be some justice here. We might be able to get this fixed," she said. "He was a very good addition to the community."

"I talk about him a lot, but I haven't talked to him in a long time."

Ernie and Carmelita Brown sat at their kitchen table, where they had sat across from Thompson on so many other afternoons. Ernie had been reading Proverbs, looking for something to preach that Sunday. Years after the settlement, the entire case was still churned up in his mind, as if behind a dam that might break at any moment. He let Carmelita tell her version of the story.

The company had underestimated the people in this area, she said. For years, people sat back and let things happen. But then they had taken a stand again. People who didn't live there always asked why she and Ernie didn't move away, or why they didn't hire a lawyer sooner. She said they wouldn't have been able to sell their house: no one would want to buy one with contaminated well water.

"So many whys," Carmelita said. Then she added her own. "Why did Don do this? Was it a money thing? . . . He did know. He had engineers come, and they told him, said, 'If you pump this in this certain spot, it's going to get into this and this and this.' See, that's what they were there for. They knew the water flow. They knew the rock strata."

Carmelita, who had endured nearly as much as anyone from contaminants in her well water, said she didn't dislike Blankenship. Her thoughts about him followed a logic with as many turns as the river has between Williamson and Matewan. She saw much that was good in the man she held most responsible for her suffering.

"Don as a person and Don as a president, CEO, two different people," she said. "When Don was a CEO, Don was a CEO. Whatever the company needed, whatever there was to benefit the company, that was Don. When Don was a person, Don was a person. He lived here. He grew up here. You can't say Don didn't love this place. He did. He graduated from Matewan. . . . He made the decision. He made the decision to put the refuse water down into the mines. Nobody else made that decision. Don made that decision. Don made it for the company. Don knew the water was bad. Why else would he have had a water line hooked up from Matewan to get city water? He knew the water was bad. He knew what was going into the water. He knew how they treated that water. Don knew all this stuff." (When Blankenship would make his failed run for US Senate a year later in 2018, Carmelita would give him her vote in the Republican primary. "Out of all the people, he was as good, if not better, than anyone running and probably a lesser evil than the rest," she said.)

When it came to Thompson, Ernie was more disappointed than his wife. He maintained that too many people who hadn't lived in the area for very long got too much settlement money. Though the amounts were confidential, rumors were rampant even before the checks were in mailboxes. Ernie recalled Blankenship's second deposition: as he'd listened to Blankenship admit to the slurry injection, he realized that the company had changed tacks. They no longer disputed whether they'd injected slurry or how much—they focused instead on arguing that the injections hadn't harmed people's health. In the end, he thought Thompson had been forced to focus more on the clients who had come down with cancer, rather than people like Ernie and Carmelita, who didn't have the most serious conditions but had gone through more than most.

"I'm not taking anything from Kevin," Carmelita said. "He worked hard. I liked him and everything. I just think he got sidetracked a little bit. . . . Kevin understood what we were going through and he knew. He pretty much lived it too for the last six or seven years. He lived it," she said. "He got to where he come in. He made hisself at home and used my phone. Even if I wasn't here, he came in and made hisself at home and used my phone. Yeah. That's how it was. He was just like one of the people. One of the family. I hold nothing against Kevin. . . . I made the best of what I could."

Carmelita had taken out several mason jars of their old well water she kept under her kitchen sink. Ernie suggested she throw them out. "No, don't throw it out. I like to look at it every now and then," she said. "I'm a keeper. You know me."

Ernie turned back to his Bible, squinting at the print in the light over the kitchen table. "An unrighteous judge gives an unrighteous judgment because he himself is unrighteous," he said, paraphrasing a verse. "Proverbs. It tells you everything you need to know in life. You can't beat it."

• • •

On a Saturday morning in late July 2017, Thompson went to the airport in Charleston. He was flying to New Orleans through Atlanta. An agent had upgraded him to first class, seat 1A, for the 6:45 a.m. flight. Moments after he sat down, he saw a man in the aisle take off a navy Brooks Brothers sport coat, fold it neatly, and place it in the overhead compartment. Don Blankenship sat in the seat beside him.

The surge of recognition in Thompson contained the tens of thousands of hours he had worked on the case, every interaction he had had with every client, and all the hours he had spent at his desk in the Mountaineer plotting ways to defeat Massey and its lawyers. The caricature of Blankenship with the cherry-red lips was still taped up in the Admiral's Den. Now the man Thompson had joked about, jeered and cursed, and even, at times, admired, was sitting a few inches away. They locked eyes and shook hands. Thompson introduced himself, just in case Blankenship wasn't able to place him. It had been six years since the two men had been in the same room together. But when Thompson mentioned Rawl, Blankenship said, "Lick Creek"—his shorthand for the water lawsuit. He knew exactly who Thompson was.

"Well, you must be doing pretty good now, if you're flyin' first class," Thompson recalled Blankenship saying.

Thompson didn't mention that he had led a team of lawyers in reaching a $150 million settlement with Eastman Chemical and the water company in the 2014 chemical spill. The settlement had been reached on the last day in October 2016, but eight months later no money had been paid out yet. Sitting next to Blankenship, Thompson was thinking more like a reporter, he recalled later. His mind was running on multiple tracks. He was disappointed with himself for not being more confrontational as they talked. But Blankenship had a certain charm. And Thompson had subjects he wanted to cover. It was a lesson he'd learned from Bruce Stanley's deposition of Blankenship: engage his intellect. Thompson didn't want to miss the opportunity, while he had Blankenship captive one final time.

"I think I convinced him on Rawl," Thompson said later. "His engineers said that it wasn't possible. I said, well, there's only one place in the world with higher lead, and that's Lake Kivu in the Congo. And what's interesting about Rawl is it's not only the highest levels of lead.

It's also the highest levels of arsenic. They're correlated. You typically don't find arsenic or lead in Appalachian water. You find iron, but not arsenic and lead, and if they're correlated, the only place you're going to find that around there is slurry. And that really fucking— That seemed to drill deep into him. He said, well, if I'd have known that, that's not what my engineers told me, if I'd have known that, I would have settled the case. That's what he told me."

Blankenship had once wielded enough power that, almost on a whim, he could have averted seven years of litigation and millions of dollars spent by each side. Yet he also told Thompson that it was his practice to starve out lawyers who sued Massey, dragging out lawsuits for ten or fifteen years. It was another point Thompson was pleased he had been able to confirm.

"What I didn't tell him was that we expected that, and at the end of the rainbow we were going to take a billion dollars and destroy the company," Thompson said.

The conversation roamed for more than an hour. Thompson brought up Ben Hatfield, who had been shot and killed in a botched robbery in May 2016 at the cemetery in Maher, ten miles north of Williamson, where he had been cleaning the grave of his wife, who had died of breast cancer in 2009. (The honorary pallbearers at her funeral had included Don Blankenship, Spike Maynard, and Gene Kitts.) Thompson and Blankenship talked about violence in Mingo County; the opioid crisis in West Virginia; the Upper Big Branch explosion; President Trump; Steve Ruby and what Blankenship viewed as the political vendetta against him; Blankenship's ideas for health care reform, which included having a government program cover people with preexisting conditions; Blankenship's girlfriend; and Blankenship's plan to run for the US Senate against Joe Manchin.

Thompson told Blankenship there were good things about him. "I didn't know anybody said any good things about me," Blankenship replied.

Thompson rattled off his list. He knew Blankenship didn't lie. He thought the CEO's use of the Massey helicopter was wise. "I complimented him on the use of the corporate air force. Because I said, you know, you're about the only corporate air force I ever saw a reason for, because from what I heard, you would leave your office over in Kentucky and if you were having a problem you would fly over and talk to the men at the face. He said, that's exactly right."

After they got off the plane, Blankenship asked Thompson if he would appear in a commercial for him if he ran for the Senate. Thompson demurred.

(In 2019, Blankenship would sue about a hundred media organizations and individuals for defamation, including Fox News and CNN, alleging that their intentional mischaracterization of him as a "felon," when he had been convicted of a misdemeanor, had cost him the primary and future business opportunities. His lawyers, including one on East Second Avenue in Williamson, were suing for $12 billion in damages. A year later, he would make a quixotic, if earnest, run for president as a candidate with the conservative Constitution Party, winning about fifty-five thousand votes in the twenty-one states where he was on the ballot.)

When they parted ways, Thompson was left to ponder his own contradictory impressions alone in the Delta Sky Club Lounge. The charge was gone from the once larger-than-life persona. Now that Blankenship was no longer CEO of one of the nation's biggest coal companies, he was no longer intimidating. But there was more to the transformation. To Thompson, there was something cartoonish about Blankenship. Up close, he seemed like a smaller man than Thompson had once thought him to be.

"I don't want to underestimate him, but he seemed so big and strong before," Thompson said. "He was a really good businessman and made astute decisions and seemed to understand how the world worked, okay? Now he clearly doesn't, unless I'm completely wrong about the world." He paused. "I don't want to say I feel sorry for him, because I don't in any way, shape, or form."

On another night in Rawl, Larry Brown sat on a swing between his double-wide trailer and his church. The hollow was surrounded by darkness, and apart from his voice, the only sounds were of the water running in the creek a few feet behind him. Remembering everything he and Brenda had been through, Brown said he still had scars on his arms and abdomen from the boils. He was certain they came from drinking contaminated well water. He recalled his daughter's miscarriages, her bout with cervical cancer, and her ongoing liver problems. But he lit up when his three-year-old granddaughter toddled over to him and held up a stick of lip balm that she pretended was lipstick. He spoke to her gently, calling her "Papaw's girl." Then he wrapped her in his long arms before sending her back to her mother's house, just a few yards from his and Brenda's.

Brown knew that in his heart Thompson had wanted to take the case to trial. He got overruled by his partners and the residents at the Embassy Suites who had wanted to settle. "I liked him from the start," Brown said. "But, you know, the main thing I got out of this—and I'm well satisfied with it—we got the water, and that means a world to me. Little kids that just been born, since we got the water in here, they never knew what we did. We made a difference."

Somewhere in the darkness beyond Brown's house, higher up the mountain, his grandfather had worked at a coal mine, where he was nearly killed twice. Brown said he believed God was on the side of the miners in those days, when the coal companies had hired detectives to evict people from their homes. And God had been on the side of the people in the water lawsuit.

Brown described a final vision. He said it happened several times, on nights like this, when he was sitting outside and heard music beyond his property in the darkness. "The more I focused on what I was hearing—it was gospel. It was singing religious. And they was saying glory to God in the highest, amen. And they were singing. And I turned wide awake, not asleep. Couldn't see nothing. It was total darkness. And all of a sudden it was people. This whole mountain was covered with people. Everywhere you see trees it was covered with people singing glory to God in the highest, amen. I went through this for eight years. I felt like I was just getting beat down. Beat down. Getting older. People was arguing over the money, calling me up, and I was saying, Come on, we got to thank God for the water. And I said, I know they didn't treat us right with the money. So they started backing off. Everybody says, I'm glad I have the water. I thank God for the water."

ACKNOWLEDGMENTS

I'm grateful to everyone who shared their stories with me for this book, especially when it meant unfolding parts of their lives that were painful. Special thanks to Carmelita and Ernie Brown, for their unvarnished accounts of growing up in Mingo County and living with their well water; to Larry and Brenda Brown, including for the memorable service I attended at their church in Rawl one night; thank you to B.I. and Debbie Sammons; Don Dillon; Bo Scott; Frank Coleman; Donetta Blankenship; and Maude Rice, all of whom welcomed me into their homes to talk about their water, the lawsuit, their health issues, and living along Route 49. Thanks to Brenda McCoy and Amber McCoy, who described past hardships and hopes for the future. James Berlin Anderson's humor and humanity as he faced the end of his life touched me deeply, and I'm glad I got to sit in his presence on his porch as the evening shadows lengthened.

I interviewed Kevin Thompson about the case and his life over a number of years in which he moved on to other cases involving environmental hazards and I had a full-time reporting job. We talked about the Rawl case in his Charleston office on many nights until I could no longer keep my eyes open, over breakfast at Tudor's Biscuit World, over dinner at Bluegrass Kitchen, and over beers at the Empty Glass or Red Carpet Lounge, where the usual suspects—including reporters like Paul Nyden, who carried their own pieces of the Massey story—eventually turned up. One weekend, I drove Thompson from Charleston to the Head of the Hooch Regatta in Chattanooga, where he rowed with the New Orleans Rowing Club, and the recordings from the six-and-a-half-hour trip each way were added to my growing collection of interviews. I believe Thompson's openness and patience with my endless questions came from his respect for journalism, his irrepressible talent for storytelling, and his desire for the entire Rawl saga to be told.

ACKNOWLEDGMENTS

I met Kathleen and Kelsey Thompson in New Orleans, where they shared personal stories about Thompson. Van Bunch, Bruce Stanley, Dave Barney, Stuart Smith, and Sean Cassidy were generous with their time and offered many insights. Stephen Wussow, Melissa Ellsworth, Nick Getzen, Eric Mathis, and Ian Henderson each had a unique perspective on the case, Thompson, and what it was like to live and work together at the Mountaineer.

I'm grateful to Ben Stout, Jack Spadaro, Scott Simonton, Dr. Carl Werntz, and others for helping me understand the local geology, the practice of slurry injection, and how to think about health outcomes in the communities. Bobby Mitchell, Katie Lautar, Vivian Stockman, and former OVEC organizers Patricia Feeney and Abe Mwara described efforts to help residents in Rawl, Lick Creek, Merrimac, and Sprigg get organized. Maria Gunnoe and filmmaker Mari-Lynn Evans have given me a richer understanding of the heavy price, both human and environmental, that the coal industry has exacted in West Virginia. I want to thank Altina Waller and Rebecca Bailey, as well as Chuck Keeney, Ryan Hardesty, and Thomas Dotson for educating me about the history of the Tug Valley. The staff at the West Virginia Department of Arts, Culture and History located records of early coal mining in the state and the Mine Wars. Other people I met in Williamson and Matewan who are not named in the book made the area's history come alive to me through stories, sometimes handed down through generations.

I want to thank Don Blankenship for inviting me into his home in Sprigg, and for giving me a tour of Delorme and pointing out the significant sites of his childhood, including the train tracks he once crossed to pump his own family's drinking water from a well. He generously extended the tour past the communities along the Tug Fork and up into Lick Creek, where he disputed that slurry injection had contaminated the area's wells. While driving up the hollow, he admitted he might not be welcome there: "I'd hate to run over somebody's dog up here. They'd probably shoot me." At the same time, I'm glad I had the opportunity to observe firsthand just how many people in Mingo County and Pike County, Kentucky, regularly approach Blankenship to pay him their respects and offer well wishes. I'm also grateful that he answered every question I put to him. I now think I should have taken him up on his offer to drive his Mercedes. I appreciate Blankenship's former colleagues who spoke to me, including E. Morgan Massey at his office in Richmond.

Thank you to my agent, David McCormick at McCormick Literary, for believing in this book and in my ability to write it. I'm indebted to Valerie Steiker, a gifted editor and all-around wonderful person, for deciding to acquire the book for Scribner. Her detailed notes, guidance, and enthusiasm throughout the process helped me find a way to tell such a wide-ranging story. I trust that our paths, which first crossed years ago at the *New Yorker*, will line up again. I'm grateful to Kathy Belden, another great editor, and to Rebekah Jett, Lisa Rivlin, and everyone else at Scribner who helped carry this book across the finish line.

Editors at the *Wall Street Journal* allowed me to take a leave to concentrate on reporting and starting to write, and I'm thankful for their support and for everything I've learned about being a journalist from fellow reporters and editors, including Matt Murray, Clare Ansberry, and most recently Shayndi Raice. As I embarked on writing, Jennie Nash offered wise thoughts about narrative structure and a big dose of encouragement. A number of people read early drafts of chapters, including *WSJ* colleagues Joe Barrett, Bob Hagerty, John Miller, and Beth Kracklauer. I'm grateful to Molly Born, who knows Williamson and Mingo County intimately, for her close reading of the entire manuscript.

I've saved a large portion of my thanks for two editorial talents who were essential to the shaping and completion of this book. I could not have pared down my original draft into a readable one without the help of the brilliant Dan Piepenbring, who helped me find the core of the story many times in a collaboration that brought a buoyancy to the task of rewriting. Ben Kalin spent weeks with me fact-checking names of people and streets, quotes, dates, ages, and myriad sources. Ben's professionalism and fact-checking expertise were indispensable.

I want to thank friends and family, including Patti Capparelli and Chuck Smith, who read early drafts. In Pittsburgh and in the mountains of West Virginia, Michael Mervosh has offered guidance and challenged me like no one else, and a circle of men continue to offer invaluable support: Andy Fisher, Joe Starkey, Jim Scharf, Clay Heberling, and Dan Valentine. Michelle Rodriguez, you came into my life at

ACKNOWLEDGMENTS

just the right moment. Thank you for bringing your light and encouragement and heart to me every day.

Thanks to my dad, Peter Maher, who told me stories and talked to me about books all of his life. And thanks to Mendel Melzer, and to my mom, Rosemary Maher, for her love and support and creative spark. Finally to my kids, Jameson and Maya, thank you for enduring my absences, whether I was in West Virginia or far away at my desk. You make every day brighter. You never tired of asking your version of "Are we there yet?" Finally I can say, yes.

A NOTE ON SOURCES

One evening in May 2010, I sat in room 409 of the Mountaineer Hotel and listened to Kevin Thompson describe his legal fight against Massey Energy. By the time it was fully dark, Thompson leaned back in his chair and pointed through a window to a string of lights on a hilltop and said they lit the driveway to the house where Don Blankenship sometimes stayed. "It's what drives me," he said of the view. That moment conveyed the sweep of the case and crystallized the story for me. Here was Thompson suing a multibillion-dollar coal company on behalf of hundreds of people from an old hotel with a *Dark Side of the Moon* poster on a wall, while Blankenship's rarefied getaway was so tantalizingly close that Thompson could see it like a beacon across the rooftops of Williamson. A shiver ran up my spine, and I knew this was a story I needed to tell.

Over the next few years, I felt uniquely positioned to tell it. As a reporter for the *Wall Street Journal* based in Pittsburgh, I was able to view the story from many angles. A month before I met Thompson, I had reported on Massey's Upper Big Branch Mine accident from the Marsh Fork Elementary School south of Charleston during the four-day search for survivors. For the *Journal*, I attended and wrote about the two congressional hearings that followed, and for months I covered the multiple civil investigations into the accident. I interviewed Blankenship several times and helped break news of the board's plans to sell the company, and then I covered Blankenship's retirement in December 2010. I wrote articles on the 2013 indictment of Judge Michael Thornsbury; I attended criminal trials of several Massey officials stemming from the Upper Big Branch investigation; and finally, I wrote about the 2014 indictment of Blankenship, his trial a year later, and his misdemeanor conviction and subsequent sentencing. When Blankenship emerged from prison in 2017, he invited me to his home in Sprigg, and he gave me a guided tour through Delorme and Lick Creek. We had breakfast at Track's End restaurant in Williamson, and a family member of his took me on a four-wheeler into the hills to see the Rawl Sales impoundment. Blankenship drove me in his Mercedes south on Route 119, past his old Belfry office, to Pikeville and the Golden Corral restaurant whose opening he was then overseeing.

While I had followed the case starting in 2010, many interviews were conducted starting in 2017 after Scribner committed to publish this book. I interviewed Thompson numerous times, mostly in the Admiral's Den, and I had transcribed more than four hundred pages before I quit typing up our conversations. I interviewed Van Bunch, Dave Barney, Bruce Stanley, and Sean Cassidy, as well as Thompson's staff, interns, and others in his orbit. I attended the August 2010 hearing in Wheeling in front of the panel of five judges, as well as a trial in a separate case Thompson had before Judge Thornsbury in Mingo County. I later attended other hearings and community meetings in Charleston where Thompson spoke. I am grateful to Larry Brown for long discussions I had with him at his home, and for the openness and perspective that Ernie and Carmelita Brown provided during interviews. I also spent hours speaking to B.I. Sammons, Don Dillon, Frank Coleman, Maude Rice, and Bo Scott at their homes, and I am grateful for their willingness to share their stories. I attempted to attend the September 2011 fairness hearing in Charleston in which Ernie, B.I., and Don Dillon were critical of Thompson, but was barred by court staff from entering the courtroom. I later secured a transcript of the hearing, and I relied on transcripts for all the other hearings in the case, along with Rawl Sales internal documents, expert reports, and depositions, including several that were taped, such as Blankenship's in 2009 and 2011. Sid Young told me about how he came to hire Blankenship and confirmed many other details about mining and growing up along Route 49. In 2014, I traveled to Charleston to cover the chemical spill on the Elk River that contaminated the drinking water for roughly three hundred thousand people, yet another disaster in which Thompson was a lead attorney for residents.

One night in 2017, I was driving through the New River Gorge area in West Virginia, when I got a call from Thompson. He told me he had just sat next to Blankenship on a plane and that the two had talked for well over an hour. I pulled over onto a dirt road and, with Thompson's permission, recorded his detailed account of their conversation.

I was fortunate to be able to view the many MiniDV tapes that Thompson had made over the years and kept in a dusty box. These included footage of water sampling at clients' homes, Thompson's hikes on James Simpkins's property back in 2004 and at Van Bunch's cabin in Tennessee in 2005, and the night in 2008 when Williamson suffered a blackout. Filippo Piscopo and Lorena Luciano generously allowed me to watch unused footage they shot for their documentary *Coal Rush*. This included scenes of Thompson, Bunch, Barney, and others in room 409, of clients like Donetta Blankenship and Larry Brown, and of Thornsbury when he helped with the recovery after the flood that delayed the trial yet again in May 2009. Several clips made me feel that I had the use of a time machine. Thanks to Piscopo and Luciano, I was able to watch Thompson march to the courthouse on East Second Avenue in July 2009 and deliver his motion to disqualify Thornsbury.

In 2018, I traveled to New Orleans to interview Kathleen and Kelsey Thompson and had lunch with Stuart Smith at his home in the French Quarter, and I interviewed Smith's former partner Mike Stag from the downtown offices overlooking the Mississippi River. I also went to Richmond, Virginia, to interview E. Morgan Massey, who shared his family history, thoughts about Blankenship, and a copy of his Massey Doctrine. I visited Point Pleasant to see Thompson's childhood home and the field where he failed to protect a tree from being uprooted; looked through microfiche files at the local library for the articles he wrote as an intern at the local newspaper; and toured the Mothman Museum. In Williamson, I interviewed many people familiar with Thornsbury, the case, and Mingo County in general. They included H. Truman Chafin and his wife, Tish Chafin, in their offices, Sheriff Lonnie Hannah in his office in the courthouse, and other current and former officials who worked with Thornsbury at the courthouse. I will not forget eating ice cream at the home of Johnie Owens—who better to recount stories of Mingo County corruption than the man who was convicted of trying to sell the sheriff's job for a hundred thousand dollars?

My intention has been to tell this story as fully as possible, which meant at a certain point placing all the narrative threads of the water lawsuit within the longer arc of coal mining and the industrialization of Mingo County.

My understanding of the Hatfield-McCoy feud was heavily influenced by Altina Waller's *Feud: Hatfields, McCoys, and Social Change in Appalachia, 1860–1900* (University of North Carolina Press, 1988), and I found a solid basis for the sociological, political, and economic context that precipitated the Matewan Massacre and subsequent violence in Rebecca Bailey's amazingly thorough *Matewan Before the Massacre: Politics, Coal, and the Roots of Conflict in a West Virginia Mining Community* (West Virginia University Press, 2008). Conversations with Waller and Bailey helped to refine my understanding of their work and the two related but distinct episodes of violence in the region. I spent several days combing through the archives at the West Virginia Department of Arts, Culture and History at the state capitol. The *New York Times* coverage from 1920–1921 provided invaluable contemporaneous descriptions of the violence between striking miners and coal operators along the Tug Fork. More recently the reporting of Ken Ward Jr. and Paul J. Nyden at the *Charleston Gazette* and Vicki Smith at the Associated Press provided a rich record of Massey Energy and Don Blankenship and their influence in West Virginia across several decades.

Every time I crossed over into West Virginia to do more reporting for this book, I felt as though I were entering a vivid world where the people I met were living characters in a story I'd been entrusted to tell. I hope I've been able to do justice to the people whose stories these are.

Chapter 1

The description of Thompson's hike, his first meeting with clients in the Rawl Church of God in Jesus Name, and his visit to the Browns' house are from interviews with Thompson, James Simpkins, Ernie and Carmelita Brown, Larry and Brenda Brown, B.I. Sammons, and others. I visited Larry's church and attended an evening service. Carmelita showed me the jars of well water she has kept all these years.

Chapter 2

For the account of the four-wheeler tour, I relied on interviews with Thompson, Van Bunch, Ernie Brown, and B.I. Sammons. Thompson's initial letter to Massey is one of many documents contained in the case record.

Chapter 3

The history of the Forgotten Communities was recounted to me in interviews, especially by Bo Scott, B.I. Sammons, and Maude Rice. Former Ohio Valley Environmental Coalition staffers Patricia Feeney and Abe Mwara also provided me with background on early organizing in the four communities. Bo Scott shared letters from government officials, as well as newspaper clippings. The 1995 state geologist's Lick Creek well study was also part of the case record, as was the engineering report that recommended a water line as the only viable solution.

Chapter 4

Details about Massey's Martin County slurry accident in 2000 are from public records and interviews with Vivian Stockman of OVEC and Jack Spadaro. I interviewed Ben Stout and visited his classroom at Wheeling Jesuit. I interviewed Larry Brown, Frank Coleman, and Don Dillon to confirm their personal experiences.

Chapter 5

Thompson's biographical details were drawn from extensive interviews with him, as well as with former classmates, family, former business partners, and his friend John Alderman. In addition to interviewing Stuart Smith, I relied on his book about his experiences as a lawyer, *Crude Justice: How I Fought Big Oil and Won, and What You Should Know About the New Environmental Attack on America* (BenBella Books, 2015). Details from the Daugherty case come from Thompson and interviews with Marc Lazenby.

Chapter 6

Barbara Smith's first and second health consultations on water quality in the four communities are part of the Rawl case record. Her April 2005 report is available at: https://www.atsdr.cdc.gov/HAC/pha/WilliamsonPrivateWell /WilliamsonPrivateWellHC040605.pdf. In an interview, Smith reiterated that investigating the movement and effects of slurry was beyond the scope of her health consultations, and she said that she was neither for nor against the coal industry. "I understand it was horrible. I understand it was nondrinkable," she said of the Lick Creek area's well water. "But the science says it was or was not a health hazard. So you have to separate those two things out."

I relied on Ben Stout's 2004 report, which Thompson added to the case record, transcripts for the April and May 2005 hearings, interviews with Donetta Blankenship about her hospitalization, and interviews with Thompson and Bunch.

Chapter 7

Coal use data are from the Energy Information Administration. Massey corporate structure information is from its annual reports filed with the Securities and Exchange Commission. Details of Blankenship's Belfry office are from his own descriptions to me, as well as newspaper accounts and the recollection of a close associate. My descriptions of the mountaintop removal fight are informed by interviews with activists like Maria Gunnoe, Vernon Haltom, and Larry Gibson, and filmmaker Mari-Lynn C. Evans, among others.

An important record of women who fought Massey and the coal industry in West Virginia, including Judy Bonds, Maria Gunnoe, and Donetta Blankenship, is contained in *Our Roots Run Deep as Ironweed: Appalachian Women and the Fight for Environmental Justice*, by Shannon Elizabeth Bell (University of Illinois Press, 2013).

Details of the Marsh Fork and Chauncey cases come from court documents. E. Morgan Massey provided me with documents that included the letter his father had written to his grandfather at the Sinton Hotel. Paul J. Nyden discussed his reporting on Massey with me and provided me with clippings of his articles. I used Kitts's deposition transcript. Kathleen and Kelsey Thompson provided details about the family's experience during Katrina.

Chapter 8

James Simpkins recounted hiring Thompson to me. I relied on Judge Thornsbury's written orders, as well as a detailed record kept by Van Bunch's firm of its hourly billings over years to track the sequence of events in the case. Water line extension details came from *Williamson Daily News* articles at the time.

Jack Spadaro provided an account of finding records at the state DEP's office, and they were corroborated by Bobby Mitchell, an activist who also went there, and Pavanne Pettigrew, a former DEP employee who oversaw the state's slurry injection program.

Chapter 9

Blankenship told me about his efforts to build the replica of the Matewan train depot. Amber McCoy described learning the area's history on field trips while she was a student. I spoke to Matewan residents who recounted stories about the massacre and feud figures handed down to them.

Rebecca Bailey describes the early history of settlement in the Tug Valley, including the sale of bearskins for use by Napoleon's grenadiers. A Norfolk and Western history with details of building the Ohio extension that was completed at Rawl can be found in *From Mine to Market: The History of Coal Transportation on the Norfolk and Western Railway*, by Joseph T. Lambie (New York University Press, 1954).

Altina Waller's *Feud* is a fascinating account of the two distinct periods of the feud, taking into account the economics, customs, and social mores of the time.

Feud investigators Thomas Dotson and Ryan Hardesty, who have dug through court records, letters, and other documentary evidence, steered me toward facts and away from sensationalized accounts. *Lies, Damned Lies, and Feud Tales: A Hatfield McCoy Feud Primer* (CreateSpace Independent Publishing Platform, 2017), by Dotson with contributions from Hardesty, debunks many feud myths.

Charles B. Keeney, an assistant professor of history at Southern West Virginia Community and Technical College, whose great-grandfather Frank Keeney was president of UMWA District 17 during the Matewan Massacre and Battle of Blair Mountain, provided valuable insights into the period. Also helpful for putting the Mine Wars in perspective was his book: *The Road to Blair Mountain: Saving a Mine Wars Battlefield from King Coal* (West Virginia University Press, 2021).

Other books on the Mine Wars period that were useful included:

Lon Savage's *Thunder in the Mountains: The West Virginia Mine War 1920–21* (University of Pittsburgh Press, 1990)

Howard B. Lee's *Bloodletting in Appalachia: The Story of West Virginia's Four Major Mine Wars and Other Thrilling Incidents on Its Coal Fields* (McClain Printing Company, 1969)

James Green's *The Devil Is Here in These Hills: West Virginia's Coal Miners and Their Battle for Freedom* (Atlantic Monthly Press, 2015)

A NOTE ON SOURCES

David Alan Corbin's *Gun Thugs, Rednecks, Radicals: A Documentary History of the West Virginia Mine Wars* (PM Press, 2011)

Rebecca J. Bailey's *Matewan Before the Massacre: Politics, Coal, and Roots of Conflict in a West Virginia Mining Community*

Several books on the mythology of Appalachian otherness helped me think about the region. They included Henry D. Shapiro's *Appalachia on Our Mind: The Southern Mountains and Mountaineers in the American Consciousness, 1870–1920* (University of North Carolina Press, 1978), and Elizabeth Catte's *What You Are Getting Wrong About Appalachia* (Belt Publishing, 2018).

The 1921 US Senate hearings on the labor conflict between the UMWA and coal operators in West Virginia, in which Sid Hatfield and others testified, is a fascinating source document. *West Virginia Coal Fields: Hearings before the Committee on Education and Labor, United States Senate, Sixty-Seventh Congress, First Session* (US Government Printing Office, 1921).

My description of the tent colonies and fighting along the Tug Fork in 1920–1921 are also drawn from about three dozen articles in the *New York Times* from November 1920 through October 1921. The description of Williamson after the fighting had ceased is from an essay in the *New York Times*, September 5, 1921.

The account of the Matewan Massacre reenactment is from video of the performance by documentary filmmaker Rory Owen Delaney. Delaney shared footage with me he shot of Thompson and Larry Brown for his film *Toxic Soup* (Man Bites Dog Films, 2010), which includes interviews with both Thompson and Brown.

Don Dillon shared with me a copy of the photograph of his father living in a tent colony.

Chapter 11

Thompson's reaction to being sued by Massey was quoted in "Attorney Responds to Coal Company," by John O'Brien in the *West Virginia Record*, May 4, 2006.

Hamrick's affidavit is contained in court filings. The story of Hamrick strangling a pit bull was recounted in a number of articles, including "Mingo Power," by Martha Bryson Hodel, Associated Press, December 18, 1988.

Huey Perry's *They'll Cut Off Your Project: A Mingo County Chronicle* (West Virginia University Press, 2011) provided background on the county's history of corruption. I interviewed Perry about Hamrick and other figures.

I attended a meeting of the Mingo County Commission and met Hubbard and other officials who worked with Judge Thornsbury.

Thompson's account of mailing a letter to Hubbard and then the *National Geographic* article to Hamrick was confirmed by Pam Patai.

The line about Blankenship suing "just about everyone" is from "'The Don' Is on a Roll—Massey CEO Suing Gov. Manchin," the *Hur Herald*, July 27, 2005, with permission of editor Bob Weaver.

The account of Bunch running the Hatfield McCoy Marathon is from interviews with Bunch, Thompson, and Ernie and Carmelita Brown. Bunch's finish is from various sites, including runhigh.com.

Details about Blankenship's 2006 trip to the French Riviera are from my reporting in 2008, which includes interviews with Bruce Stanley and others familiar with the trip.

Thompson and Larry Brown described their perceptions of intimidation by Rawl Sales in interviews with me.

Chapter 12

The detail about Ben Hatfield's great-grandfather finding the bodies of the three McCoys and returning them to their parents is from local feud historian Ryan Hardesty.

Chapter 13

Thompson's at times difficult working relationship with Stuart Smith is from multiple interviews with Thompson.

Stephen Wussow described in interviews his hiring process and early days of working with Thompson in room 409.

Dave Barney in multiple interviews described his decision to set up a law firm with Thompson and their working relationship and cases.

Chapter 14

I attended a speech Blankenship made to the Tug Valley Chamber of Commerce in 2017, as well as events in his 2018 Senate primary campaign.

In interviews with Blankenship in the summer of 2017, he recounted his childhood in Delorme; his math talent; his brother George's return from Vietnam; his discovery that he had a different father from his siblings; his experience working in coal mines while he went to college; his early career; his purchase of the blue Chevrolet pickup truck; his hiring at Rawl Sales; his productivity improvements and handling of the 1985 strike; the Upper Big Branch accident; his criminal case; and the water lawsuit, among other things.

Interviews with James Gardner, Wilma Steele, Clay Mullins, E. Morgan Massey, Jeff Wilson, and others provided different views on Blankenship.

Blankenship has maintained that the UBB explosion was the result of MSHA requiring a ventilation plan that cut airflow in the mine by half and that MSHA shouldn't be allowed to investigate its own conduct leading up to accidents. He was also insistent that his trial had been unfair because the judge issued a gag order that prevented him from speaking publicly, and he has argued that prosecutors and MSHA withheld exculpatory evidence at his trial. The fullest account of his argument can be found in Blankenship's 2020 self-published book, *Obama's Deadliest Cover-Up: They All Have Blood on Their Hands*. In 2019, a US magistrate judge in southern West Virginia recommended throwing out Blankenship's conviction because evidence had been withheld. The federal judge who oversaw the trial denied Blankenship's request to overturn the conviction.

Blankenship was adamant in denying that getting a water line to his house from Matewan had anything to do with slurry injection or the lawsuit. He said he believed the water quality in the area had been poor for a long time as a result of decades of mining.

Chapter 16

Melissa Ellsworth provided details about her working with Thompson in multiple interviews.

Details of the site inspection were confirmed through interviews with Thompson, Bunch, Ellsworth, Wussow, Eric Mathis, and Scott Simonton, as well as photographs and video taken during the tour.

Some details of the operation in room 409 came from my visit to the office in 2010, as well from interviews with Nick Getzen, Wussow, and others.

Filippo Piscopo and Lorena Luciano described their time in Mingo County to me in separate interviews. As stated earlier, they made available unused footage from their film *Coal Rush* (Film2 Productions, 2012), which also informed my reporting.

I interviewed James Berlin Anderson at his home about growing up in Rawl, the case, coal mining, the history of Williamson, and his health.

Bunch's reference to Williamson as "Toon Town" comes from interviews with him.

The pressure-cooker environment of Williamson was described to me by multiple people, including Thompson, Wussow, Mathis, Ellsworth, and Ian "Thor" Henderson.

Chapter 17

I acquired my own copies of the photographs of Blankenship and Maynard vacationing together. The story was broken by Adam Liptak at the *New York Times*, on January 15, 2008, in "Motion Ties W. Virginia Justice to Coal Executive."

Thompson and others working in room 409 described their concern following Blankenship's encounter with an ABC cameraman in the parking lot of Blankenship's Belfry office.

Thompson provided me with copies of his opening statement at various stages. The story of him leaving a message for Dan Stickler about the seersucker suit comes from Thompson.

The account of Thompson's deteriorating finances and growing anxiety in the summer of 2008 is from interviews with Thompson and others, as well as video Thompson shot, including of the night that he and Allen Sowards drank beers in the Mountaineer lobby.

Chapter 18

For details about the state senate hearings on coal slurry, I watched video of the hearings in which Donetta Blankenship and Deborah Sammons provided testimony about their families' health issues related to their well water, and a USGS official testified about studies into potential adverse health effects from exposure to coal. Chris Hamilton testified about the state coal association's view on the Rawl case and regulating slurry injection.

The Associated Press article on slurry injection, "Critics Question Safety of Storing Coal Slurry," March 21, 2009, was written by Vicki Smith.

The search for the black Dodge Charger was recounted in interviews by Thompson, Frank Coleman, Wussow, Ellsworth, and Henderson.

Chapter 19

The account of Thompson demanding financing from Smith comes primarily from interviews with Thompson and Mathis. Smith and Mike Stag in separate interviews confirmed that Thompson had threatened to leave with his graphics if they didn't invest more in the Rawl case.

Chapter 20

Thompson's impressions during Blankenship's deposition come from interviews with Thompson. Bunch described his conclusion about the deposition in an interview.

Chapter 21

The bench conference between the judge and lawyers at the April 27 hearing that is not on the record, in which Thompson said there was a deal and Stickler said there wasn't one, is from Thompson's recollection.

Details about the April 27 community meeting at Bo Scott's church are from an interview with Brenda McCoy, as well as a photograph of the meeting provided by Thompson.

A NOTE ON SOURCES

Vicki Smith's story on the massive settlement day: "Judge Seeks to Resolve Coal Slurry Pollution Case," Associated Press, May 1, 2009.

I interviewed Virginia and Russell Prince at their home to discuss the death of their daughter Chastity Dawn Prince from kidney cancer, which the family blamed on her exposure to the water in Rawl.

Thompson described in interviews his exchange with Bunch when Thompson refused to wear his suit jacket.

The account of a man who had a seizure in the courtroom during the settlement conference is partly from a subsequent hearing before Judge Thornsbury in which Thompson recounted the episode in open court.

Settlement offers were described in Vicki Smith's May 1 article.

Details of Thompson lying on his floor fielding calls are from interviews with Thompson and Sean Cassidy.

Chapter 22

The interaction between Getzen and Donetta Blankenship appears in *Coal Rush*.

The discussion between Bunch and Thompson about whether clients will be able to sue for future illnesses is in unused footage shot by Piscopo and Luciano.

Thompson's interactions with the judge's clerk are from interviews with Thompson, and he described them in recusal motions filed to the state Supreme Court.

Bunch and Barney recounted to me that the judge had cleared the courtroom for the medical monitoring trust hearing, and the fact that the details of the trust were sealed is reflected in the hearing transcript.

Chapter 23

In an interview in their offices in Williamson, Truman and Tish Chafin described the two political factions in the courthouse and how Thornsbury had been appointed circuit court judge with help from Spike Maynard and Chafin himself.

Thornsbury's statements about the opportunity presented by the corruption sweep in the 1980s were in "Election Brings New Candidates to Corruption-Plagued Mingo County," by Martha Bryson Hodel, Associated Press, May 9, 1988.

Carmelita's views on politics in Williamson are from an interview with her.

Thornsbury's statements to a man he sentenced to ten years in prison: "Man Sentenced to Up to 10 Years in Prison," Associated Press, June 19, 2004.

A NOTE ON SOURCES

Chapter 24

Blankenship said in an interview that he didn't know Thornsbury well but that Williamson was a small town and it wasn't unusual that they would be at the same restaurant at the same time.

Thompson's statement that he wished he had fallen off the four-wheeler in 2004 is from interviews with Thompson and Carmelita and Ernie Brown.

I interviewed Lonnie Hannah in his office in the courthouse, and he confirmed his conversation with Thompson before the judge was disqualified from the case.

Chapter 25

Dr. Christopher Beckett explained his business relationship with the judge in an interview. The account of the exodus is from interviews with Thompson, Wussow, and Ellsworth.

Chapter 26

In interviews, Thompson described Stuart Smith's fiftieth birthday party at the House of Blues.

Details of Mary Dillon's illness and her funeral are from interviews with Don Dillon.

Thompson's impressions of the response in Mingo County to the Upper Big Branch accident come from interviews with him.

Thompson told me he was able to keep his house of out foreclosure when Bruce Stanley came on board and Reed Smith invested in the case.

I was present in the Admiral's Den when Thompson joked about Stanley controlling the weather. I also observed Thompson describing his impressions of the five judges, including his nicknames for them.

Chapter 27

I was present in room 409 during Thompson's preparations, went to dinner at El Azul, and drove up to the civic center with Van Bunch, and then was present in the auditorium.

In the fall of 2010, I wrote stories with Joann S. Lublin and Anupreeta Das about the Massey board's decision to sell the company. "Massey's Directors Mull Sale, Options," the *Wall Street Journal*, October 19, 2010, and "Alpha Stokes Buyout Interest in Rival Massey," the *Wall Street Journal*, November 6, 2010.

Admiral Inman's communications with Alpha executives about a sale of Massey are from emails and other documents in the shareholder litigation.

The story about Blankenship going to a Bob Evans restaurant on the day his retirement was announced was from Nick Getzen and Thompson.

Chapter 28

Thompson's similarities to Stickler were recounted to me by Thompson and several people who work for him and were familiar with these exchanges between him and Stickler and his staff.

Chapter 29

Ernie Brown's belief that Stickler was going to crush Thompson like a stink bug and his thoughts about the pending trial were communicated to me in interviews.

The mine map vault search was described to me by Thompson and Andrew Davis, a Thompson Barney intern at the time, as well as Bo Scott; Rob Goodwin, a surveyor Thompson asked to help with the search; and a Reed Smith paralegal.

Chapter 30

Details of the settlement process were provided by Thompson.

The $35 million settlement was reported by Vicki Smith at the Associated Press in "Letter Reveals Massey Offering $35M to Settle Coal Slurry Lawsuit in W.Va.," August 9, 2011.

Bruce Stanley provided his views on the settlement to me. Thompson gave me his account of meeting with people at the field house to discuss the settlement. The exchange between Stickler and Thompson is from interviews with Thompson. I was in the Admiral's Den when Thompson and others were reviewing the events of the day and reflecting on the end of the case.

Epilogue

All quotes in the epilogue come from interviews with the people who are quoted.

INDEX

INDEX

Thompson's recusal motion against
Judge Thornsbury and, 211
Thornsbury and, 208–9
Brown, Charity, 12
Brown, Christopher, 12
Brown, Ernie, 4, 5, 7, 105, 151
appearance of, 5, 10
black well water, 50
Blankenship depositions, 180, 255–56,
257, 299
disability of, 10–11
health problems and bad water, 11–12
health survey circulated by, 26–27
home of, sulfur smell and, 9, 16, 26
lawyer Bunch meeting with, 15–16
life after Rawl settlement, 298, 299
Rawl lawsuit and, 48, 103, 175, 177,
178, 195, 198, 200, 240, 253–54, 260
Rawl lawsuit settlement and (2011),
267, 273, 274–75, 277
Rawl Sales, information about, 31
Rawl Sales test of well water, results
(1997), 123
Scott's friendship with, 23
Stout well testing and report, 26, 46
takes Thompson and Bunch to Sprouse
Creek impoundment, 15–16
Thompson hired as his lawyer, 8
Thompson meeting with, 9–12
Thompson's recusal motion against
Judge Thornsbury and, 211
Thornsbury and, 208
well testing and, 201–2
Brown, Larry, 4, 115, 151
affidavit in Massey's defamation suit
against Thompson, 107
appearance, 5
Blankenship deposition and, 180, 189
born-again experience, 28
creek running black (Jan. 14, 2009),
175
distributing and tracking court-ordered
water, 107, 113, 117
health problems and bad water, 7, 27,
302–3
intimidation of, 165
life after Rawl settlement, 302–4
monthly income, 103
mountaintop vision, 48, 185
OVEC and, 25–26
as pastor, 5, 11, 28, 52
Rawl lawsuit and, 175, 195, 198, 240
as Rawl lawsuit key plaintiff, 27–28, 31

Rawl lawsuit motions for bottled water
and, 48, 52, 103
Thompson hired by, 8
Thompson's initial meeting with, 5–8
Thompson's recusal motion against
Judge Thornsbury and, 211
trial date delayed and, 78
vision of, after lawsuit, 303
Bunch, Van, 14, 57, 153
background, 14
Blankenship depositions and, 180, 187,
189, 258
Charleston chemical spill case,
284–85
court-sanctioned tour of Rawl prep
plant, 147–49
Ernie Brown takes Thompson and, to
Sprouse Creek impoundment,
15–16
Hatfield McCoy Marathon, 104–5
Massey Energy corporate getaway and,
158
meeting with Ernie and Carmelita
Brown, 15
Rawl lawsuit, 14–17, 31, 57, 74, 78, 103,
104, 106, 150, 151, 159, 192, 194–95,
198–99, 262, 266
Rawl lawsuit ends, 276
Rawl lawsuit fee expectation, 196
Rawl lawsuit funding and, 163, 267
Rawl lawsuit Mass Litigation Panel
hearing, 233
Rawl lawsuit mediation (2010), 236,
237, 238, 240
Rawl lawsuit medical monitoring plan,
31, 193, 203, 204–5
Rawl lawsuit settlement, final deal
(2011), 266–70, 272, 274, 275
runner-up, Trial Lawyer of the Year
Award, 280
Thornsbury and, 207, 213, 219
Bunnell, Joseph E., 165
study of coal slurry on liver cells,
165–67
Burnwell Coal and Coke Company, 88
Bush, George W., 75–76
Byrd, Robert, 23
death of, 230
as "King of Pork," 23
UBB mine explosion hearing,
questioning Blankenship, 228,
229–30
W. Va.'s drinking water problem and, 23

325

INDEX

INDEX

INDEX

INDEX

INDEX

INDEX

Obama, Barack, 223, 227
oil and gas industry
  ExxonMobil radioactive
    contamination, Smith landmark
    lawsuit and record judgment, 40–41
  pollution lawsuits against, 41
  Smith's landmark case against Chevron,
    40
OVEC (Ohio Valley Environmental
  Coalition), 25–26, 110, 147, 150
Owens, Johnie, 98–99, 207

Parsley, Thelma, 30, 31, 62, 180, 265
Patai, Pam, 99, 276, 277
Phillips, Baxter, 143
Piscopo, Filippo, 150, 202, 280
Pittston Coal, Buffalo Creek disaster
  (1972), 26
Point Pleasant, W. Va., 4, 6, 33, 37
  the Mothman and, 37–38
  Silver Bridge collapse, 38
Powell, Bill, 43
Prenter, W. Va., 165
Prince, Chastity Dawn, 27, 198
Prince, Virginia, 198
Princeton, W. Va., 41
Public Justice, 280, 283

Quillen, Mike, 244

Rawl, W. Va., xi, 5, 7, 10, 95, 294
  arsenic and lead in wells, 46, 300–301
  Church of God in Jesus Name, meeting
    at, 5
  Coleman's home in, 28
  Dillon family in, 88
  flooding in, 202
  health problems and bad water, 7, 29,
    99, 294, 297
  highway sign pleading for a water
    system, 24
  leaking of coal slurry in, 7, 25
  "Rawl syndrome," 154
  settlement money and, 296
  Simonton on the water at, 50–51
  striking miners, violence and (1921),
    91–92
  Thompson's initial meeting in,
    5–8
  Thompson's need to prove bad water
    caused bad health, 66
  underground coal fire, 15, 17
  water contamination levels, 46

water line completion to, 117
wells gone bad in, 5
Rawl lawsuit against Massey Energy
  accomplishments of, 275
  amount sought from Massey, 159
  animations and videos developed, 150,
    151
  assistants hired by Thompson, 114,
    147, 149
  bad water and residents' health, 26–27,
    31, 110–12, 150–51, 152, 164, 165,
    185–86, 234, 237–38, 252–53
  Blankenship depositions, 146–47, 163,
    164, 180–89, 255–60
  Blankenship subpoena, 71
  building a case, information needed, 28
  Bunch as partner with Thompson in,
    14–17, 31, 57, 74, 78, 103, 104, 106,
    150, 151, 159, 163, 192, 194–96,
    198–99, 262, 266, 267, 276
  Bunnell report on coal slurry and liver
    cells, 165–67
  charges against Massey in, 31–32
  Charleston office (the Admiral's Den),
    214, 247–48
  Cisco depositions, 190
  as a class action, 8, 17, 56, 74
  court-sanctioned tour of Rawl prep
    plant, 147–49
  damages and property loss figures, 21
  "The Depo War," 109–10, 116, 117
  digging into Rawl Sales' past, 75
  disappointment in lack of a trial, 270,
    272
  discovery documents, 54, 115, 116,
    119, 164, 178, 261, 287
  documentary made on, 150, 202, 280
  Esmer deposition, 123–25
  Evans appointed judge, then recused,
    219, 231, 232
  "the exodus" from Williamson, 213–14,
    216, 217
  experts for, 50–51, 75–77
  filing of lawsuit (Sept. 16, 2004), 31
  former Rawl Sales officials deposed,
    260–61
  funds for lawsuit, 114, 158, 163, 175,
    217, 232, 267–68, 284
  Hamrick hire and double-cross,
    97–100, 153, 177, 178, 207
  Hatfield deposition, 108–9
  Jackson Kelly's motion for sanctions,
    272

INDEX

INDEX

ABOUT THE AUTHOR

Kris Maher is a staff reporter for the *Wall Street Journal* who writes about environmental issues, coal mining, politics, regional economics, and other topics. He lives in Pittsburgh with his son and daughter.